**The Quran With
Tafsir Ibn Kathir
Part 9 of 30:
Al A'raf 088 To
Al Anfal 040**

The Quran With Tafsir Ibn Kathir
Part 9 of 30:
Al A'raf 088 To
Al Anfal 040

With
Arabic Script, Transliteration of Arabic, Meaning in English
and Ibn Kathir's Abridged Tafsir (Explanation)

Muhammad Saed Abdul-Rahman

BSc, DipHE

© Muhammad Saed Abdul-Rahman, 2012
ISBN 978-1-86179-852-7

All Rights reserved

British Library Cataloguing in Publication Data. A Catalogue record for this book is available from the British Library

Designed, Typeset and produced by:
MSA Publication Limited, 4 Bello Close, Herne Hill,
London SE24 9BW
United Kingdom

Cover design: Houriyah Abdul-Rahman

TABLE OF CONTENTS

TABLE OF CONTENTS V
PRELUDE XIII
    OPENING SERMAN XIII
    OUR MISSION XIV
    BIOGRAPHY OF HAFIZ IBN KATHIR (701 H - 774 H) XIV
        Ibn Kathir's Teachers xiv
        Ibn Kathir's Students xv
        Ibn Kathir's Books xv
        Ibn Kathir's Death xvi

PREFACE XVII
    ABOUT THIS BOOK XVII
    PERFORMING PROSTRATION WHILE READING THE QUR'AN XVII

PART 9 FULL ARABIC TEXT 1

CHAPTER 7: AL-ARAF (THE HEIGHTS), VERSES 088 - 206 12
    Surah: 7 Ayah: 88 & Ayah: 89 12
        Tafsir Ibn Kathir 13
        Allah describes the way the disbelievers answered His Prophet Shu`ayb and those who believed in him, by threatening them with expulsion from their village, or with forceful reversion to the disbeliever's religion. 13
    Surah: 7 Ayah: 90, Ayah: 91 & Ayah: 92 13
        Tafsir Ibn Kathir 14
    Surah: 7 Ayah: 93 15
        Tafsir Ibn Kathir 15
    Surah: 7 Ayah: 94 & Ayah: 95 15
        Tafsir Ibn Kathir 16
        Afflictions that struck Earlier Nations 16
    Surah: 7 Ayah: 96, Ayah: 97, Ayah: 98 & Ayah: 99 17
        Tafsir Ibn Kathir 18
        Blessings come with Faith, while Kufr brings Torment 18
    Surah: 7 Ayah: 100 19
        Tafsir Ibn Kathir 19
        Ibn `Abbas commented on Allah's statement, ... 19
    Surah: 7 Ayah: 101 & Ayah: 102 20
        Tafsir Ibn Kathir 20
    Surah: 7 Ayah: 103 22
        Tafsir Ibn Kathir 22
        Story of Prophet Musa, upon him be Peace, and Fir`awn 22
    Surah: 7 Ayah: 104, Ayah: 105 & Ayah: 106 22

- Tafsir Ibn Kathir 23
- *Surah: 7 Ayah: 107 & Ayah: 108 .... 24*
  - Tafsir Ibn Kathir 24
- *Surah: 7 Ayah: 109 & Ayah: 110 .... 24*
  - Tafsir Ibn Kathir 25
    - Fir`awn's People say that Musa is a Magician! 25
- *Surah: 7 Ayah: 111 & Ayah: 112 .... 25*
  - Tafsir Ibn Kathir 25
- *Surah: 7 Ayah: 113 & Ayah: 114 .... 26*
  - Tafsir Ibn Kathir 26
    - The Magicians convene and change Their Ropes into Snakes before Musa 26
- *Surah: 7 Ayah: 115 & Ayah: 116 .... 26*
  - Tafsir Ibn Kathir 27
- *Surah: 7 Ayah: 117, Ayah: 118, Ayah: 119, Ayah: 120, Ayah: 121 & Ayah: 122 .... 27*
  - Tafsir Ibn Kathir 28
    - Musa defeats the Magicians, Who believe in Him 28
- *Surah: 7 Ayah: 123, Ayah: 124, Ayah: 125 & Ayah: 126 .... 29*
  - Tafsir Ibn Kathir 30
    - Fir`awn threatens the Magicians after They believed in Musa and Their Response to Him
      30
- *Surah: 7 Ayah: 127, Ayah: 128 & Ayah: 129 .... 31*
  - Tafsir Ibn Kathir 32
    - Fir`awn vows to kill the Children of Israel, Who complain to Musa; Allah promises Them Victory 32
- *Surah: 7 Ayah: 130 & Ayah: 131 .... 33*
  - Tafsir Ibn Kathir 33
    - Fir`awn and His People suffer Years of Drought 33
- *Surah: 7 Ayah: 132, Ayah: 133, Ayah: 134 & Ayah: 135 .... 34*
  - Tafsir Ibn Kathir 35
    - Allah punishes the People of Fir`awn because of Their Rebellion 35
- *Surah: 7 Ayah: 136 & Ayah: 137 .... 37*
  - Tafsir Ibn Kathir 38
    - The People of Fir`awn drown in the Sea; the Children of Israel inherit the Holy Land 38
- *Surah: 7 Ayah: 138 & Ayah: 139 .... 38*
  - Tafsir Ibn Kathir 39
    - The Children of Israel safely cross the Sea, but still held on to the Idea of Idol Worshipping 39
- *Surah: 7 Ayah: 140 & Ayah: 141 .... 40*
  - Tafsir Ibn Kathir 40
    - Reminding the Children of Israel of Allah's Blessings for Them 40
- *Surah: 7 Ayah: 142 .... 40*
  - Tafsir Ibn Kathir 41
    - Musa fasts and worships Allah for Forty Days 41
- *Surah: 7 Ayah: 143 .... 41*

Table of Contents

- Tafsir Ibn Kathir 42
  - Musa asks to see Allah 42
- *Surah: 7 Ayah: 144 & Ayah: 145* 44
  - Tafsir Ibn Kathir 44
    - Allah chooses Musa and gives Him the Tablets 44
- *Surah: 7 Ayah: 146 & Ayah: 147* 45
  - Tafsir Ibn Kathir 46
    - Arrogant People will be deprived of Allah's Ayat 46
- *Surah: 7 Ayah: 148 & Ayah: 149* 47
  - Tafsir Ibn Kathir 47
    - Story of worshipping the Calf 47
- *Surah: 7 Ayah: 150 & Ayah: 151* 48
  - Tafsir Ibn Kathir 49
- *Surah: 7 Ayah: 152 & Ayah: 153* 50
  - Tafsir Ibn Kathir 50
- *Surah: 7 Ayah: 154* 51
  - Tafsir Ibn Kathir 52
    - Musa picked up the Tablets when His Anger subsided 52
- *Surah: 7 Ayah: 155 & Ayah: 156* 52
  - Tafsir Ibn Kathir 53
    - Seventy Men from the Children of Israel go for the appointed Meeting Place that Allah designated, Allah later on destroys Them 53
    - Allah's Mercy is for Those Who have Taqwa and believe in Allah's Ayat and His Messenger 55
- *Surah: 7 Ayah: 157* 56
  - Tafsir Ibn Kathir 57
    - The Description of that Messenger 57
- *Surah: 7 Ayah: 158* 60
  - Tafsir Ibn Kathir 60
    - Muhammad's Message is Universal 60
- *Surah: 7 Ayah: 159* 62
  - Tafsir Ibn Kathir 62
- *Surah: 7 Ayah: 160, Ayah: 161 & Ayah: 162* 63
  - Tafsir Ibn Kathir 64
- *Surah: 7 Ayah: 163* 64
  - Tafsir Ibn Kathir 64
    - The Jews transgress the Sanctity of the Sabbath 64
- *Surah: 7 Ayah: 164, Ayah: 165 & Ayah: 166* 65
  - Tafsir Ibn Kathir 66
    - Those Who breached the Sabbath were turned into Monkeys, but Those Who prohibited Their Actions were saved 66
- *Surah: 7 Ayah: 167* 67
  - Tafsir Ibn Kathir 67
    - Eternal Humiliation placed on the Jews 67

Surah: 7 Ayah: 168, Ayah: 169 & Ayah: 170 68
   Tafsir Ibn Kathir 69
      The Children of Israel scatter throughout the Land 69
Surah: 7 Ayah: 171 71
   Tafsir Ibn Kathir 71
      Raising Mount Tur over the Jews, because of Their Rebellion 71
Surah: 7 Ayah: 172, Ayah: 173 & Ayah: 174 72
   Tafsir Ibn Kathir 72
      The Covenant taken from the Descendants of Adam 72
Surah: 7 Ayah: 175, Ayah: 176 & Ayah: 177 75
   Tafsir Ibn Kathir 76
      Story Bal`am bin Ba`ura 76
Surah: 7 Ayah: 178 78
   Tafsir Ibn Kathir 79
Surah: 7 Ayah: 179 79
   Tafsir Ibn Kathir 80
      Disbelief and the Divine Decree 80
Surah: 7 Ayah: 180 81
   Tafsir Ibn Kathir 81
      Allah's Most Beautiful Names 81
Surah: 7 Ayah: 181 83
   Tafsir Ibn Kathir 83
Surah: 7 Ayah: 182 & Ayah: 183 83
   Tafsir Ibn Kathir 84
Surah: 7 Ayah: 184 84
   Tafsir Ibn Kathir 84
Surah: 7 Ayah: 185 85
   Tafsir Ibn Kathir 86
Surah: 7 Ayah: 186 86
   Tafsir Ibn Kathir 86
Surah: 7 Ayah: 187 86
   Tafsir Ibn Kathir 87
      The Last Hour and its Portents 87
Surah: 7 Ayah: 188 93
   Tafsir Ibn Kathir 93
      The Messenger does not know the Unseen, and He cannot bring Benefit or Harm even to Himself 93
Surah: 7 Ayah: 189 & Ayah: 190 94
   Tafsir Ibn Kathir 94
      All Mankind are the Offspring of Adam 94
Surah: 7 Ayah: 191, Ayah: 192, Ayah: 193, Ayah: 194, Ayah: 195, Ayah: 196, Ayah: 197 & Ayah: 198 96
   Tafsir Ibn Kathir 97
      Idols do not create, help, or have Power over Anything 97

Table of Contents

Surah: 7 Ayah: 199 & Ayah: 200 100
   Tafsir Ibn Kathir 100
      Showing Forgiveness 100

Surah: 7 Ayah: 201 & Ayah: 202 102
   Tafsir Ibn Kathir 102
      The Whispering of Shaytan and the People of Taqwa 102
      A Brethren of Devils among Mankind lure to Falsehood 103

Surah: 7 Ayah: 203 103
   Tafsir Ibn Kathir 104
      Idolators ask to witness Miracles 104

Surah: 7 Ayah: 204 104
   Tafsir Ibn Kathir 104
      The Order to listen to the Qur'an 104

Surah: 7 Ayah: 205 & Ayah: 206 105
   Tafsir Ibn Kathir 105
      Remembering Allah in the Mornings and Afternoons 105

INTRODUCTION TO CHAPTER (SURAH) 8: AL-ANFAL (SPOILS OF WAR, BOOTY) 106

   IBN KATHIR'S INTRODUCTION 106

CHAPTER (SURAH) 8: AL-ANFAL (SPOILS OF WAR, BOOTY), VERSES 001–040 106

Surah: 8 Ayah: 1 107
   Tafsir Ibn Kathir 107
      Meaning of Anfal 107
      The Reason behind revealing Ayah 8:1 107
      Another Reason behind revealing the Ayah 8:1 108

Surah: 8 Ayah: 2, Ayah: 3 & Ayah: 4 109
   Tafsir Ibn Kathir 110
      Qualities of the Faithful and Truthful Believers 110
      (The believers are only those who, when Allah is mentioned, feel a fear in their hearts) 110
      Faith increases when the Qur'an is recited 110
      The Reality of Tawakkul 111
      Deeds of Faithful Believers 111
      The Reality of Faith 111
      The Fruits of Perfect Faith 112

Surah: 8 Ayah: 5, Ayah: 6, Ayah: 7 & Ayah: 8 112
   Tafsir Ibn Kathir 113
      Following the Messenger is Better for the Believers 113

Surah: 8 Ayah: 9 & Ayah: 10 116
   Tafsir Ibn Kathir 116
      Muslims invoke Allah for Help, Allah sends the Angels to help Them 116

Surah: 8 Ayah: 11, Ayah: 12, Ayah: 13 & Ayah: 14 119
   Tafsir Ibn Kathir 120
      Slumber overcomes Muslims 120

- Rain falls on the Eve of Badr 121
- Allah commands the Angels to fight and support the Believers 122

Surah: 8 Ayah: 15 & Ayah: 16 123
- Tafsir Ibn Kathir 124
- Fleeing from Battle is prohibited, and its Punishment 124

Surah: 8 Ayah: 17 & Ayah: 18 125
- Tafsir Ibn Kathir 126
- Allah's Signs displayed during Badr, And throwing Sand in the Eyes of the Disbelievers 126

Surah: 8 Ayah: 19 127
- Tafsir Ibn Kathir 127
- The Response to the Disbelievers Who ask for a Judgement 127

Surah: 8 Ayah: 20, Ayah: 21, Ayah: 22 & Ayah: 23 129
- Tafsir Ibn Kathir 129
- The Command to obey Allah and His Messenger 129

Surah: 8 Ayah: 24 130
- Tafsir Ibn Kathir 131
- The Command to answer and obey Allah and His Messenger 131
- Allah comes in between a Person and His Heart 132

Surah: 8 Ayah: 25 133
- Tafsir Ibn Kathir 133
- Warning against an encompassing Fitnah 133

Surah: 8 Ayah: 26 136
- Tafsir Ibn Kathir 136
- Reminding Muslims of Their previous State of Weakness and Subjugation which changed into Might and Triumph 136

Surah: 8 Ayah: 27 & Ayah: 28 137
- Tafsir Ibn Kathir 137
- Reason behind revealing This Ayah, and the prohibition of Betrayal 137

Surah: 8 Ayah: 29 139
- Tafsir Ibn Kathir 139

Surah: 8 Ayah: 30 140
- Tafsir Ibn Kathir 140
- The Makkans plot to kill the Prophet , imprison Him or expel Him from Makkah 140

Surah: 8 Ayah: 31, Ayah: 32 & Ayah: 33 141
- Tafsir Ibn Kathir 142
- The Quraysh claimed They can produce Something similar to the Qur'an ... 142
- The Idolators ask for Allah's Judgment and Torment! 143
- The Presence of the Prophet , and the Idolators' asking For forgiveness, were the Shelters against receiving Allah's immediate Torment 144

Surah: 8 Ayah: 34 & Ayah: 35 145
- Tafsir Ibn Kathir 145
- The Idolators deserved Allah's Torment after Their Atrocities 145

Surah: 8 Ayah: 36 & Ayah: 37 147
- Tafsir Ibn Kathir 148

Table of Contents

The Disbelievers spend Their Wealth to hinder Others from Allah's Path, but this will only cause Them Grief 148

Surah: 8 Ayah: 38, Ayah: 39 & Ayah: 40 .... *149*

Tafsir Ibn Kathir 150

Encouraging the Disbelievers to seek Allah's Forgiveness, warning Them against Disbelief 150

The Order to fight to eradicate Shirk and Kufr 150

PRELUDE

Opening Serman

Indeed, all praise is due to Allah. We praise Him and seek His help and forgiveness. We seek refuge with Allah from our soul's evil and our wrong doings. He whom Allah guides, no one can misguide; and he whom He misguides, no one can guide

I bear witness that there is no (true) god except Allah – alone without a partner, and I bear witness that Muhammad (peace and blessings of Allah be upon him) is His 'abd (servant) and messenger.

$$\text{يَٰٓأَيُّهَا ٱلَّذِينَ ءَامَنُوا۟ ٱتَّقُوا۟ ٱللَّهَ حَقَّ تُقَاتِهِۦ وَلَا تَمُوتُنَّ إِلَّا وَأَنتُم مُّسْلِمُونَ}$$

O you who believe! Fear Allâh (by doing all that He has ordered and by abstaining from all that He has forbidden) as He should be feared. (Obey Him, be thankful to Him, and remember Him always), and die not except in a state of Islâm (as Muslims (with complete submission to Allâh)).

$$\text{يَٰٓأَيُّهَا ٱلنَّاسُ ٱتَّقُوا۟ رَبَّكُمُ ٱلَّذِى خَلَقَكُم مِّن نَّفْسٍ وَٰحِدَةٍ وَخَلَقَ مِنْهَا زَوْجَهَا وَبَثَّ مِنْهُمَا رِجَالًا كَثِيرًا وَنِسَآءً وَٱتَّقُوا۟ ٱللَّهَ ٱلَّذِى تَسَآءَلُونَ بِهِۦ وَٱلْأَرْحَامَ إِنَّ ٱللَّهَ كَانَ عَلَيْكُمْ رَقِيبًا}$$

O mankind! Be dutiful to your Lord, Who created you from a single person (Adam), and from him (Adam) He created his wife (Hawwâ (Eve)) and from them both He created many men and women; and fear Allâh through Whom you demand (your mutual rights), and (do not cut the relations of) the wombs (kinship). Surely, Allâh is Ever an All-Watcher over you.

$$\text{يُصْلِحْ لَكُمْ أَعْمَٰلَكُمْ وَيَغْفِرْ لَكُمْ ذُنُوبَكُمْ وَمَن يُطِعِ ٱللَّهَ وَرَسُولَهُۥ فَقَدْ فَازَ فَوْزًا عَظِيمًا}$$

He will direct you to do righteous good deeds and will forgive you your sins. And whosoever obeys Allâh and His Messenger (peace be upon him), he has indeed achieved a great achievement (i.e. he will be saved from the Hell-fire and will be admitted to Paradise).

Indeed, the best speech is Allah's Book and the best guidance is Muhammad's () guidance. The worst affairs (of religion) are those innovated (by people), for every such innovation is an act of misguidance leading to the Fire

Our Mission

Our mission is to gather in one place, for the English-speaking public, all relevant information needed to make the Qur'an more understandable and easier to study. This book tries to do this by providing the following:

1. The Arabic Text for those who are able to read Arabic
2. Transliteration of the Arabic text for those who are unable to read the Arabic script. This will give them a sample of the sound of the Qur'an, which they could not otherwise comprehend from reading the English meaning.
3. The meaning of the qur'an (translated by Dr. Muhammad Taqi-ud-Din Al-Hilali, Ph.D. and Dr. Muhammad Muhsin Khan)
4. Explanation (abridged Tafsir) by Ibn Kathir (translated by Safi-ur-Rahman al-Mubarakpuri)

We hope that by doing this an ordinary English-speaker will be able to pick up a copy of this book and study and comprehend The Glorious Qur'an in a way that is acceptable to the understanding of the Rightly-guided Muslim Ummah (Community).

Biography of Hafiz Ibn Kathir (701 H - 774 H)

By the Honored Shaykh `Abdul-Qadir Al-Arna'ut, may Allah protect him.

He is the respected Imam, Abu Al-Fida', `Imad Ad-Din Isma il bin 'Umar bin Kathir Al-Qurashi Al-Busrawi - Busraian in origin; Dimashqi in training, learning and residence.

Ibn Kathir was born in the city of Busra in 701 H. His father was the Friday speaker of the village, but he died while Ibn Kathir was only four years old. Ibn Kathir's brother, Shaykh Abdul-Wahhab, reared him and taught him until he moved to Damascus in 706 H., when he was five years old.

Ibn Kathir's Teachers

Ibn Kathir studied Fiqh - Islamic jurisprudence - with Burhan Ad-Din, Ibrahim bin `Abdur-Rahman Al-Fizari, known as Ibn Al-Firkah (who died in 729 H). Ibn Kathir heard Hadiths from `Isa bin Al-Mutim, Ahmad bin Abi Talib, (Ibn Ash-Shahnah) (who died in 730 H), Ibn Al-Hajjar, (who died in 730 H), and the Hadith narrator of Ash-Sham (modern day Syria and surrounding areas); Baha Ad-Din Al-Qasim bin Muzaffar bin `Asakir (who died in 723 H), and Ibn Ash-Shirdzi, Ishaq bin Yahya Al-Ammuddi, also known as `Afif Ad-Din, the Zahiriyyah Shaykh who died in 725 H, and Muhammad bin Zarrad. He remained with Jamal Ad-Din, Yusuf bin Az-Zaki AlMizzi who died in 724 H, he benefited from his knowledge and also married his daughter. He also read with Shaykh Al-Islam, Taqi Ad-Din Ahmad bin `Abdul-Halim bin `Abdus-Salam bin Taymiyyah who died in 728 H. He also read with the Imam Hafiz and historian Shams Ad-Din, Muhammad bin Ahmad bin Uthman bin Qaymaz Adh-Dhahabi, who died in 748 H. Also, Abu Musa Al-Qarafai, Abu Al-Fath Ad-Dabbusi and

'Ali bin `Umar As-Suwani and others who gave him permission to transmit the knowledge he learned with them in Egypt.

In his book, Al-Mu jam Al-Mukhtas, Al-Hafiz Adh-Dhaliabi wrote that Ibn Kathir was, "The Imam, scholar of jurisprudence, skillful scholar of Hadith, renowned Faqih and scholar of Tafsir who wrote several beneficial books."

Further, in Ad-Durar Al-Kdminah, Al-Hafiz Ibn Hajar AlAsqalani said, "Ibn Kathir worked on the subject of the Hadith in the areas of texts and chains of narrators. He had a good memory, his books became popular during his lifetime, and people benefited from them after his death."

Also, the renowned historian Abu Al-Mahasin, Jamal Ad-Din Yusuf bin Sayf Ad-Din (Ibn Taghri Bardi), said in his book, AlManhal As-Safi, "He is the Shaykh, the Imam, the great scholar `Imad Ad-Din Abu Al-Fida'. He learned extensively and was very active in collecting knowledge and writing. He was excellent in the areas of Fiqh, Tafsfr and Hadith. He collected knowledge, authored (books), taught, narrated Hadith and wrote. He had immense knowledge in the fields of Hadith, Tafsir, Fiqh, the Arabic language, and so forth. He gave Fatawa (religious verdicts) and taught until he died, may Allah grant him mercy. He was known for his precision and vast knowledge, and as a scholar of history, Hadith and Tafsir."

Ibn Kathir's Students

Ibn Hajji was one of Ibn Kathir's students, and he described Ibn Kathir: "He had the best memory of the Hadith texts. He also had the most knowledge concerning the narrators and authenticity, his contemporaries and teachers admitted to these qualities. Every time I met him I gained some benefit from him."

Also, Ibn Al-`Imad Al-Hanbali said in his book, Shadhardt Adh-Dhahab, "He is the renowned Hafiz `Imad Ad-Din, whose memory was excellent, whose forgetfulness was miniscule, whose understanding was adequate, and who had good knowledge in the Arabic language." Also, Ibn Habib said about Ibn Kathir, "He heard knowledge and collected it and wrote various books. He brought comfort to the ears with his Fatwas and narrated Hadith and brought benefit to other people. The papers that contained his Fatwas were transmitted to the various (Islamic) provinces. Further, he was known for his precision and encompassing knowledge."

Ibn Kathir's Books

1 - One of the greatest books that Ibn Kathir wrote was his Tafsir of the Noble Qur'an, which is one of the best Tafsir that rely on narrations [of Ahadith, the Tafsir of the Companions, etc.]. The Tafsir by Ibn Kathir was printed many times and several scholars have summarized it.

2- The History Collection known as Al-Biddyah, which was printed in 14 volumes under the name Al-Bidayah wanNihdyah, and contained the stories of the Prophets and previous nations, the Prophet's Seerah (life story) and Islamic history until his time. He also added a book Al-Fitan, about the Signs of the Last Hour.

3- At-Takmil ft Ma`rifat Ath-Thiqat wa Ad-Du'afa wal Majdhil which Ibn Kathir collected from the books of his two Shaykhs Al-Mizzi and Adh-Dhahabi; Al-Kdmal and Mizan Al-Ftiddl. He added several benefits regarding the subject of Al-Jarh and AtT'adil.

4- Al-Hadi was-Sunan ft Ahadith Al-Masdnfd was-Sunan which is also known by, Jami` Al-Masdnfd. In this book, Ibn Kathir collected the narrations of Imams Ahmad bin Hanbal, Al-Bazzar, Abu Ya`la Al-Mawsili, Ibn Abi Shaybah and from the six collections of Hadith: the Two Sahihs [Al-Bukhari and Muslim] and the Four Sunan [Abu Dawud, At-Tirmidhi, AnNasa and Ibn Majah]. Ibn Kathir divided this book according to areas of Fiqh.

5-Tabaqat Ash-Shaf iyah which also contains the virtues of Imam Ash-Shafi.

6- Ibn Kathir wrote references for the Ahadith of Adillat AtTanbfh, from the Shafi school of Fiqh.

7- Ibn Kathir began an explanation of Sahih Al-Bukhari, but he did not finish it.

8- He started writing a large volume on the Ahkam (Laws), but finished only up to the Hajj rituals.

9- He summarized Al-Bayhaqi's 'Al-Madkhal. Many of these books were not printed.

10- He summarized `Ulum Al-Hadith, by Abu `Amr bin AsSalah and called it Mukhtasar `Ulum Al-Hadith. Shaykh Ahmad Shakir, the Egyptian Muhaddith, printed this book along with his commentary on it and called it Al-Ba'th Al-Hathfth fi Sharh Mukhtasar `Ulum Al-Hadith.

11- As-Sfrah An-Nabawiyyah, which is contained in his book Al-Biddyah, and both of these books are in print.

12- A research on Jihad called Al-Ijtihad ft Talabi Al-Jihad, which was printed several times.

Ibn Kathir's Death

Al-Hafiz Ibn Hajar Al-Asgalani said, "Ibn Kathir lost his sight just before his life ended. He died in Damascus in 774 H." May Allah grant mercy upon Ibn Kathir and make him among the residents of His Paradise.

PREFACE

In the name of Allah, Most Gracious, Most Merciful.

About this book

The previous publication of this book included some background information to the chapters of the Qur'an by an Islamic scholar known as Abul Ala Maududi. This information was used to shed more light on the chapters by giving a summery of why each chapter was given its name, It's period of revelation and the circumstances surrounding its revelatiom. However, some Muslims objected to the inclusion of the contributions of Maududi.

In this new publication of Tafsir Ibn Kathir, we have removed all traces of the contribution of Abul Ala Maududi. Personally, I do not know the reasons for the objections to Maududi, but this work concerns only the tafsir of Ibn Kathir, so we have not included anything from Maududi in it. We have also corrected all the typing and formatting errors found in the previous publication. We have not alter the structure of the book. The reader is still able to read the full Arabic Text of the thirty Parts of the Qur'an and follow its meanings in the English language. The transliteration of the Arabic text should also give the reader a taste of the sound of the original Arabic.

May Almighty Allah accept this effort from us, and make it a source of blessings for us in this world and in the next. I bear witness that there is none worthy of worship but Allah and I bear witness that Muhammad (may the peace and blessings of Allah be upon him) is the slave and messenger of Allah.

Performing Prostration While Reading the Qur'an

Question:

Could you please give a list of the Qur'anic verses when a prostration is recommended? What happens if we read these verses and not perform a prostration?

A. Jalil

Answer:

There are 15 verses in the Qur'an that mention prostration before God Almighty as a good action by God-fearing believers. Therefore, it is strongly recommended to perform such a prostration when we read or listen to any of these verses, whether during prayer or in any situation.

Some scholars are of the view that even if one has not performed ablution, one should prostrate oneself. These verses are given here, starting with the Arabic title of the surah which is followed by two numbers, the first indicating the surah, and the second indicating the verse,: Al-Araf 7: 206; Al-Raad 13: 15; Al-Nahl 16: 50; Al-Isra 17: 109; Maryam 19: 58; Al-Hajj 22: 18 & 22: 77; Al-Furqan 25: 60; Al-Naml 27: 26;

Al-Sajdah 32: 15; Saad 38: 25; Fussilat 41: 38; Al-Najm 53: 62; Al-Inshiqaq 84: 21 and Al-Alaq 96: 19.

If you do not perform a prostration when you read or listen to any of these verses, you have done badly because you miss out on the reward of performing a prostration for God. You incur no sin and violate no divine order.

Reference:
http://archive.arabnews.com/?page=5&section=0&article=97811&d=1&m=7&y=2007

The Glorious Qur'an Juz' 9 (Part 9): Chapter (Surah) 7: Al-Araf (The Heights) 088 To Chapter (Surah) 8: Al-Anfal (Spoils Of War, Booty) 040

PART 9 FULL ARABIC TEXT

Chapter (Surah) 7: Al-A'raf 088-206

﴿ ٭ قَالَ ٱلْمَلَأُ ٱلَّذِينَ ٱسْتَكْبَرُوا۟ مِن قَوْمِهِۦ لَنُخْرِجَنَّكَ يَـٰشُعَيْبُ وَٱلَّذِينَ ءَامَنُوا۟ مَعَكَ مِن قَرْيَتِنَآ أَوْ لَتَعُودُنَّ فِى مِلَّتِنَا ۚ قَالَ أَوَلَوْ كُنَّا كَـٰرِهِينَ ۝ قَدِ ٱفْتَرَيْنَا عَلَى ٱللَّهِ كَذِبًا إِنْ عُدْنَا فِى مِلَّتِكُم بَعْدَ إِذْ نَجَّىٰنَا ٱللَّهُ مِنْهَا ۚ وَمَا يَكُونُ لَنَآ أَن نَّعُودَ فِيهَآ إِلَّآ أَن يَشَآءَ ٱللَّهُ رَبُّنَا ۚ وَسِعَ رَبُّنَا كُلَّ شَىْءٍ عِلْمًا ۚ عَلَى ٱللَّهِ تَوَكَّلْنَا ۚ رَبَّنَا ٱفْتَحْ بَيْنَنَا وَبَيْنَ قَوْمِنَا بِٱلْحَقِّ وَأَنتَ خَيْرُ ٱلْفَـٰتِحِينَ ۝ وَقَالَ ٱلْمَلَأُ ٱلَّذِينَ كَفَرُوا۟ مِن قَوْمِهِۦ لَئِنِ ٱتَّبَعْتُمْ شُعَيْبًا إِنَّكُمْ إِذًا لَّخَـٰسِرُونَ ۝ فَأَخَذَتْهُمُ ٱلرَّجْفَةُ فَأَصْبَحُوا۟ فِى دَارِهِمْ جَـٰثِمِينَ ۝ ٱلَّذِينَ كَذَّبُوا۟ شُعَيْبًا كَأَن لَّمْ يَغْنَوْا۟ فِيهَا ۚ ٱلَّذِينَ كَذَّبُوا۟ شُعَيْبًا كَانُوا۟ هُمُ ٱلْخَـٰسِرِينَ ۝ فَتَوَلَّىٰ عَنْهُمْ وَقَالَ يَـٰقَوْمِ لَقَدْ أَبْلَغْتُكُمْ رِسَـٰلَـٰتِ رَبِّى وَنَصَحْتُ لَكُمْ ۖ فَكَيْفَ ءَاسَىٰ عَلَىٰ قَوْمٍ كَـٰفِرِينَ ۝ وَمَآ أَرْسَلْنَا فِى قَرْيَةٍ مِّن نَّبِىٍّ إِلَّآ أَخَذْنَآ أَهْلَهَا بِٱلْبَأْسَآءِ وَٱلضَّرَّآءِ لَعَلَّهُمْ يَضَّرَّعُونَ ۝ ثُمَّ بَدَّلْنَا مَكَانَ ٱلسَّيِّئَةِ ٱلْحَسَنَةَ حَتَّىٰ عَفَوا۟ وَّقَالُوا۟ قَدْ مَسَّ ءَابَآءَنَا ٱلضَّرَّآءُ وَٱلسَّرَّآءُ فَأَخَذْنَـٰهُم بَغْتَةً وَهُمْ لَا يَشْعُرُونَ ۝ وَلَوْ أَنَّ أَهْلَ ٱلْقُرَىٰٓ ءَامَنُوا۟ وَٱتَّقَوْا۟ لَفَتَحْنَا عَلَيْهِم بَرَكَـٰتٍ مِّنَ ٱلسَّمَآءِ وَٱلْأَرْضِ وَلَـٰكِن كَذَّبُوا۟ فَأَخَذْنَـٰهُم بِمَا كَانُوا۟ يَكْسِبُونَ ۝ أَفَأَمِنَ أَهْلُ ٱلْقُرَىٰٓ أَن يَأْتِيَهُم بَأْسُنَا بَيَـٰتًا وَهُمْ نَآئِمُونَ ۝ أَوَأَمِنَ أَهْلُ

ٱلْقُرَىٰٓ أَن يَأْتِيَهُم بَأْسُنَا ضُحًى وَهُمْ يَلْعَبُونَ ۝ أَفَأَمِنُوا۟ مَكْرَ ٱللَّهِ ۚ فَلَا يَأْمَنُ مَكْرَ ٱللَّهِ إِلَّا ٱلْقَوْمُ ٱلْخَـٰسِرُونَ ۝ أَوَلَمْ يَهْدِ لِلَّذِينَ يَرِثُونَ ٱلْأَرْضَ مِنۢ بَعْدِ أَهْلِهَآ أَن لَّوْ نَشَآءُ أَصَبْنَـٰهُم بِذُنُوبِهِمْ ۚ وَنَطْبَعُ عَلَىٰ قُلُوبِهِمْ فَهُمْ لَا يَسْمَعُونَ ۝ تِلْكَ ٱلْقُرَىٰ نَقُصُّ عَلَيْكَ مِنْ أَنۢبَآئِهَا ۚ وَلَقَدْ جَآءَتْهُمْ رُسُلُهُم بِٱلْبَيِّنَـٰتِ فَمَا كَانُوا۟ لِيُؤْمِنُوا۟ بِمَا كَذَّبُوا۟ مِن قَبْلُ ۚ كَذَٰلِكَ يَطْبَعُ ٱللَّهُ عَلَىٰ قُلُوبِ ٱلْكَـٰفِرِينَ ۝ وَمَا وَجَدْنَا لِأَكْثَرِهِم مِّنْ عَهْدٍ ۖ وَإِن وَجَدْنَآ أَكْثَرَهُمْ لَفَـٰسِقِينَ ۝ ثُمَّ بَعَثْنَا مِنۢ بَعْدِهِم مُّوسَىٰ بِـَٔايَـٰتِنَآ إِلَىٰ فِرْعَوْنَ وَمَلَإِيْهِۦ فَظَلَمُوا۟ بِهَا ۖ فَٱنظُرْ كَيْفَ كَانَ عَـٰقِبَةُ ٱلْمُفْسِدِينَ ۝ وَقَالَ مُوسَىٰ يَـٰفِرْعَوْنُ إِنِّى رَسُولٌ مِّن رَّبِّ ٱلْعَـٰلَمِينَ ۝ حَقِيقٌ عَلَىٰٓ أَن لَّآ أَقُولَ عَلَى ٱللَّهِ إِلَّا ٱلْحَقَّ ۚ قَدْ جِئْتُكُم بِبَيِّنَةٍ مِّن رَّبِّكُمْ فَأَرْسِلْ مَعِىَ بَنِىٓ إِسْرَٰٓءِيلَ ۝ قَالَ إِن كُنتَ جِئْتَ بِـَٔايَةٍ فَأْتِ بِهَآ إِن كُنتَ مِنَ ٱلصَّـٰدِقِينَ ۝ فَأَلْقَىٰ عَصَاهُ فَإِذَا هِىَ ثُعْبَانٌ مُّبِينٌ ۝ وَنَزَعَ يَدَهُۥ فَإِذَا هِىَ بَيْضَآءُ لِلنَّـٰظِرِينَ ۝ قَالَ ٱلْمَلَأُ مِن قَوْمِ فِرْعَوْنَ إِنَّ هَـٰذَا لَسَـٰحِرٌ عَلِيمٌ ۝ يُرِيدُ أَن يُخْرِجَكُم مِّنْ أَرْضِكُمْ ۖ فَمَاذَا تَأْمُرُونَ ۝ قَالُوٓا۟ أَرْجِهْ وَأَخَاهُ وَأَرْسِلْ فِى ٱلْمَدَآئِنِ حَـٰشِرِينَ ۝ يَأْتُوكَ بِكُلِّ سَـٰحِرٍ عَلِيمٍ ۝ وَجَآءَ ٱلسَّحَرَةُ فِرْعَوْنَ قَالُوٓا۟ إِنَّ لَنَا لَأَجْرًا إِن كُنَّا نَحْنُ ٱلْغَـٰلِبِينَ ۝ قَالَ نَعَمْ وَإِنَّكُمْ لَمِنَ ٱلْمُقَرَّبِينَ ۝ قَالُوا۟ يَـٰمُوسَىٰٓ إِمَّآ أَن تُلْقِىَ وَإِمَّآ أَن نَّكُونَ نَحْنُ ٱلْمُلْقِينَ ۝ قَالَ أَلْقُوا۟ ۖ فَلَمَّآ أَلْقَوْا۟ سَحَرُوٓا۟ أَعْيُنَ ٱلنَّاسِ وَٱسْتَرْهَبُوهُمْ وَجَآءُو بِسِحْرٍ عَظِيمٍ ۝ ۞ وَأَوْحَيْنَآ إِلَىٰ مُوسَىٰٓ أَنْ أَلْقِ عَصَاكَ ۖ فَإِذَا هِىَ تَلْقَفُ مَا يَأْفِكُونَ ۝ فَوَقَعَ ٱلْحَقُّ وَبَطَلَ مَا كَانُوا۟ يَعْمَلُونَ ۝ فَغُلِبُوا۟ هُنَالِكَ وَٱنقَلَبُوا۟ صَـٰغِرِينَ ۝ وَأُلْقِىَ ٱلسَّحَرَةُ سَـٰجِدِينَ ۝ قَالُوٓا۟ ءَامَنَّا بِرَبِّ ٱلْعَـٰلَمِينَ

﴿ رَبِّ مُوسَىٰ وَهَٰرُونَ ۝ قَالَ فِرْعَوْنُ ءَامَنتُم بِهِۦ قَبْلَ أَنْ ءَاذَنَ لَكُمْ ۖ إِنَّ هَٰذَا لَمَكْرٌ مَّكَرْتُمُوهُ فِى ٱلْمَدِينَةِ لِتُخْرِجُوا۟ مِنْهَآ أَهْلَهَا ۖ فَسَوْفَ تَعْلَمُونَ ۝ لَأُقَطِّعَنَّ أَيْدِيَكُمْ وَأَرْجُلَكُم مِّنْ خِلَٰفٍ ثُمَّ لَأُصَلِّبَنَّكُمْ أَجْمَعِينَ ۝ قَالُوٓا۟ إِنَّآ إِلَىٰ رَبِّنَا مُنقَلِبُونَ ۝ وَمَا تَنقِمُ مِنَّآ إِلَّآ أَنْ ءَامَنَّا بِـَٔايَٰتِ رَبِّنَا لَمَّا جَآءَتْنَا ۚ رَبَّنَآ أَفْرِغْ عَلَيْنَا صَبْرًا وَتَوَفَّنَا مُسْلِمِينَ ۝ وَقَالَ ٱلْمَلَأُ مِن قَوْمِ فِرْعَوْنَ أَتَذَرُ مُوسَىٰ وَقَوْمَهُۥ لِيُفْسِدُوا۟ فِى ٱلْأَرْضِ وَيَذَرَكَ وَءَالِهَتَكَ ۚ قَالَ سَنُقَتِّلُ أَبْنَآءَهُمْ وَنَسْتَحْىِۦ نِسَآءَهُمْ وَإِنَّا فَوْقَهُمْ قَٰهِرُونَ ۝ قَالَ مُوسَىٰ لِقَوْمِهِ ٱسْتَعِينُوا۟ بِٱللَّهِ وَٱصْبِرُوٓا۟ ۖ إِنَّ ٱلْأَرْضَ لِلَّهِ يُورِثُهَا مَن يَشَآءُ مِنْ عِبَادِهِۦ ۖ وَٱلْعَٰقِبَةُ لِلْمُتَّقِينَ ۝ قَالُوٓا۟ أُوذِينَا مِن قَبْلِ أَن تَأْتِيَنَا وَمِنۢ بَعْدِ مَا جِئْتَنَا ۚ قَالَ عَسَىٰ رَبُّكُمْ أَن يُهْلِكَ عَدُوَّكُمْ وَيَسْتَخْلِفَكُمْ فِى ٱلْأَرْضِ فَيَنظُرَ كَيْفَ تَعْمَلُونَ ۝ وَلَقَدْ أَخَذْنَآ ءَالَ فِرْعَوْنَ بِٱلسِّنِينَ وَنَقْصٍ مِّنَ ٱلثَّمَرَٰتِ لَعَلَّهُمْ يَذَّكَّرُونَ ۝ فَإِذَا جَآءَتْهُمُ ٱلْحَسَنَةُ قَالُوا۟ لَنَا هَٰذِهِۦ ۖ وَإِن تُصِبْهُمْ سَيِّئَةٌ يَطَّيَّرُوا۟ بِمُوسَىٰ وَمَن مَّعَهُۥٓ ۗ أَلَآ إِنَّمَا طَٰٓئِرُهُمْ عِندَ ٱللَّهِ وَلَٰكِنَّ أَكْثَرَهُمْ لَا يَعْلَمُونَ ۝ وَقَالُوا۟ مَهْمَا تَأْتِنَا بِهِۦ مِنْ ءَايَةٍ لِّتَسْحَرَنَا بِهَا فَمَا نَحْنُ لَكَ بِمُؤْمِنِينَ ۝ فَأَرْسَلْنَا عَلَيْهِمُ ٱلطُّوفَانَ وَٱلْجَرَادَ وَٱلْقُمَّلَ وَٱلضَّفَادِعَ وَٱلدَّمَ ءَايَٰتٍ مُّفَصَّلَٰتٍ فَٱسْتَكْبَرُوا۟ وَكَانُوا۟ قَوْمًا مُّجْرِمِينَ ۝ وَلَمَّا وَقَعَ عَلَيْهِمُ ٱلرِّجْزُ قَالُوا۟ يَٰمُوسَى ٱدْعُ لَنَا رَبَّكَ بِمَا عَهِدَ عِندَكَ ۖ لَئِن كَشَفْتَ عَنَّا ٱلرِّجْزَ لَنُؤْمِنَنَّ لَكَ وَلَنُرْسِلَنَّ مَعَكَ بَنِىٓ إِسْرَٰٓءِيلَ ۝ فَلَمَّا كَشَفْنَا عَنْهُمُ ٱلرِّجْزَ إِلَىٰٓ أَجَلٍ هُم بَٰلِغُوهُ إِذَا هُمْ يَنكُثُونَ ۝ فَٱنتَقَمْنَا مِنْهُمْ فَأَغْرَقْنَٰهُمْ فِى ٱلْيَمِّ بِأَنَّهُمْ كَذَّبُوا۟ بِـَٔايَٰتِنَا وَكَانُوا۟ عَنْهَا غَٰفِلِينَ ۝ وَأَوْرَثْنَا ٱلْقَوْمَ ٱلَّذِينَ كَانُوا۟ يُسْتَضْعَفُونَ مَشَٰرِقَ

ٱلْأَرْضِ وَمَغَٰرِبَهَا ٱلَّتِى بَٰرَكْنَا فِيهَا ۖ وَتَمَّتْ كَلِمَتُ رَبِّكَ ٱلْحُسْنَىٰ عَلَىٰ بَنِىٓ إِسْرَٰٓءِيلَ بِمَا صَبَرُوا۟ ۖ وَدَمَّرْنَا مَا كَانَ يَصْنَعُ فِرْعَوْنُ وَقَوْمُهُۥ وَمَا كَانُوا۟ يَعْرِشُونَ ۝١٣٧ وَجَٰوَزْنَا بِبَنِىٓ إِسْرَٰٓءِيلَ ٱلْبَحْرَ فَأَتَوْا۟ عَلَىٰ قَوْمٍ يَعْكُفُونَ عَلَىٰٓ أَصْنَامٍ لَّهُمْ ۚ قَالُوا۟ يَٰمُوسَى ٱجْعَل لَّنَآ إِلَٰهًا كَمَا لَهُمْ ءَالِهَةٌ ۚ قَالَ إِنَّكُمْ قَوْمٌ تَجْهَلُونَ ۝١٣٨ إِنَّ هَٰٓؤُلَآءِ مُتَبَّرٌ مَّا هُمْ فِيهِ وَبَٰطِلٌ مَّا كَانُوا۟ يَعْمَلُونَ ۝١٣٩ قَالَ أَغَيْرَ ٱللَّهِ أَبْغِيكُمْ إِلَٰهًا وَهُوَ فَضَّلَكُمْ عَلَى ٱلْعَٰلَمِينَ ۝١٤٠ وَإِذْ أَنجَيْنَٰكُم مِّنْ ءَالِ فِرْعَوْنَ يَسُومُونَكُمْ سُوٓءَ ٱلْعَذَابِ ۖ يُقَتِّلُونَ أَبْنَآءَكُمْ وَيَسْتَحْيُونَ نِسَآءَكُمْ ۚ وَفِى ذَٰلِكُم بَلَآءٌ مِّن رَّبِّكُمْ عَظِيمٌ ۝١٤١ ۞ وَوَٰعَدْنَا مُوسَىٰ ثَلَٰثِينَ لَيْلَةً وَأَتْمَمْنَٰهَا بِعَشْرٍ فَتَمَّ مِيقَٰتُ رَبِّهِۦٓ أَرْبَعِينَ لَيْلَةً ۚ وَقَالَ مُوسَىٰ لِأَخِيهِ هَٰرُونَ ٱخْلُفْنِى فِى قَوْمِى وَأَصْلِحْ وَلَا تَتَّبِعْ سَبِيلَ ٱلْمُفْسِدِينَ ۝١٤٢ وَلَمَّا جَآءَ مُوسَىٰ لِمِيقَٰتِنَا وَكَلَّمَهُۥ رَبُّهُۥ قَالَ رَبِّ أَرِنِىٓ أَنظُرْ إِلَيْكَ ۚ قَالَ لَن تَرَىٰنِى وَلَٰكِنِ ٱنظُرْ إِلَى ٱلْجَبَلِ فَإِنِ ٱسْتَقَرَّ مَكَانَهُۥ فَسَوْفَ تَرَىٰنِى ۚ فَلَمَّا تَجَلَّىٰ رَبُّهُۥ لِلْجَبَلِ جَعَلَهُۥ دَكًّا وَخَرَّ مُوسَىٰ صَعِقًا ۚ فَلَمَّآ أَفَاقَ قَالَ سُبْحَٰنَكَ تُبْتُ إِلَيْكَ وَأَنَا۠ أَوَّلُ ٱلْمُؤْمِنِينَ ۝١٤٣ قَالَ يَٰمُوسَىٰٓ إِنِّى ٱصْطَفَيْتُكَ عَلَى ٱلنَّاسِ بِرِسَٰلَٰتِى وَبِكَلَٰمِى فَخُذْ مَآ ءَاتَيْتُكَ وَكُن مِّنَ ٱلشَّٰكِرِينَ ۝١٤٤ وَكَتَبْنَا لَهُۥ فِى ٱلْأَلْوَاحِ مِن كُلِّ شَىْءٍ مَّوْعِظَةً وَتَفْصِيلًا لِّكُلِّ شَىْءٍ فَخُذْهَا بِقُوَّةٍ وَأْمُرْ قَوْمَكَ يَأْخُذُوا۟ بِأَحْسَنِهَا ۚ سَأُو۟رِيكُمْ دَارَ ٱلْفَٰسِقِينَ ۝١٤٥ سَأَصْرِفُ عَنْ ءَايَٰتِىَ ٱلَّذِينَ يَتَكَبَّرُونَ فِى ٱلْأَرْضِ بِغَيْرِ ٱلْحَقِّ وَإِن يَرَوْا۟ كُلَّ ءَايَةٍ لَّا يُؤْمِنُوا۟ بِهَا وَإِن يَرَوْا۟ سَبِيلَ ٱلرُّشْدِ لَا يَتَّخِذُوهُ سَبِيلًا وَإِن يَرَوْا۟ سَبِيلَ ٱلْغَىِّ يَتَّخِذُوهُ سَبِيلًا ۚ ذَٰلِكَ بِأَنَّهُمْ كَذَّبُوا۟ بِـَٔايَٰتِنَا وَكَانُوا۟ عَنْهَا غَٰفِلِينَ ۝١٤٦ وَٱلَّذِينَ كَذَّبُوا۟ بِـَٔايَٰتِنَا وَلِقَآءِ ٱلْءَاخِرَةِ

حَبِطَتْ أَعْمَـٰلُهُمْ ۚ هَلْ يُجْزَوْنَ إِلَّا مَا كَانُوا۟ يَعْمَلُونَ ۝ وَٱتَّخَذَ قَوْمُ مُوسَىٰ مِنۢ بَعْدِهِۦ مِنْ حُلِيِّهِمْ عِجْلًا جَسَدًا لَّهُۥ خُوَارٌ ۚ أَلَمْ يَرَوْا۟ أَنَّهُۥ لَا يُكَلِّمُهُمْ وَلَا يَهْدِيهِمْ سَبِيلًا ۘ ٱتَّخَذُوهُ وَكَانُوا۟ ظَـٰلِمِينَ ۝ وَلَمَّا سُقِطَ فِىٓ أَيْدِيهِمْ وَرَأَوْا۟ أَنَّهُمْ قَدْ ضَلُّوا۟ قَالُوا۟ لَئِن لَّمْ يَرْحَمْنَا رَبُّنَا وَيَغْفِرْ لَنَا لَنَكُونَنَّ مِنَ ٱلْخَـٰسِرِينَ ۝ وَلَمَّا رَجَعَ مُوسَىٰٓ إِلَىٰ قَوْمِهِۦ غَضْبَـٰنَ أَسِفًا قَالَ بِئْسَمَا خَلَفْتُمُونِى مِنۢ بَعْدِىٓ ۖ أَعَجِلْتُمْ أَمْرَ رَبِّكُمْ ۖ وَأَلْقَى ٱلْأَلْوَاحَ وَأَخَذَ بِرَأْسِ أَخِيهِ يَجُرُّهُۥٓ إِلَيْهِ ۚ قَالَ ٱبْنَ أُمَّ إِنَّ ٱلْقَوْمَ ٱسْتَضْعَفُونِى وَكَادُوا۟ يَقْتُلُونَنِى فَلَا تُشْمِتْ بِىَ ٱلْأَعْدَآءَ وَلَا تَجْعَلْنِى مَعَ ٱلْقَوْمِ ٱلظَّـٰلِمِينَ ۝ قَالَ رَبِّ ٱغْفِرْ لِى وَلِأَخِى وَأَدْخِلْنَا فِى رَحْمَتِكَ ۖ وَأَنتَ أَرْحَمُ ٱلرَّٰحِمِينَ ۝ إِنَّ ٱلَّذِينَ ٱتَّخَذُوا۟ ٱلْعِجْلَ سَيَنَالُهُمْ غَضَبٌ مِّن رَّبِّهِمْ وَذِلَّةٌ فِى ٱلْحَيَوٰةِ ٱلدُّنْيَا ۚ وَكَذَٰلِكَ نَجْزِى ٱلْمُفْتَرِينَ ۝ وَٱلَّذِينَ عَمِلُوا۟ ٱلسَّيِّئَاتِ ثُمَّ تَابُوا۟ مِنۢ بَعْدِهَا وَءَامَنُوٓا۟ إِنَّ رَبَّكَ مِنۢ بَعْدِهَا لَغَفُورٌ رَّحِيمٌ ۝ وَلَمَّا سَكَتَ عَن مُّوسَى ٱلْغَضَبُ أَخَذَ ٱلْأَلْوَاحَ ۖ وَفِى نُسْخَتِهَا هُدًى وَرَحْمَةٌ لِّلَّذِينَ هُمْ لِرَبِّهِمْ يَرْهَبُونَ ۝ وَٱخْتَارَ مُوسَىٰ قَوْمَهُۥ سَبْعِينَ رَجُلًا لِّمِيقَـٰتِنَا ۖ فَلَمَّآ أَخَذَتْهُمُ ٱلرَّجْفَةُ قَالَ رَبِّ لَوْ شِئْتَ أَهْلَكْتَهُم مِّن قَبْلُ وَإِيَّـٰىَ ۖ أَتُهْلِكُنَا بِمَا فَعَلَ ٱلسُّفَهَآءُ مِنَّآ ۖ إِنْ هِىَ إِلَّا فِتْنَتُكَ تُضِلُّ بِهَا مَن تَشَآءُ وَتَهْدِى مَن تَشَآءُ ۖ أَنتَ وَلِيُّنَا فَٱغْفِرْ لَنَا وَٱرْحَمْنَا ۖ وَأَنتَ خَيْرُ ٱلْغَـٰفِرِينَ ۝ ۞ وَٱكْتُبْ لَنَا فِى هَـٰذِهِ ٱلدُّنْيَا حَسَنَةً وَفِى ٱلْـَٔاخِرَةِ إِنَّا هُدْنَآ إِلَيْكَ ۚ قَالَ عَذَابِىٓ أُصِيبُ بِهِۦ مَنْ أَشَآءُ ۖ وَرَحْمَتِى وَسِعَتْ كُلَّ شَىْءٍ ۚ فَسَأَكْتُبُهَا لِلَّذِينَ يَتَّقُونَ وَيُؤْتُونَ ٱلزَّكَوٰةَ وَٱلَّذِينَ هُم بِـَٔايَـٰتِنَا يُؤْمِنُونَ ۝ ٱلَّذِينَ يَتَّبِعُونَ ٱلرَّسُولَ ٱلنَّبِىَّ ٱلْأُمِّىَّ ٱلَّذِى يَجِدُونَهُۥ مَكْتُوبًا عِندَهُمْ فِى ٱلتَّوْرَىٰةِ وَٱلْإِنجِيلِ يَأْمُرُهُم بِٱلْمَعْرُوفِ وَيَنْهَىٰهُمْ عَنِ

ٱلْمُنكَرَ وَيُحِلُّ لَهُمُ ٱلطَّيِّبَـٰتِ وَيُحَرِّمُ عَلَيْهِمُ ٱلْخَبَـٰٓئِثَ وَيَضَعُ عَنْهُمْ إِصْرَهُمْ وَٱلْأَغْلَـٰلَ ٱلَّتِى كَانَتْ عَلَيْهِمْ ۚ فَٱلَّذِينَ ءَامَنُوا۟ بِهِۦ وَعَزَّرُوهُ وَنَصَرُوهُ وَٱتَّبَعُوا۟ ٱلنُّورَ ٱلَّذِىٓ أُنزِلَ مَعَهُۥٓ ۙ أُو۟لَـٰٓئِكَ هُمُ ٱلْمُفْلِحُونَ ۝١٥٧ قُلْ يَـٰٓأَيُّهَا ٱلنَّاسُ إِنِّى رَسُولُ ٱللَّهِ إِلَيْكُمْ جَمِيعًا ٱلَّذِى لَهُۥ مُلْكُ ٱلسَّمَـٰوَٰتِ وَٱلْأَرْضِ ۖ لَآ إِلَـٰهَ إِلَّا هُوَ يُحْىِۦ وَيُمِيتُ ۖ فَـَٔامِنُوا۟ بِٱللَّهِ وَرَسُولِهِ ٱلنَّبِىِّ ٱلْأُمِّىِّ ٱلَّذِى يُؤْمِنُ بِٱللَّهِ وَكَلِمَـٰتِهِۦ وَٱتَّبِعُوهُ لَعَلَّكُمْ تَهْتَدُونَ ۝١٥٨ وَمِن قَوْمِ مُوسَىٰٓ أُمَّةٌ يَهْدُونَ بِٱلْحَقِّ وَبِهِۦ يَعْدِلُونَ ۝١٥٩ وَقَطَّعْنَـٰهُمُ ٱثْنَتَىْ عَشْرَةَ أَسْبَاطًا أُمَمًا ۚ وَأَوْحَيْنَآ إِلَىٰ مُوسَىٰٓ إِذِ ٱسْتَسْقَىٰهُ قَوْمُهُۥٓ أَنِ ٱضْرِب بِّعَصَاكَ ٱلْحَجَرَ ۖ فَٱنۢبَجَسَتْ مِنْهُ ٱثْنَتَا عَشْرَةَ عَيْنًا ۖ قَدْ عَلِمَ كُلُّ أُنَاسٍ مَّشْرَبَهُمْ ۚ وَظَلَّلْنَا عَلَيْهِمُ ٱلْغَمَـٰمَ وَأَنزَلْنَا عَلَيْهِمُ ٱلْمَنَّ وَٱلسَّلْوَىٰ ۖ كُلُوا۟ مِن طَيِّبَـٰتِ مَا رَزَقْنَـٰكُمْ ۚ وَمَا ظَلَمُونَا وَلَـٰكِن كَانُوٓا۟ أَنفُسَهُمْ يَظْلِمُونَ ۝١٦٠ وَإِذْ قِيلَ لَهُمُ ٱسْكُنُوا۟ هَـٰذِهِ ٱلْقَرْيَةَ وَكُلُوا۟ مِنْهَا حَيْثُ شِئْتُمْ وَقُولُوا۟ حِطَّةٌ وَٱدْخُلُوا۟ ٱلْبَابَ سُجَّدًا نَّغْفِرْ لَكُمْ خَطِيٓـَٔـٰتِكُمْ ۚ سَنَزِيدُ ٱلْمُحْسِنِينَ ۝١٦١ فَبَدَّلَ ٱلَّذِينَ ظَلَمُوا۟ مِنْهُمْ قَوْلًا غَيْرَ ٱلَّذِى قِيلَ لَهُمْ فَأَرْسَلْنَا عَلَيْهِمْ رِجْزًا مِّنَ ٱلسَّمَآءِ بِمَا كَانُوا۟ يَظْلِمُونَ ۝١٦٢ وَسْـَٔلْهُمْ عَنِ ٱلْقَرْيَةِ ٱلَّتِى كَانَتْ حَاضِرَةَ ٱلْبَحْرِ إِذْ يَعْدُونَ فِى ٱلسَّبْتِ إِذْ تَأْتِيهِمْ حِيتَانُهُمْ يَوْمَ سَبْتِهِمْ شُرَّعًا وَيَوْمَ لَا يَسْبِتُونَ ۙ لَا تَأْتِيهِمْ ۚ كَذَٰلِكَ نَبْلُوهُم بِمَا كَانُوا۟ يَفْسُقُونَ ۝١٦٣ وَإِذْ قَالَتْ أُمَّةٌ مِّنْهُمْ لِمَ تَعِظُونَ قَوْمًا ۙ ٱللَّهُ مُهْلِكُهُمْ أَوْ مُعَذِّبُهُمْ عَذَابًا شَدِيدًا ۖ قَالُوا۟ مَعْذِرَةً إِلَىٰ رَبِّكُمْ وَلَعَلَّهُمْ يَتَّقُونَ ۝١٦٤ فَلَمَّا نَسُوا۟ مَا ذُكِّرُوا۟ بِهِۦٓ أَنجَيْنَا ٱلَّذِينَ يَنْهَوْنَ عَنِ ٱلسُّوٓءِ وَأَخَذْنَا ٱلَّذِينَ ظَلَمُوا۟ بِعَذَابٍۭ بَـِٔيسٍۭ بِمَا كَانُوا۟ يَفْسُقُونَ ۝١٦٥ فَلَمَّا عَتَوْا۟ عَن مَّا نُهُوا۟ عَنْهُ قُلْنَا

هُمْ كُونُوا۟ قِرَدَةً خَـٰسِـِٔينَ ۝ وَإِذْ تَأَذَّنَ رَبُّكَ لَيَبْعَثَنَّ عَلَيْهِمْ إِلَىٰ يَوْمِ ٱلْقِيَـٰمَةِ مَن يَسُومُهُمْ سُوٓءَ ٱلْعَذَابِ ۗ إِنَّ رَبَّكَ لَسَرِيعُ ٱلْعِقَابِ ۖ وَإِنَّهُۥ لَغَفُورٌ رَّحِيمٌ ۝ وَقَطَّعْنَـٰهُمْ فِى ٱلْأَرْضِ أُمَمًا ۖ مِّنْهُمُ ٱلصَّـٰلِحُونَ وَمِنْهُمْ دُونَ ذَٰلِكَ ۖ وَبَلَوْنَـٰهُم بِٱلْحَسَنَـٰتِ وَٱلسَّيِّـَٔاتِ لَعَلَّهُمْ يَرْجِعُونَ ۝ فَخَلَفَ مِنۢ بَعْدِهِمْ خَلْفٌ وَرِثُوا۟ ٱلْكِتَـٰبَ يَأْخُذُونَ عَرَضَ هَـٰذَا ٱلْأَدْنَىٰ وَيَقُولُونَ سَيُغْفَرُ لَنَا وَإِن يَأْتِهِمْ عَرَضٌ مِّثْلُهُۥ يَأْخُذُوهُ ۚ أَلَمْ يُؤْخَذْ عَلَيْهِم مِّيثَـٰقُ ٱلْكِتَـٰبِ أَن لَّا يَقُولُوا۟ عَلَى ٱللَّهِ إِلَّا ٱلْحَقَّ وَدَرَسُوا۟ مَا فِيهِ ۗ وَٱلدَّارُ ٱلْـَٔاخِرَةُ خَيْرٌ لِّلَّذِينَ يَتَّقُونَ ۗ أَفَلَا تَعْقِلُونَ ۝ وَٱلَّذِينَ يُمَسِّكُونَ بِٱلْكِتَـٰبِ وَأَقَامُوا۟ ٱلصَّلَوٰةَ إِنَّا لَا نُضِيعُ أَجْرَ ٱلْمُصْلِحِينَ ۝ ۞ وَإِذْ نَتَقْنَا ٱلْجَبَلَ فَوْقَهُمْ كَأَنَّهُۥ ظُلَّةٌ وَظَنُّوٓا۟ أَنَّهُۥ وَاقِعٌۢ بِهِمْ خُذُوا۟ مَآ ءَاتَيْنَـٰكُم بِقُوَّةٍ وَٱذْكُرُوا۟ مَا فِيهِ لَعَلَّكُمْ تَتَّقُونَ ۝ وَإِذْ أَخَذَ رَبُّكَ مِنۢ بَنِىٓ ءَادَمَ مِن ظُهُورِهِمْ ذُرِّيَّتَهُمْ وَأَشْهَدَهُمْ عَلَىٰٓ أَنفُسِهِمْ أَلَسْتُ بِرَبِّكُمْ ۖ قَالُوا۟ بَلَىٰ ۛ شَهِدْنَآ ۛ أَن تَقُولُوا۟ يَوْمَ ٱلْقِيَـٰمَةِ إِنَّا كُنَّا عَنْ هَـٰذَا غَـٰفِلِينَ ۝ أَوْ تَقُولُوٓا۟ إِنَّمَآ أَشْرَكَ ءَابَآؤُنَا مِن قَبْلُ وَكُنَّا ذُرِّيَّةً مِّنۢ بَعْدِهِمْ ۖ أَفَتُهْلِكُنَا بِمَا فَعَلَ ٱلْمُبْطِلُونَ ۝ وَكَذَٰلِكَ نُفَصِّلُ ٱلْـَٔايَـٰتِ وَلَعَلَّهُمْ يَرْجِعُونَ ۝ وَٱتْلُ عَلَيْهِمْ نَبَأَ ٱلَّذِىٓ ءَاتَيْنَـٰهُ ءَايَـٰتِنَا فَٱنسَلَخَ مِنْهَا فَأَتْبَعَهُ ٱلشَّيْطَـٰنُ فَكَانَ مِنَ ٱلْغَاوِينَ ۝ وَلَوْ شِئْنَا لَرَفَعْنَـٰهُ بِهَا وَلَـٰكِنَّهُۥٓ أَخْلَدَ إِلَى ٱلْأَرْضِ وَٱتَّبَعَ هَوَىٰهُ ۚ فَمَثَلُهُۥ كَمَثَلِ ٱلْكَلْبِ إِن تَحْمِلْ عَلَيْهِ يَلْهَثْ أَوْ تَتْرُكْهُ يَلْهَث ۚ ذَّٰلِكَ مَثَلُ ٱلْقَوْمِ ٱلَّذِينَ كَذَّبُوا۟ بِـَٔايَـٰتِنَا ۚ فَٱقْصُصِ ٱلْقَصَصَ لَعَلَّهُمْ يَتَفَكَّرُونَ ۝ سَآءَ مَثَلًا ٱلْقَوْمُ ٱلَّذِينَ كَذَّبُوا۟ بِـَٔايَـٰتِنَا وَأَنفُسَهُمْ كَانُوا۟ يَظْلِمُونَ ۝ مَن يَهْدِ ٱللَّهُ فَهُوَ ٱلْمُهْتَدِى ۖ وَمَن يُضْلِلْ فَأُو۟لَـٰٓئِكَ هُمُ ٱلْخَـٰسِرُونَ ۝ وَلَقَدْ ذَرَأْنَا لِجَهَنَّمَ كَثِيرًا مِّنَ ٱلْجِنِّ

وَالْإِنسِ ۖ لَهُمْ قُلُوبٌ لَّا يَفْقَهُونَ بِهَا وَلَهُمْ أَعْيُنٌ لَّا يُبْصِرُونَ بِهَا وَلَهُمْ ءَاذَانٌ لَّا يَسْمَعُونَ بِهَا ۚ أُو۟لَٰٓئِكَ كَٱلْأَنْعَٰمِ بَلْ هُمْ أَضَلُّ ۚ أُو۟لَٰٓئِكَ هُمُ ٱلْغَٰفِلُونَ ۞ وَلِلَّهِ ٱلْأَسْمَآءُ ٱلْحُسْنَىٰ فَٱدْعُوهُ بِهَا ۖ وَذَرُوا۟ ٱلَّذِينَ يُلْحِدُونَ فِىٓ أَسْمَٰٓئِهِۦ ۚ سَيُجْزَوْنَ مَا كَانُوا۟ يَعْمَلُونَ ۞ وَمِمَّنْ خَلَقْنَآ أُمَّةٌ يَهْدُونَ بِٱلْحَقِّ وَبِهِۦ يَعْدِلُونَ ۞ وَٱلَّذِينَ كَذَّبُوا۟ بِـَٔايَٰتِنَا سَنَسْتَدْرِجُهُم مِّنْ حَيْثُ لَا يَعْلَمُونَ ۞ وَأُمْلِى لَهُمْ ۚ إِنَّ كَيْدِى مَتِينٌ ۞ أَوَلَمْ يَتَفَكَّرُوا۟ ۗ مَا بِصَاحِبِهِم مِّن جِنَّةٍ ۚ إِنْ هُوَ إِلَّا نَذِيرٌ مُّبِينٌ ۞ أَوَلَمْ يَنظُرُوا۟ فِى مَلَكُوتِ ٱلسَّمَٰوَٰتِ وَٱلْأَرْضِ وَمَا خَلَقَ ٱللَّهُ مِن شَىْءٍ وَأَنْ عَسَىٰٓ أَن يَكُونَ قَدِ ٱقْتَرَبَ أَجَلُهُمْ ۖ فَبِأَىِّ حَدِيثٍۭ بَعْدَهُۥ يُؤْمِنُونَ ۞ مَن يُضْلِلِ ٱللَّهُ فَلَا هَادِىَ لَهُۥ ۚ وَيَذَرُهُمْ فِى طُغْيَٰنِهِمْ يَعْمَهُونَ ۞ يَسْـَٔلُونَكَ عَنِ ٱلسَّاعَةِ أَيَّانَ مُرْسَىٰهَا ۖ قُلْ إِنَّمَا عِلْمُهَا عِندَ رَبِّى ۖ لَا يُجَلِّيهَا لِوَقْتِهَآ إِلَّا هُوَ ۚ ثَقُلَتْ فِى ٱلسَّمَٰوَٰتِ وَٱلْأَرْضِ ۚ لَا تَأْتِيكُمْ إِلَّا بَغْتَةً ۗ يَسْـَٔلُونَكَ كَأَنَّكَ حَفِىٌّ عَنْهَا ۖ قُلْ إِنَّمَا عِلْمُهَا عِندَ ٱللَّهِ وَلَٰكِنَّ أَكْثَرَ ٱلنَّاسِ لَا يَعْلَمُونَ ۞ قُل لَّآ أَمْلِكُ لِنَفْسِى نَفْعًا وَلَا ضَرًّا إِلَّا مَا شَآءَ ٱللَّهُ ۚ وَلَوْ كُنتُ أَعْلَمُ ٱلْغَيْبَ لَٱسْتَكْثَرْتُ مِنَ ٱلْخَيْرِ وَمَا مَسَّنِىَ ٱلسُّوٓءُ ۚ إِنْ أَنَا۠ إِلَّا نَذِيرٌ وَبَشِيرٌ لِّقَوْمٍ يُؤْمِنُونَ ۞ ۞ هُوَ ٱلَّذِى خَلَقَكُم مِّن نَّفْسٍ وَٰحِدَةٍ وَجَعَلَ مِنْهَا زَوْجَهَا لِيَسْكُنَ إِلَيْهَا ۖ فَلَمَّا تَغَشَّىٰهَا حَمَلَتْ حَمْلًا خَفِيفًا فَمَرَّتْ بِهِۦ ۖ فَلَمَّآ أَثْقَلَت دَّعَوَا ٱللَّهَ رَبَّهُمَا لَئِنْ ءَاتَيْتَنَا صَٰلِحًا لَّنَكُونَنَّ مِنَ ٱلشَّٰكِرِينَ ۞ فَلَمَّآ ءَاتَىٰهُمَا صَٰلِحًا جَعَلَا لَهُۥ شُرَكَآءَ فِيمَآ ءَاتَىٰهُمَا ۚ فَتَعَٰلَى ٱللَّهُ عَمَّا يُشْرِكُونَ ۞ أَيُشْرِكُونَ مَا لَا يَخْلُقُ شَيْـًٔا وَهُمْ يُخْلَقُونَ ۞ وَلَا يَسْتَطِيعُونَ لَهُمْ نَصْرًا وَلَآ أَنفُسَهُمْ يَنصُرُونَ ۞ وَإِن تَدْعُوهُمْ إِلَى ٱلْهُدَىٰ لَا يَتَّبِعُوكُمْ ۚ سَوَآءٌ عَلَيْكُمْ أَدَعَوْتُمُوهُمْ أَمْ أَنتُمْ صَٰمِتُونَ ۞

إِنَّ ٱلَّذِينَ تَدْعُونَ مِن دُونِ ٱللَّهِ عِبَادٌ أَمْثَالُكُمْ ۖ فَٱدْعُوهُمْ فَلْيَسْتَجِيبُوا۟ لَكُمْ إِن كُنتُمْ صَـٰدِقِينَ ۝١٩٤ أَلَهُمْ أَرْجُلٌ يَمْشُونَ بِهَآ ۖ أَمْ لَهُمْ أَيْدٍ يَبْطِشُونَ بِهَآ ۖ أَمْ لَهُمْ أَعْيُنٌ يُبْصِرُونَ بِهَآ ۖ أَمْ لَهُمْ ءَاذَانٌ يَسْمَعُونَ بِهَا ۗ قُلِ ٱدْعُوا۟ شُرَكَآءَكُمْ ثُمَّ كِيدُونِ فَلَا تُنظِرُونِ ۝١٩٥ إِنَّ وَلِـِّىَ ٱللَّهُ ٱلَّذِى نَزَّلَ ٱلْكِتَـٰبَ ۖ وَهُوَ يَتَوَلَّى ٱلصَّـٰلِحِينَ ۝١٩٦ وَٱلَّذِينَ تَدْعُونَ مِن دُونِهِۦ لَا يَسْتَطِيعُونَ نَصْرَكُمْ وَلَآ أَنفُسَهُمْ يَنصُرُونَ ۝١٩٧ وَإِن تَدْعُوهُمْ إِلَى ٱلْهُدَىٰ لَا يَسْمَعُوا۟ ۖ وَتَرَىٰهُمْ يَنظُرُونَ إِلَيْكَ وَهُمْ لَا يُبْصِرُونَ ۝١٩٨ خُذِ ٱلْعَفْوَ وَأْمُرْ بِٱلْعُرْفِ وَأَعْرِضْ عَنِ ٱلْجَـٰهِلِينَ ۝١٩٩ وَإِمَّا يَنزَغَنَّكَ مِنَ ٱلشَّيْطَـٰنِ نَزْغٌ فَٱسْتَعِذْ بِٱللَّهِ ۚ إِنَّهُۥ سَمِيعٌ عَلِيمٌ ۝٢٠٠ إِنَّ ٱلَّذِينَ ٱتَّقَوْا۟ إِذَا مَسَّهُمْ طَـٰٓئِفٌ مِّنَ ٱلشَّيْطَـٰنِ تَذَكَّرُوا۟ فَإِذَا هُم مُّبْصِرُونَ ۝٢٠١ وَإِخْوَٰنُهُمْ يَمُدُّونَهُمْ فِى ٱلْغَىِّ ثُمَّ لَا يُقْصِرُونَ ۝٢٠٢ وَإِذَا لَمْ تَأْتِهِم بِـَٔايَةٍ قَالُوا۟ لَوْلَا ٱجْتَبَيْتَهَا ۚ قُلْ إِنَّمَآ أَتَّبِعُ مَا يُوحَىٰٓ إِلَىَّ مِن رَّبِّى ۚ هَـٰذَا بَصَآئِرُ مِن رَّبِّكُمْ وَهُدًى وَرَحْمَةٌ لِّقَوْمٍ يُؤْمِنُونَ ۝٢٠٣ وَإِذَا قُرِئَ ٱلْقُرْءَانُ فَٱسْتَمِعُوا۟ لَهُۥ وَأَنصِتُوا۟ لَعَلَّكُمْ تُرْحَمُونَ ۝٢٠٤ وَٱذْكُر رَّبَّكَ فِى نَفْسِكَ تَضَرُّعًا وَخِيفَةً وَدُونَ ٱلْجَهْرِ مِنَ ٱلْقَوْلِ بِٱلْغُدُوِّ وَٱلْـَٔاصَالِ وَلَا تَكُن مِّنَ ٱلْغَـٰفِلِينَ ۝٢٠٥ إِنَّ ٱلَّذِينَ عِندَ رَبِّكَ لَا يَسْتَكْبِرُونَ عَنْ عِبَادَتِهِۦ وَيُسَبِّحُونَهُۥ وَلَهُۥ يَسْجُدُونَ ۩ ۝٢٠٦

(Al-A'raf 088-206)

Chapter (Surah) 8: Al-Anfal 001-040

بِسْمِ ٱللَّهِ ٱلرَّحْمَـٰنِ ٱلرَّحِيمِ

﴿ يَسْـَٔلُونَكَ عَنِ ٱلْأَنفَالِ ۖ قُلِ ٱلْأَنفَالُ لِلَّهِ وَٱلرَّسُولِ ۖ فَٱتَّقُوا۟ ٱللَّهَ وَأَصْلِحُوا۟ ذَاتَ بَيْنِكُمْ ۖ وَأَطِيعُوا۟ ٱللَّهَ وَرَسُولَهُۥٓ إِن كُنتُم مُّؤْمِنِينَ ۝١ إِنَّمَا ٱلْمُؤْمِنُونَ ٱلَّذِينَ إِذَا ذُكِرَ ٱللَّهُ وَجِلَتْ قُلُوبُهُمْ وَإِذَا تُلِيَتْ عَلَيْهِمْ ءَايَـٰتُهُۥ زَادَتْهُمْ إِيمَـٰنًا وَعَلَىٰ رَبِّهِمْ

يَتَوَكَّلُونَ ۞ ٱلَّذِينَ يُقِيمُونَ ٱلصَّلَوٰةَ وَمِمَّا رَزَقْنَٰهُمْ يُنفِقُونَ ۞ أُوْلَٰٓئِكَ هُمُ ٱلْمُؤْمِنُونَ حَقًّا ۚ لَّهُمْ دَرَجَٰتٌ عِندَ رَبِّهِمْ وَمَغْفِرَةٌ وَرِزْقٌ كَرِيمٌ ۞ كَمَآ أَخْرَجَكَ رَبُّكَ مِنۢ بَيْتِكَ بِٱلْحَقِّ وَإِنَّ فَرِيقًا مِّنَ ٱلْمُؤْمِنِينَ لَكَٰرِهُونَ ۞ يُجَٰدِلُونَكَ فِى ٱلْحَقِّ بَعْدَ مَا تَبَيَّنَ كَأَنَّمَا يُسَاقُونَ إِلَى ٱلْمَوْتِ وَهُمْ يَنظُرُونَ ۞ وَإِذْ يَعِدُكُمُ ٱللَّهُ إِحْدَى ٱلطَّآئِفَتَيْنِ أَنَّهَا لَكُمْ وَتَوَدُّونَ أَنَّ غَيْرَ ذَاتِ ٱلشَّوْكَةِ تَكُونُ لَكُمْ وَيُرِيدُ ٱللَّهُ أَن يُحِقَّ ٱلْحَقَّ بِكَلِمَٰتِهِۦ وَيَقْطَعَ دَابِرَ ٱلْكَٰفِرِينَ ۞ لِيُحِقَّ ٱلْحَقَّ وَيُبْطِلَ ٱلْبَٰطِلَ وَلَوْ كَرِهَ ٱلْمُجْرِمُونَ ۞ إِذْ تَسْتَغِيثُونَ رَبَّكُمْ فَٱسْتَجَابَ لَكُمْ أَنِّى مُمِدُّكُم بِأَلْفٍ مِّنَ ٱلْمَلَٰٓئِكَةِ مُرْدِفِينَ ۞ وَمَا جَعَلَهُ ٱللَّهُ إِلَّا بُشْرَىٰ وَلِتَطْمَئِنَّ بِهِۦ قُلُوبُكُمْ ۚ وَمَا ٱلنَّصْرُ إِلَّا مِنْ عِندِ ٱللَّهِ ۚ إِنَّ ٱللَّهَ عَزِيزٌ حَكِيمٌ ۞ إِذْ يُغَشِّيكُمُ ٱلنُّعَاسَ أَمَنَةً مِّنْهُ وَيُنَزِّلُ عَلَيْكُم مِّنَ ٱلسَّمَآءِ مَآءً لِّيُطَهِّرَكُم بِهِۦ وَيُذْهِبَ عَنكُمْ رِجْزَ ٱلشَّيْطَٰنِ وَلِيَرْبِطَ عَلَىٰ قُلُوبِكُمْ وَيُثَبِّتَ بِهِ ٱلْأَقْدَامَ ۞ إِذْ يُوحِى رَبُّكَ إِلَى ٱلْمَلَٰٓئِكَةِ أَنِّى مَعَكُمْ فَثَبِّتُوا۟ ٱلَّذِينَ ءَامَنُوا۟ ۚ سَأُلْقِى فِى قُلُوبِ ٱلَّذِينَ كَفَرُوا۟ ٱلرُّعْبَ فَٱضْرِبُوا۟ فَوْقَ ٱلْأَعْنَاقِ وَٱضْرِبُوا۟ مِنْهُمْ كُلَّ بَنَانٍ ۞ ذَٰلِكَ بِأَنَّهُمْ شَآقُّوا۟ ٱللَّهَ وَرَسُولَهُۥ ۚ وَمَن يُشَاقِقِ ٱللَّهَ وَرَسُولَهُۥ فَإِنَّ ٱللَّهَ شَدِيدُ ٱلْعِقَابِ ۞ ذَٰلِكُمْ فَذُوقُوهُ وَأَنَّ لِلْكَٰفِرِينَ عَذَابَ ٱلنَّارِ ۞ يَٰٓأَيُّهَا ٱلَّذِينَ ءَامَنُوٓا۟ إِذَا لَقِيتُمُ ٱلَّذِينَ كَفَرُوا۟ زَحْفًا فَلَا تُوَلُّوهُمُ ٱلْأَدْبَارَ ۞ وَمَن يُوَلِّهِمْ يَوْمَئِذٍ دُبُرَهُۥٓ إِلَّا مُتَحَرِّفًا لِّقِتَالٍ أَوْ مُتَحَيِّزًا إِلَىٰ فِئَةٍ فَقَدْ بَآءَ بِغَضَبٍ مِّنَ ٱللَّهِ وَمَأْوَىٰهُ جَهَنَّمُ ۖ وَبِئْسَ ٱلْمَصِيرُ ۞ فَلَمْ تَقْتُلُوهُمْ وَلَٰكِنَّ ٱللَّهَ قَتَلَهُمْ ۚ وَمَا رَمَيْتَ إِذْ رَمَيْتَ وَلَٰكِنَّ ٱللَّهَ رَمَىٰ ۚ وَلِيُبْلِىَ ٱلْمُؤْمِنِينَ مِنْهُ بَلَآءً حَسَنًا ۚ إِنَّ ٱللَّهَ سَمِيعٌ عَلِيمٌ ۞ ذَٰلِكُمْ وَأَنَّ ٱللَّهَ مُوهِنُ كَيْدِ ٱلْكَٰفِرِينَ ۞ إِن تَسْتَفْتِحُوا۟ فَقَدْ جَآءَكُمُ ٱلْفَتْحُ ۖ وَإِن تَنتَهُوا۟ فَهُوَ

خَيْرٌ لَّكُمْ ۖ وَإِن تَعُودُوا۟ نَعُدْ وَلَن تُغْنِىَ عَنكُمْ فِئَتُكُمْ شَيْـًٔا وَلَوْ كَثُرَتْ وَأَنَّ ٱللَّهَ مَعَ ٱلْمُؤْمِنِينَ ۝ يَـٰٓأَيُّهَا ٱلَّذِينَ ءَامَنُوٓا۟ أَطِيعُوا۟ ٱللَّهَ وَرَسُولَهُۥ وَلَا تَوَلَّوْا۟ عَنْهُ وَأَنتُمْ تَسْمَعُونَ ۝ وَلَا تَكُونُوا۟ كَٱلَّذِينَ قَالُوا۟ سَمِعْنَا وَهُمْ لَا يَسْمَعُونَ ۝ ۞ إِنَّ شَرَّ ٱلدَّوَآبِّ عِندَ ٱللَّهِ ٱلصُّمُّ ٱلْبُكْمُ ٱلَّذِينَ لَا يَعْقِلُونَ ۝ وَلَوْ عَلِمَ ٱللَّهُ فِيهِمْ خَيْرًا لَّأَسْمَعَهُمْ ۖ وَلَوْ أَسْمَعَهُمْ لَتَوَلَّوا۟ وَّهُم مُّعْرِضُونَ ۝ يَـٰٓأَيُّهَا ٱلَّذِينَ ءَامَنُوا۟ ٱسْتَجِيبُوا۟ لِلَّهِ وَلِلرَّسُولِ إِذَا دَعَاكُمْ لِمَا يُحْيِيكُمْ ۖ وَٱعْلَمُوٓا۟ أَنَّ ٱللَّهَ يَحُولُ بَيْنَ ٱلْمَرْءِ وَقَلْبِهِۦ وَأَنَّهُۥٓ إِلَيْهِ تُحْشَرُونَ ۝ وَٱتَّقُوا۟ فِتْنَةً لَّا تُصِيبَنَّ ٱلَّذِينَ ظَلَمُوا۟ مِنكُمْ خَآصَّةً ۖ وَٱعْلَمُوٓا۟ أَنَّ ٱللَّهَ شَدِيدُ ٱلْعِقَابِ ۝ وَٱذْكُرُوٓا۟ إِذْ أَنتُمْ قَلِيلٌ مُّسْتَضْعَفُونَ فِى ٱلْأَرْضِ تَخَافُونَ أَن يَتَخَطَّفَكُمُ ٱلنَّاسُ فَـَٔاوَىٰكُمْ وَأَيَّدَكُم بِنَصْرِهِۦ وَرَزَقَكُم مِّنَ ٱلطَّيِّبَـٰتِ لَعَلَّكُمْ تَشْكُرُونَ ۝ يَـٰٓأَيُّهَا ٱلَّذِينَ ءَامَنُوا۟ لَا تَخُونُوا۟ ٱللَّهَ وَٱلرَّسُولَ وَتَخُونُوٓا۟ أَمَـٰنَـٰتِكُمْ وَأَنتُمْ تَعْلَمُونَ ۝ وَٱعْلَمُوٓا۟ أَنَّمَآ أَمْوَٰلُكُمْ وَأَوْلَـٰدُكُمْ فِتْنَةٌ وَأَنَّ ٱللَّهَ عِندَهُۥٓ أَجْرٌ عَظِيمٌ ۝ يَـٰٓأَيُّهَا ٱلَّذِينَ ءَامَنُوٓا۟ إِن تَتَّقُوا۟ ٱللَّهَ يَجْعَل لَّكُمْ فُرْقَانًا وَيُكَفِّرْ عَنكُمْ سَيِّـَٔاتِكُمْ وَيَغْفِرْ لَكُمْ ۗ وَٱللَّهُ ذُو ٱلْفَضْلِ ٱلْعَظِيمِ ۝ وَإِذْ يَمْكُرُ بِكَ ٱلَّذِينَ كَفَرُوا۟ لِيُثْبِتُوكَ أَوْ يَقْتُلُوكَ أَوْ يُخْرِجُوكَ ۚ وَيَمْكُرُونَ وَيَمْكُرُ ٱللَّهُ ۖ وَٱللَّهُ خَيْرُ ٱلْمَـٰكِرِينَ ۝ وَإِذَا تُتْلَىٰ عَلَيْهِمْ ءَايَـٰتُنَا قَالُوا۟ قَدْ سَمِعْنَا لَوْ نَشَآءُ لَقُلْنَا مِثْلَ هَـٰذَآ ۙ إِنْ هَـٰذَآ إِلَّآ أَسَـٰطِيرُ ٱلْأَوَّلِينَ ۝ وَإِذْ قَالُوا۟ ٱللَّهُمَّ إِن كَانَ هَـٰذَا هُوَ ٱلْحَقَّ مِنْ عِندِكَ فَأَمْطِرْ عَلَيْنَا حِجَارَةً مِّنَ ٱلسَّمَآءِ أَوِ ٱئْتِنَا بِعَذَابٍ أَلِيمٍ ۝ وَمَا كَانَ ٱللَّهُ لِيُعَذِّبَهُمْ وَأَنتَ فِيهِمْ ۚ وَمَا كَانَ ٱللَّهُ مُعَذِّبَهُمْ وَهُمْ يَسْتَغْفِرُونَ ۝ وَمَا لَهُمْ أَلَّا يُعَذِّبَهُمُ ٱللَّهُ وَهُمْ يَصُدُّونَ عَنِ ٱلْمَسْجِدِ ٱلْحَرَامِ وَمَا كَانُوٓا۟ أَوْلِيَآءَهُۥٓ ۚ إِنْ أَوْلِيَآؤُهُۥٓ إِلَّا ٱلْمُتَّقُونَ وَلَـٰكِنَّ أَكْثَرَهُمْ لَا يَعْلَمُونَ ۝

وَمَا كَانَ صَلَاتُهُمْ عِندَ ٱلْبَيْتِ إِلَّا مُكَآءً وَتَصْدِيَةً ۚ فَذُوقُوا۟ ٱلْعَذَابَ بِمَا كُنتُمْ تَكْفُرُونَ ۝ إِنَّ ٱلَّذِينَ كَفَرُوا۟ يُنفِقُونَ أَمْوَٰلَهُمْ لِيَصُدُّوا۟ عَن سَبِيلِ ٱللَّهِ ۚ فَسَيُنفِقُونَهَا ثُمَّ تَكُونُ عَلَيْهِمْ حَسْرَةً ثُمَّ يُغْلَبُونَ ۗ وَٱلَّذِينَ كَفَرُوٓا۟ إِلَىٰ جَهَنَّمَ يُحْشَرُونَ ۝ لِيَمِيزَ ٱللَّهُ ٱلْخَبِيثَ مِنَ ٱلطَّيِّبِ وَيَجْعَلَ ٱلْخَبِيثَ بَعْضَهُۥ عَلَىٰ بَعْضٍ فَيَرْكُمَهُۥ جَمِيعًا فَيَجْعَلَهُۥ فِى جَهَنَّمَ ۚ أُو۟لَـٰٓئِكَ هُمُ ٱلْخَـٰسِرُونَ ۝ قُل لِّلَّذِينَ كَفَرُوٓا۟ إِن يَنتَهُوا۟ يُغْفَرْ لَهُم مَّا قَدْ سَلَفَ وَإِن يَعُودُوا۟ فَقَدْ مَضَتْ سُنَّتُ ٱلْأَوَّلِينَ ۝ وَقَـٰتِلُوهُمْ حَتَّىٰ لَا تَكُونَ فِتْنَةٌ وَيَكُونَ ٱلدِّينُ كُلُّهُۥ لِلَّهِ ۚ فَإِنِ ٱنتَهَوْا۟ فَإِنَّ ٱللَّهَ بِمَا يَعْمَلُونَ بَصِيرٌ ۝ وَإِن تَوَلَّوْا۟ فَٱعْلَمُوٓا۟ أَنَّ ٱللَّهَ مَوْلَىٰكُمْ ۚ نِعْمَ ٱلْمَوْلَىٰ وَنِعْمَ ٱلنَّصِيرُ ۝

(Al-Anfal 001-040)

CHAPTER 7: AL-ARAF (THE HEIGHTS), VERSES 088 - 206

Surah: 7 Ayah: 88 & Ayah: 89

۞ قَالَ ٱلْمَلَأُ ٱلَّذِينَ ٱسْتَكْبَرُوا۟ مِن قَوْمِهِۦ لَنُخْرِجَنَّكَ يَـٰشُعَيْبُ وَٱلَّذِينَ ءَامَنُوا۟ مَعَكَ مِن قَرْيَتِنَآ أَوْ لَتَعُودُنَّ فِى مِلَّتِنَا ۚ قَالَ أَوَلَوْ كُنَّا كَـٰرِهِينَ ۝

88. The chiefs of those who were arrogant among his people said: "We shall certainly drive you out, O Shu'aib, and those who have believed with you from our town, or else you (all) shall return to our religion." He said: "Even though we hate it!?"

قَدِ ٱفْتَرَيْنَا عَلَى ٱللَّهِ كَذِبًا إِنْ عُدْنَا فِى مِلَّتِكُم بَعْدَ إِذْ نَجَّىٰنَا ٱللَّهُ مِنْهَا ۚ وَمَا يَكُونُ لَنَآ أَن نَّعُودَ فِيهَآ إِلَّآ أَن يَشَآءَ ٱللَّهُ رَبُّنَا ۚ وَسِعَ رَبُّنَا كُلَّ شَىْءٍ عِلْمًا ۚ عَلَى ٱللَّهِ تَوَكَّلْنَا ۚ رَبَّنَا ٱفْتَحْ بَيْنَنَا وَبَيْنَ قَوْمِنَا بِٱلْحَقِّ وَأَنتَ خَيْرُ ٱلْفَـٰتِحِينَ ۝

89. "We should have invented a lie against Allâh if we returned to your religion, after Allâh has rescued us from it. And it is not for us to return to it unless Allâh, our Lord, should will. Our Lord comprehends all things in His Knowledge. In Allâh (Alone) we put our trust. Our Lord! Judge between us and our people in truth, for You are the Best of those who give judgment."

Transliteration

88. Qala almalao allatheena istakbaroo min qawmihi lanukhrijannaka ya shuAAaybu waallatheena amanoo maAAaka min qaryatina aw lataAAoodunna fee millatina qala awa law kunna kariheena 89. Qadi iftarayna AAala Allahi kathiban in AAudna fee millatikum baAAda ith najjana Allahu minha wama yakoonu lana an naAAooda feeha illa an yashaa Allahu rabbuna wasiAAa rabbuna kulla shay-in AAilman AAala Allahi tawakkalna rabbana iftah baynana wabayna qawmina bialhaqqi waanta khayru alfatiheena

Tafsir Ibn Kathir

Allah describes the way the disbelievers answered His Prophet Shu`ayb and those who believed in him, by threatening them with expulsion from their village, or with forceful reversion to the disbeliever's religion.

The chiefs spoke the words mentioned here to the Messenger Shu`ayb, but intended it for those who followed his religion too. The statement,

("Even though we hate it"), means, would you force us to do that, even though we hate what you are calling us to Certainly if we revert to your religion and accept your ways, we will have uttered a tremendous lie against Allah by calling partners as rivals to Him,

(And it is not for us to return to it unless Allah, our Lord, should will.) This part of the Ayah refers all matters to Allah's will, and certainly, He has perfect knowledge of all matters and His observation encompasses all things,

(In Allah (Alone) we put our trust.), concerning all our affairs, what we practice of them and what we ignore,

(Our Lord! Judge between us and our people in truth) judge between us and our people and give us victory over them,

(for You are the best of those who give judgment) and You are the Most Just Who never wrongs any in His judgment.

Surah: 7 Ayah: 90, Ayah: 91 & Ayah: 92

﴿ وَقَالَ ٱلۡمَلَأُ ٱلَّذِينَ كَفَرُواْ مِن قَوۡمِهِۦ لَئِنِ ٱتَّبَعۡتُمۡ شُعَيۡبًا إِنَّكُمۡ إِذًا لَّخَٰسِرُونَ ۝ ﴾

90. The chiefs of those who disbelieved among his people said (to their people): "If you follow Shu'aib, be sure then you will be the losers!"

﴿ فَأَخَذَتۡهُمُ ٱلرَّجۡفَةُ فَأَصۡبَحُواْ فِي دَارِهِمۡ جَٰثِمِينَ ۝ ﴾

91. So the earthquake seized them and they lay (dead), prostrate in their homes.

﴿ ٱلَّذِينَ كَذَّبُواْ شُعَيْبًا كَأَن لَّمْ يَغْنَوْاْ فِيهَا ٱلَّذِينَ كَذَّبُواْ شُعَيْبًا كَانُواْ هُمُ ٱلْخَسِرِينَ ۝ ﴾

92. Those who belied Shu'aib, became as if they had never dwelt there (in their homes). Those who belied Shu'aib, they were the losers.

Transliteration

90. Waqala almalao allatheena kafaroo min qawmihi la-ini ittabaAAtum shuAAayban innakum ithan lakhasiroona 91. Faakhathat-humu alrrajfatu faasbahoo fee darihim jathimeena 92. Allatheena kaththaboo shuAAayban kaan lam yaghnaw feeha allatheena kaththaboo shuAAayban kanoo humu alkhasireena

Tafsir Ibn Kathir

Allah describes the enormity of disbelief, rebellion, transgression and misguidance (of Shu`ayb's people) and the defiance of truth encrypted in their hearts. They vowed, saying,

("If you follow Shu`ayb, be sure then you will be the losers!") Allah answered them,

(So the earthquake seized them and they lay (dead), prostrate in their homes) Allah said that the earthquake shook them, as punishment for threatening to expel Shu`ayb and his followers. Allah mentioned their end again in Suah Hud,

(And when Our commandment came, We saved Shu`ayb and those who believed with him by a mercy from Us. And the Sayhah (loud cry) seized the wrongdoers, and they lay (dead) prostrate in their homes.) (11:94) This Ayah mentions the Sayhah (cry) that struck them after they mocked Shu`ayb, saying,

(Does your Salah (prayer) command you...) so it was befitting to mention here the cry that made them silence. In Surat Ash-Shu`ara', Allah said,

(But they belied him, so the torment of the Day of Shadow (a gloomy cloud) seized them. Indeed that was the torment of a Great Day) (26:189) because they challenged Shu`ayb,

("So cause a piece of the heaven to fall on us, if you are of the truthful!") (26:187). Therefore, Allah stated that each of these forms of punishment struck them on the Day of the Shadow. First,

(So the torment of the Day of Shadow (a gloomy cloud) seized them) (26:189) when a gloomy cloud came over them (containing) fire, flames and a tremendous light. Next, a cry from the sky descended on them and a tremor shook them from beneath. Consequently, their souls were captured, their lives were taken and their bodies became idle,

(and they lay (dead), prostrate in their homes). Allah said next,

(They became as if they had never dwelt there) meaning, after the torment seized them, it looked as if they never dwelled in the land from which they wanted to expel their Messenger Shu`ayb and his followers. Here, Allah refuted their earlier statement,

(Those who belied Shu`ayb, they were the losers.)

Surah: 7 Ayah: 93

﴿ فَتَوَلَّىٰ عَنْهُمْ وَقَالَ يَـٰقَوْمِ لَقَدْ أَبْلَغْتُكُمْ رِسَـٰلَـٰتِ رَبِّى وَنَصَحْتُ لَكُمْ ۖ فَكَيْفَ ءَاسَىٰ عَلَىٰ قَوْمٍ كَـٰفِرِينَ ۝ ﴾

93. Then he (Shu'aib) turned from them and said: "O my people! I have indeed conveyed my Lord's Messages unto you and I have given you good advice. Then how can I sorrow for the disbelieving people's (destruction)."

Transliteration

93. Fatawalla AAanhum waqala ya qawmi laqad ablaghtukum risalati rabbee wanasahtu lakum fakayfa asa AAala qawmin kafireena

Tafsir Ibn Kathir

Prophet Shu`ayb, peace be upon him, turned away from his people after the torment, punishment and destruction struck them, admonishing and censuring them by saying to them,

("O my people! I have indeed conveyed my Lord's Messages unto you and I have given you good advice.") Shu`ayb said, I have conveyed to you what I was sent with, so I will not feel any sorrow for you since you disbelieved in what I brought you,

("Then how can I grieve over pepple who are disbelievers")

Surah: 7 Ayah: 94 & Ayah: 95

﴿ وَمَآ أَرْسَلْنَا فِى قَرْيَةٍ مِّن نَّبِىٍّ إِلَّآ أَخَذْنَآ أَهْلَهَا بِٱلْبَأْسَآءِ وَٱلضَّرَّآءِ لَعَلَّهُمْ يَضَّرَّعُونَ ۝ ﴾

94. And We sent no Prophet unto any town (and they denied him), but We seized its people with suffering from extreme poverty (or loss of wealth) and loss of health (and calamities), so that they might humiliate themselves (and repent to Allâh).

﴿ ثُمَّ بَدَّلْنَا مَكَانَ ٱلسَّيِّئَةِ ٱلْحَسَنَةَ حَتَّىٰ عَفَوا وَّقَالُوا قَدْ مَسَّ ءَابَآءَنَا ٱلضَّرَّآءُ وَٱلسَّرَّآءُ فَأَخَذْنَـٰهُم بَغْتَةً وَهُمْ لَا يَشْعُرُونَ ۝ ﴾

95. Then We changed the evil for the good, until they increased in number and in wealth, and said: "Our fathers were touched with evil (loss of health and

calamities) and with good (prosperity)." So We seized them all of a sudden while they were unaware.

Transliteration

94. Wama arsalna fee qaryatin min nabiyyin illa akhathna ahlaha bialba/sa-i waalddarra-i laAAallahum yaddarraAAoona   95. Thumma baddalna makana alssayyi-ati alhasanata hatta AAafaw waqaloo qad massa abaana alddarrao waalssarrao faakhathnahum baghtatan wahum la yashAAuroona

Tafsir Ibn Kathir

Afflictions that struck Earlier Nations

Allah mentions the Ba'sa' and Darra' that struck the earlier nations to whom He sent Prophets. Ba'sa', refers to the physical sicknesses and ailments that they suffered, while Darra', refers to the poverty and humiliation that they experienced,

(so that they might humble themselves) supplicate, humble themselves and invoke Allah, that He might remove the afflictions that they suffered from. This Ayah indicates that Allah sent down severe afflictions to them so that they might invoke Him, but they did not do what He ordered them. Therefore, He changed the affliction into prosperity to test them,

(Then We changed the evil for the good,) Therefore, Allah changed the hardship into prosperity, disease and sickness into health and well-being, and poverty into richness in provision, so that they might be thankful to Allah for this, but they did none of that. Allah's statement,

(until they `Afaw) refers to increase in numbers, wealth and offspring. Allah said next,

(. . and they said: "Our fathers were touched with evil and with good." So We seized them all of a sudden while they were unaware.) He tested them with this (afflictions) and that (ease and abundance) so that they may humble themselves and repent to Him. However, they failed both tests, for neither this nor that compelled them to change their ways. They said, "We suffered Ba'sa' and Darra', but prosperity came afterwards, just as like our forefathers in earlier times." "Therefore," they said, "it is a cycle where we sometimes suffer a hardship and at other times, we enjoy a bounty." However, they did not comprehend Allah's wisdom, nor the fact that He is testing them in both cases. To the contrary, the believers are grateful to Allah in good times and practice patience in hard times. In the Sahih, there is a Hadith that says,

«عَجَبًا لِلْمُؤْمِنِ لَا يَقْضِي اللهُ لَهُ قَضَاءً إِلَّا كَانَ خَيْرًا لَهُ، وَإِنْ أَصَابَتْهُ ضَرَّاءُ صَبَرَ فَكَانَ خَيْرًا لَهُ، وَإِنْ أَصَابَتْهُ سَرَّاءُ شَكَرَ فَكَانَ خَيْرًا لَهُ»

(The matter of the believer is amazing, for nothing that Allah decrees for him, but it is better for him. If a Darra' (harm) strikes him, he is patient, and this is better for him, if he is given Sarra' (prosperity), he thanks (Allah) for it and this is better for him.)

The believer, therefore, is aware of the test behind the afflictions whether it may be prosperity or adversity that Allah sends to him, as well as the blessings. Similarly, in another Hadith,

«لَا يَزَالُ الْبَلَاءُ بِالْمُؤْمِنِ حَتَّى يَخْرُجَ نَقِيًّا مِنْ ذُنُوبِهِ، وَالْمُنَافِقِ مِثْلَهُ كَمَثَلِ الْحِمَارِ لَا يَدْرِي فِيمَ رَبَطَهُ أَهْلُهُ وَلَا فِيمَ أَرْسَلُوهُ»

(The believer will continue to be tested by afflictions until he ends up pure from sin. And the parable of the hypocrite is that of a donkey, it does not know why its owners tied it or released it.) Allah said next,

(So We seized them all of a sudden while they were unaware.) meaning, We struck them with punishment all of a sudden, while they were unaware. A Hadith describes sudden death,

«مَوْتُ الْفَجْأَةِ رَحْمَةٌ لِلْمُؤْمِنِ وَأَخْذَةُ أَسَفٍ لِلْكَافِرِ»

(Sudden death is a mercy for the believer, but a sorrowful punishment for the disbeliever.)

Surah: 7 Ayah: 96, Ayah: 97, Ayah: 98 & Ayah: 99

﴿ وَلَوْ أَنَّ أَهْلَ ٱلْقُرَىٰٓ ءَامَنُوا۟ وَٱتَّقَوْا۟ لَفَتَحْنَا عَلَيْهِم بَرَكَـٰتٍ مِّنَ ٱلسَّمَآءِ وَٱلْأَرْضِ وَلَـٰكِن كَذَّبُوا۟ فَأَخَذْنَـٰهُم بِمَا كَانُوا۟ يَكْسِبُونَ ﴾

96. And if the people of the towns had believed and had the Taqwâ (piety), certainly, We should have opened for them blessings from the heaven and the earth, but they belied (the Messengers). So We took them (with punishment) for what they used to earn (polytheism and crimes).

﴿ أَفَأَمِنَ أَهْلُ ٱلْقُرَىٰٓ أَن يَأْتِيَهُم بَأْسُنَا بَيَـٰتًا وَهُمْ نَآئِمُونَ ﴾

97. Did the people of the towns then feel secure against the coming of Our Punishment by night while they were asleep?

﴿ أَوَأَمِنَ أَهْلُ ٱلْقُرَىٰٓ أَن يَأْتِيَهُم بَأْسُنَا ضُحًى وَهُمْ يَلْعَبُونَ ﴾

98. Or, did the people of the towns then feel secure against the coming of Our Punishment in the forenoon while they were playing?

﴿ أَفَأَمِنُوا۟ مَكْرَ ٱللَّهِ فَلَا يَأْمَنُ مَكْرَ ٱللَّهِ إِلَّا ٱلْقَوْمُ ٱلْخَـٰسِرُونَ ﴾

99. Did they then feel secure against the Plan of Allâh? None feels secure from the Plan of Allâh except the people who are the losers.

Transliteration

96. Walaw anna ahla alqura amanoo waittaqaw lafatahna AAalayhim barakatin mina alssama-i waal-ardi walakin kaththaboo faakhathnahum bima kanoo yaksiboona 97. Afaamina ahlu alqura an ya/tiyahum ba/suna bayatan wahum na-imoona 98. Awa amina ahlu alqura an ya/tiyahum ba/suna duhan wahum yalAAaboona 99. Afaaminoo makra Allahi fala ya/manu makra Allahi illa alqawmu alkhasiroona

Tafsir Ibn Kathir

Blessings come with Faith, while Kufr brings Torment

Allah mentions here the little faith of the people of the towns to whom He sent Messengers. In another instance, Allah said,

(Was there any town (community) that believed (after seeing the punishment), and its faith (at that moment) saved it (from the punishment) -- Except the people of Yunus; when they believed, We removed from them the torment of disgrace in the life of the (present) world, and permitted them to enjoy for a while.) (10:98) This Ayah indicates that no city believed in its entirety, except the city of Prophet Yunus, for they all believed after they were stricken by punishment. Allah said (about Prophet Yunus),

(And We sent him to a hundred thousand (people) or even more. And they believed; so We gave them enjoyment for a while.) (37:147-148) Allah said in another Ayah,

(And We did not send a warner to a township....) (34:34) Allah said here,

(And if the people of the towns had believed and had Taqwa. ..) meaning their hearts had faith in what the Messenger brought them, believed and obeyed him, and had Taqwa by performing the acts of obedience and abstaining from the prohibitions,

(We should have opened for them blessings from the heaven and the earth,) in reference to the rain that falls from the sky and the vegetation of the earth. Allah said,

(but they belied (the Messengers). So We took them (with punishment) for what they used to earn.) They denied their Messengers, so that We punished them and sent destruction on them as a result of the sins and wickedness that they earned. Allah then said, while warning and threatening against defying His orders and daring to commit His prohibitions,

(Did the people of the towns then feel secure),meaning the disbelievers among them,

(that should come to them our punishment), Our torment and punishing example,

(Bayatan) during the night,

(while they were asleep Or, did the people of the towns then feel secure against the coming of Our punishment in the forenoon while they were playing) while they are busy in their affairs and unaware.

(Did they then feel secure against Allah's plan) His torment, vengeance, and His power to destroy them while they are inattentive and heedless,

(None feels secure from Allah's plan except the people who are the losers.) Al-Hasan Al-Basri said, "The believer performs the acts of worship, all the while feeling fear, in fright and anxiety. The Fajir (wicked sinner, or disbeliever) commits the acts of disobedience while feeling safe (from Allah's torment)!"

Surah: 7 Ayah: 100

﴿ أَوَلَمْ يَهْدِ لِلَّذِينَ يَرِثُونَ ٱلْأَرْضَ مِنۢ بَعْدِ أَهْلِهَآ أَن لَّوْ نَشَآءُ أَصَبْنَـٰهُم بِذُنُوبِهِمْ ۚ وَنَطْبَعُ عَلَىٰ قُلُوبِهِمْ فَهُمْ لَا يَسْمَعُونَ ۝ ﴾

100. Is it not clear to those who inherit the earth in succession from its (previous) possessors, that had We willed, We would have punished them for their sins. And We seal up their hearts so that they hear not?

Transliteration

100. Awa lam yahdi lillatheena yarithoona al-arda min baAAdi ahliha an law nashao asabnahum bithunoobihim wanatbaAAu AAala quloobihim fahum la yasmaAAoona

Tafsir Ibn Kathir

Ibn `Abbas commented on Allah's statement,

(Is it not a guidance for those who inherit the earth from its previous inhabitants. ..) "(Allah says,) did We not make clear to them that had We willed, We would have punished them because of their sins" Mujahid and several others said similarly. Abu Ja`far bin Jarir At-Tabari explained this Ayah, "Allah says, `Did We not make clear to those who succeeded on the earth after destroying the previous nations who used to dwell in that land. Then they followed their own ways, and behaved as they did and were unruly with their Lord. (Did We not make clear to them) that,

(that had We willed, We would have punished them for their sins.) by bringing them the same end that was decreed for those before them,

(And We seal up their hearts), We place a cover over their heart,

(so that they hear not), words of advice or reminding'" I say that similarly, Allah said,

(Is it not a guidance for them: how many generations We have destroyed before them, in whose dwellings they walk Verily, in this are signs indeed for men of understanding.) (20:128)

(Is it not a guidance for them: how many generations We have destroyed before them in whose dwellings they do walk about Verily, therein indeed are signs. Would they not then listen) (32:26) and,

(Had you not sworn aforetime that you would not leave (the world for the Hereafter). And you dwelt in the dwellings of men who wronged themselves)(14:44-45) Also, Allah said,

(And how many a generation before them have We destroyed! Can you find a single one of them or hear even a whisper of them) (19:98) meaning, do you see any of them or hear their voices There are many other Ayat that testify that Allah's torment strikes His enemies, while His bounty reaches His faithful believers. Thereafter comes Allah's statement, and He is the Most Truthful, the Lord of all that exists,

Surah: 7 Ayah: 101 & Ayah: 102

﴿ تِلْكَ ٱلْقُرَىٰ نَقُصُّ عَلَيْكَ مِنْ أَنۢبَآئِهَا ۚ وَلَقَدْ جَآءَتْهُمْ رُسُلُهُم بِٱلْبَيِّنَـٰتِ فَمَا كَانُوا۟ لِيُؤْمِنُوا۟ بِمَا كَذَّبُوا۟ مِن قَبْلُ ۚ كَذَٰلِكَ يَطْبَعُ ٱللَّهُ عَلَىٰ قُلُوبِ ٱلْكَـٰفِرِينَ ۝ ﴾

101. Those were the towns whose story We relate unto you (O Muhammad (peace be upon him)) And there came indeed to them their Messengers with clear proofs, but they were not such as to believe in that which they had rejected before. Thus Allâh does seal up the hearts of the disbelievers (from every kind of religious guidance).

﴿ وَمَا وَجَدْنَا لِأَكْثَرِهِم مِّنْ عَهْدٍ ۖ وَإِن وَجَدْنَآ أَكْثَرَهُمْ لَفَـٰسِقِينَ ۝ ﴾

102. And most of them We found not (true) to their covenant, but most of them We found indeed Fâsiqûn (rebellious, disobedient to Allâh).

Transliteration

101. Tilka alqura naqussu AAalayka min anba-iha walaqad jaat-hum rusuluhum bialbayyinati fama kanoo liyu/minoo bima kaththaboo min qablu kathalika yatbaAAu Allahu AAala quloobi alkafireena   102. Wama wajadna li-aktharihim min AAahdin wa-in wajadna aktharahum lafasiqeena

Tafsir Ibn Kathir

After narrating the stories of the people of Prophets Nuh, Hud, Salih, Lut and Shu`ayb, destroying the disbelievers, saving the believers, warning these nations by explaining the truth to them with the evidence sent in the words of His Messengers, may Allah's peace and blessings be on them all, Allah said;

(Those were the towns that We relate to you) O Muhammad,

(their story), and news,

(And there came indeed to them their Messengers with clear proofs,) and evidences of the truth of what they brought them. Allah said in other Ayah,

(And We never punish until We have sent a Messenger (to give warning).) (17:15), and,

(That is some of the news of the towns which We relate unto you; of them, some are standing, and some have been reaped. We wronged them not, but they wronged themselves.) (11:100-101) Allah said

(but they were not such who would believe in what they had rejected before.) meaning they would not have later on believed in what the Messengers brought them, because they denied the truth when it first came to them (although they recognized it), according to the Tafsir of Ibn `Atiyyah. This explanation is sound, and is supported by Allah's statement,

(And what will make you perceive that if it came, they will not believe And We shall turn their hearts and their eyes away (from guidance), as they refused to believe therein for the first time.) (6:109-110) This is why Allah said here,

(Thus Allah does seal up the hearts of the disbelievers. And most of them We found not...) meaning, We did not find most of the previous nations,

(true to their covenant, but most of them We found to indeed be rebellious.) This Ayah means, We found most of them to be rebellious, deviating away from obedience and compliance. The covenant mentioned here is the Fitrah that Allah instilled in them while still in their fathers' loins, and taking their covenant, that He is their Lord, King, and that there is no deity worthy of worship except Him,. They affirmed this covenant and testified against themselves to this fact. However, they defied this covenant, threw it behind their backs and worshipped others besides Allah, having no proof or plea, nor support from rationality or by divine law. Surely, the pure Fitrah defies these actions, while all the honorable Messengers, from beginning to end, forbade them. Muslim collected the Hadith,

«يَقُولُ اللهُ تَعَالَى إِنِّي خَلَقْتُ عِبَادِي حُنَفَاءَ فَجَاءَتْهُمُ الشَّيَاطِينُ فَاجْتَالَتْهُمْ عَنْ دِينِهِمْ وَحَرَّمَتْ عَلَيْهِمْ مَا أَحْلَلْتُ لَهُم»

(Allah said, "I created My servants Hunafa' (monotheists), but the devils came to them and deviated them from their religion and prohibited them what I allowed them.") It is recorded in the Two Sahihs,

«كُلُّ مَوْلُودٍ يُولَدُ عَلَى الْفِطْرَةِ فَأَبَوَاهُ يُهَوِّدَانِهِ وَيُنَصِّرَانِهِ وَيُمَجِّسَانِه»

(Every child is born upon the Fitrah, it is only his parents who turn him into a Jew, a Christian or a Zoroastrian.)

Surah: 7 Ayah: 103

﴿ ثُمَّ بَعَثْنَا مِنْ بَعْدِهِم مُّوسَىٰ بِـَٔايَـٰتِنَآ إِلَىٰ فِرْعَوْنَ وَمَلَإِيْهِۦ فَظَلَمُواْ بِهَا ۖ فَٱنظُرْ كَيْفَ كَانَ عَـٰقِبَةُ ٱلْمُفْسِدِينَ ۝ ﴾

103. Then after them We sent Mûsâ (Moses) with Our Signs to Fir'aun (Pharaoh) and his chiefs, but they wrongfully rejected them. So see how was the end of the Mufsidûn (mischief-makers, corrupts).

Transliteration

103. Thumma baAAathna min baAAdihim moosa bi-ayatina ila firAAawna wamala-ihi fathalamoo biha faonuthur kayfa kana AAaqibatu almufsideena

Tafsir Ibn Kathir

Story of Prophet Musa, upon him be Peace, and Fir`awn

Allah said,

(Then after them We sent), after the Messengers whom We mentioned, such as Nuh, Hud, Salih Lut and Shu`ayb (may Allah's peace and blessings be on them and the rest of Allah's Prophets), We sent,

(Musa with Our signs) proofs and clear evidences, to Fir`awn, who was ruler of Egypt during the time of Musa,

(and his chiefs) the people of Fir`awn,

(but they wrongfully rejected them), they denied and disbelieved in the signs, out of injustice and stubbornness on their part. Allah said about them in another Ayah,

(And they belied them (those Ayat) wrongfully and arrogantly, though they were themselves convinced thereof. So see what was the end of the evildoers.)(27:14) The Ayah says, `those who hindered from the path of Allah and belied in His Messengers, look how We punished them, We caused them to drown, all of them, while Musa and his people were watching.' Public drowning added disgrace to the punishment that Fir`awn and his people suffered, while adding comfort to the hearts of Allah's party, Musa and those people who believed in him.

Surah: 7 Ayah: 104, Ayah: 105 & Ayah: 106

﴿ وَقَالَ مُوسَىٰ يَـٰفِرْعَوْنُ إِنِّى رَسُولٌ مِّن رَّبِّ ٱلْعَـٰلَمِينَ ۝ ﴾

104. And Mûsâ (Moses) said: "O Fir'aun (Pharaoh)! Verily, I am a Messenger from the Lord of the 'Alamîn (mankind, jinn and all that exists).

$$\left\{ \text{حَقِيقٌ عَلَىٰٓ أَن لَّآ أَقُولَ عَلَى ٱللَّهِ إِلَّا ٱلْحَقَّ ۚ قَدْ جِئْتُكُم بِبَيِّنَةٍ مِّن رَّبِّكُمْ فَأَرْسِلْ مَعِيَ بَنِىٓ إِسْرَٰٓءِيلَ} \right\}$$

105. "Proper it is for me that I say nothing concerning Allâh but the truth. Indeed I have come unto you from your Lord with a clear proof. So let the Children of Israel depart along with me."

$$\left\{ \text{قَالَ إِن كُنتَ جِئْتَ بِـَٔايَةٍ فَأْتِ بِهَآ إِن كُنتَ مِنَ ٱلصَّـٰدِقِينَ} \right\}$$

106. (Fir'aun (Pharaoh)) said: "If you have come with a sign, show it forth, if you are one of those who tell the truth."

Transliteration

104. Waqala moosa ya firAAawnu innee rasoolun min rabbi alAAalameena   105. Haqeequn AAala an la aqoola AAala Allahi illa alhaqqa qad ji/tukum bibayyinatin min rabbikum faarsil maAAiya banee isra-eela   106. Qala in kunta ji/ta bi-ayatin fa/ti biha in kunta mina alssadiqeena

Tafsir Ibn Kathir

Allah mentions a debate that took place between Musa and Fir`awn, and Musa's refuting Fir`awn with the unequivocal proof and clear miracles, in the presence of Fir`awn and his people, the Copts of Egypt. Allah said,

(And Musa said: "O Fir`awn! Verily, I am a Messenger from the Lord of all that exists".) meaning Musa said, `the one Who sent me is the Creator, Lord and King of all things,'

("Proper it is for me that I say nothing concerning Allah but the truth. ") `It is incumbent and a duty for me to convey only the Truth from Him, because of what I know of His might and power.'

("Indeed I have come unto you from your Lord with a clear proof.") `I brought unequivocal evidence that Allah gave me to prove that I am conveying the truth to you,'

("So let the Children of Israel depart along with me.") means, release them from your slavery and subjugation. Let them worship your Lord and their Lord. They are from the offspring of an honorable Prophet, Isra'il, who is Ya`qub son of Ishaq son of Ibrahim, the Khalil (intimate friend) of Allah.

((Fir`awn) said: "If you have come with a sign, show it forth, if you are one of those who tell the truth.") Fir`awn said, `I will not believe in what you have said nor entertain your request'. Therefore, he said, `if you have proof, then produce it for us to see, so that we know if your claim is true.'

Surah: 7 Ayah: 107 & Ayah: 108

﴿ فَأَلْقَىٰ عَصَاهُ فَإِذَا هِيَ ثُعْبَانٌ مُبِينٌ ۝ ﴾

107. Then (Mûsâ (Moses)) threw his stick and behold! it was a serpent, manifest!

﴿ وَنَزَعَ يَدَهُ فَإِذَا هِيَ بَيْضَاءُ لِلنَّاظِرِينَ ۝ ﴾

108. And he drew out his hand, and behold! it was white (with radiance) for the beholders.

Transliteration

107. Faalqa AAasahu fa-itha hiya thuAAbanun mubeenun 108. WanazaAAa yadahu fa-itha hiya baydao lilnnathireena

Tafsir Ibn Kathir

`Ali bin Abi Talhah reported that Ibn `Abbas commented on Allah's statement,

(a (Thu`ban) serpent, manifest), refers to "The male snake." As-Suddi and Ad-Dahhak said similarly. A report from Ibn `Abbas said,

"(Then (Musa) threw his staff), and it turned into a huge snake that opened its mouth and rushed towards Fir`awn. When Fir`awn saw the snake rushing towards him, he jumped from his throne and cried to Musa for help, so that Musa would remove the snake from his way. Musa did that." As-Suddi commented,

(and behold! It was a (Thu`ban) serpent, manifest!) "This (Thu`ban) refers to male snakes. The snake opened its mouth and headed towards Fir`awn to swallow him, placing its lower jaw on the ground and its upper jaw reaching the (top of the) wall of the palace. When Fir`awn saw the snake, he was frightened, so he jumped and wet himself and he never wet himself before this incident. He cried, `O Musa! Take it away and I will believe in you and release the Children of Israel to you.' So Musa, peace be on him, took it, and it became a staff again."

(And he drew out his hand, and behold! it was white (with radiance) for the beholders.) Musa took his hand out of his cloak after he inserted his hand in it and it was shining, not because of leprosy or sickness. Allah said in another Ayah,

(And put your hand into your bosom, it will come forth white without hurt.) (27:12) Ibn `Abbas said, "without hurt', means, `not because of leprosy'. Musa inserted his hand again in his sleeve and it returned back to its normal color." Mujahid and several others said similarly.

Surah: 7 Ayah: 109 & Ayah: 110

﴿ قَالَ ٱلْمَلَأُ مِن قَوْمِ فِرْعَوْنَ إِنَّ هَـٰذَا لَسَـٰحِرٌ عَلِيمٌ ۝ ﴾

109. The chiefs of the people of Fir'aun (Pharaoh) said: "This is indeed a well-versed sorcerer;

﴿ يُرِيدُ أَن يُخْرِجَكُم مِّنْ أَرْضِكُمْ فَمَاذَا تَأْمُرُونَ ۞ ﴾

110. "He wants to get you out of your land, so what do you advise?"

Transliteration

109. Qala almalao min qawmi firAAawna inna hatha lasahirun AAaleemun 110. Yureedu an yukhrijakum min ardikum famatha ta/muroona

Tafsir Ibn Kathir

Fir`awn's People say that Musa is a Magician!

The chiefs and noblemen of the people of Fir`awn agreed with Fir`awn's statement about Musa. After Fir`awn felt safe and returned to his throne, he said to the chiefs of his people,

(This is indeed a well-versed sorcerer) and they agreed. They held counsel to decide what they should do about Musa. They conspired to extinguish the light that he brought and bring down his word. They plotted to portray Musa as a liar and fake. They feared that he might lure people to his side by his magic, they claimed, and thus prevail over them and drive them away from their land. What they feared occured, just as Allah said,

(And We let Fir`awn and Haman and their hosts receive from them that which they feared.) (28:6) After they conferred about Musa, they agreed on a plot, as Allah said about them,

Surah: 7 Ayah: 111 & Ayah: 112

﴿ قَالُوا أَرْجِهْ وَأَخَاهُ وَأَرْسِلْ فِي الْمَدَائِنِ حَاشِرِينَ ۞ ﴾

111. They said: "Put him and his brother off (for a time), and send callers to the cities to collect -

﴿ يَأْتُوكَ بِكُلِّ سَاحِرٍ عَلِيمٍ ۞ ﴾

112. "That they bring up to you all well-versed sorcerers."

Transliteration

111. Qaloo arjih waakhahu waarsil fee almada-ini hashireena   112. Ya/tooka bikulli sahirin AAaleemin

Tafsir Ibn Kathir

Ibn `Abbas commented,

("Put him off"), means, "delay him (for a time)."

("and send to the cities"), areas and provinces of your kingdom -- O Fir`awn,

("to collect") to gather magicians from various lands. At this time, magic was the trade of the day and it was widespread and popular. They had the idea that what Musa brought was a type of magic similar to the magic that the sorcerers of their time practiced. Because of this incorrect assumption, they brought all the magicians in order to defeat the miracles that he showed them. Allah said about Fir`awn,

(Then verily, we can produce magic the like thereof; so appoint a meeting between us and you, which neither we nor you shall fail to keep, in an open place where both shall have a just and equal chance." (Musa) said: "Your appointed meeting is the day of the festival, and let the people assemble when the sun has risen (forenoon)." So Fir`awn withdrew, devised his plot and then came back.) (20:58-60). Allah said,

Surah: 7 Ayah: 113 & Ayah: 114

﴿ وَجَاءَ ٱلسَّحَرَةُ فِرْعَوْنَ قَالُوٓاْ إِنَّ لَنَا لَأَجْرًا إِن كُنَّا نَحْنُ ٱلْغَٰلِبِينَ ۝ ﴾

113. And so the sorcerers came to Fir'aun (Pharaoh). They said: "Indeed there will be a (good) reward for us if we are the victors."

﴿ قَالَ نَعَمْ وَإِنَّكُمْ لَمِنَ ٱلْمُقَرَّبِينَ ۝ ﴾

114. He said: "Yes, and moreover you will (in that case) be of the nearest (to me)."

Transliteration

113. Wajaa alssaharatu firAAawna qaloo inna lana laajran in kunna nahnu alghalibeena 114. Qala naAAam wa-innakum lamina almuqarrabeena

Tafsir Ibn Kathir

The Magicians convene and change Their Ropes into Snakes before Musa

Allah describes the conversation that took place between Fir`awn and the magicians he collected to defeat Musa, peace be upon him. Fir`awn told them that he will reward them and give them tremendous provisions. He made them hope in acquiring what they wished for and to make them among his private audience and best associates. When they were assured of the cursed Fir`awn's promises,

Surah: 7 Ayah: 115 & Ayah: 116

﴿ قَالُواْ يَٰمُوسَىٰٓ إِمَّآ أَن تُلْقِىَ وَإِمَّآ أَن نَّكُونَ نَحْنُ ٱلْمُلْقِينَ ۝ ﴾

115. They said: "O Mûsâ (Moses)! Either you throw (first), or shall we have the (first) throw?"

Chapter 7: Al-Araf (The Heights), Verses 088-206

﴿ قَالَ أَلْقُواْ فَلَمَّآ أَلْقَوْاْ سَحَرُوٓاْ أَعْيُنَ ٱلنَّاسِ وَٱسْتَرْهَبُوهُمْ وَجَآءُو بِسِحْرٍ عَظِيمٍ ۝ ﴾

116. He (Mûsâ (Moses)) said: "Throw you (first)." So when they threw, they bewitched the eyes of the people, and struck terror into them, and they displayed a great magic.

Transliteration

115. Qaloo ya moosa imma an tulqiya wa-imma an nakoona nahnu almulqeena 116. Qala alqoo falamma alqaw saharoo aAAyuna alnnasi waistarhaboohum wajaoo bisihrin AAatheemin

Tafsir Ibn Kathir

The magicians challenged Musa, when they said,

(Either you throw (first), or shall we have the (first) throw) before you. In another Ayah, they said,

(Or we be the first to throw) (20:65). Musa said to them, you throw first. It was said that the wisdom behind asking them to throw first, is that - Allah knows best - the people might witness the magicians' sorcery first. When the magicians had cast their spell and captured the eyes, the clear and unequivocal truth came, at a time when they all anticipated and waited for it to come, thus making the truth even more impressive to their hearts. This is what happened. Allah said,

(So when they threw, they bewitched the eyes of the people, and struck terror into them,) meaning, they deceived the eyes and made them think that thet trick was real, when it was only an illusion, just as Allah said,

(So Musa conceived fear in himself. We (Allah) said: "Fear not! Surely, you will have the upper hand. And throw that which is in your right hand! It will swallow up that which they have made. That which they have made is only a magician's trick, and the magician will never be successful, to whatever amount (of skill) he may attain") (20:67-69). Ibn `Abbas commented that the magicians threw, "Thick ropes and long sticks, and they appeared to be crawling, an illusion that they created with their magic."

Surah: 7 Ayah: 117, Ayah: 118, Ayah: 119, Ayah: 120, Ayah: 121 & Ayah: 122

﴿ ۞ وَأَوْحَيْنَآ إِلَىٰ مُوسَىٰٓ أَنْ أَلْقِ عَصَاكَ فَإِذَا هِىَ تَلْقَفُ مَا يَأْفِكُونَ ۝ ﴾

117. And We inspired Mûsâ (Moses) (saying): "Throw your stick," and behold! It swallowed up straight away all the falsehoods which they showed.

﴿ فَوَقَعَ ٱلْحَقُّ وَبَطَلَ مَا كَانُوا۟ يَعْمَلُونَ ۝ ﴾

118. Thus truth was confirmed, and all that they did was made of no effect.

﴿ فَغُلِبُوا۟ هُنَالِكَ وَٱنقَلَبُوا۟ صَـٰغِرِينَ ۝ ﴾

119. So they were defeated there and returned disgraced.

﴿ وَأُلْقِىَ ٱلسَّحَرَةُ سَـٰجِدِينَ ۝ ﴾

120. And the sorcerers fell down prostrate.

﴿ قَالُوٓا۟ ءَامَنَّا بِرَبِّ ٱلْعَـٰلَمِينَ ۝ ﴾

121. They said: "We believe in the Lord of the 'Alamîn (mankind, jinn and all that exists).

﴿ رَبِّ مُوسَىٰ وَهَـٰرُونَ ۝ ﴾

122. "The Lord of Mûsâ (Moses) and Hârûn (Aaron)."

Transliteration

117. Waawhayna ila moosa an alqi AAasaka fa-itha hiya talqafu ma ya/fikoona 118. FawaqaAAa alhaqqu wabatala ma kanoo yaAAmaloona 119. Faghuliboo hunalika wainqalaboo saghireena   120. Waolqiya alssaharatu sajideena 121. Qaloo amanna birabbi alAAalameena   122. Rabbi moosa waharoona

Tafsir Ibn Kathir

Musa defeats the Magicians, Who believe in Him

Allah states that at that tremendous moment, in which Allah differentiated between Truth and Falsehood, He sent a revelation to His servant and Messenger Musa, peace be upon him, ordering him to throw the stick that he held in his right hand,

(It swallowed straight away) and devoured,

(all the falsehood which they showed.) the magic that they caused the illusion with, of magic with which they caused making it appear real, whereas it was not real at all. Ibn `Abbas said that Musa's stick swallowed all the ropes and sticks that the magicians threw. The magicians realized that this was from heaven and was by no means magic. They fell in prostration and proclaimed,

("We believe in the Lord of all that exists. The Lord of Musa and Harun). Muhammad bin Ishaq commented, "It followed the ropes and sticks one after another, until nothing that the sorcerers threw remained. Musa then held it in his hand, and it became a stick again just as it was before. The magicians fell in prostration and proclaimed, `We believe in the Lord of all that exists, the Lord of Musa and Harun. Had Musa been a magician, he would not have prevailed over us. '" Al-Qasim bin Abi

Bazzah commented, "Allah revealed to Musa to throw his stick. When he threw his stick, it became a huge, manifest snake that opened its mouth and swallowed the magicians' ropes and sticks. On that, the magicians fell in prostration. They did not raise their heads before seeing the Paradise, the Fire, and the recompense of their inhabitants."

Surah: 7 Ayah: 123, Ayah: 124, Ayah: 125 & Ayah: 126

﴿ قَالَ فِرْعَوْنُ ءَامَنتُم بِهِۦ قَبْلَ أَنْ ءَاذَنَ لَكُمْ إِنَّ هَـٰذَا لَمَكْرٌ مَّكَرْتُمُوهُ فِى ٱلْمَدِينَةِ لِتُخْرِجُواْ مِنْهَآ أَهْلَهَا فَسَوْفَ تَعْلَمُونَ ۝ ﴾

123. Fir'aun (Pharaoh) said: "You have believed in him (Mûsâ (Moses)) before I give you permission. Surely, this is a plot which you have plotted in the city to drive out its people, but you shall come to know.

﴿ لَأُقَطِّعَنَّ أَيْدِيَكُمْ وَأَرْجُلَكُم مِّنْ خِلَٰفٍ ثُمَّ لَأُصَلِّبَنَّكُمْ أَجْمَعِينَ ۝ ﴾

124. "Surely, I will cut off your hands and your feet from opposite sides, then I will crucify you all."

﴿ قَالُوٓاْ إِنَّآ إِلَىٰ رَبِّنَا مُنقَلِبُونَ ۝ ﴾

125. They said: "Verily, we are returning to our Lord.

﴿ وَمَا تَنقِمُ مِنَّآ إِلَّآ أَنْ ءَامَنَّا بِـَٔايَٰتِ رَبِّنَا لَمَّا جَآءَتْنَا رَبَّنَآ أَفْرِغْ عَلَيْنَا صَبْرًا وَتَوَفَّنَا مُسْلِمِينَ ۝ ﴾

126. "And you take vengeance on us only because we believed in the Ayât (proofs, evidences, lessons, signs, etc.) of our Lord when they reached us! Our Lord! pour out on us patience, and cause us to die as Muslims."

Transliteration

123. Qala firAAawnu amantum bihi qabla an athana lakum inna hatha lamakrun makartumoohu fee almadeenati litukhrijoo minha ahlaha fasawfa taAAlamoona 124. LaoqatiAAanna aydiyakum waarjulakum min khilafin thumma laosallibannakum ajmaAAeena 125. Qaloo inna ila rabbina munqaliboona 126. Wama tanqimu minna illa an amanna bi-ayati rabbina lamma jaatna rabbana afrigh AAalayna sabran watawaffana muslimeena

Tafsir Ibn Kathir

Fir`awn threatens the Magicians after They believed in Musa and Their Response to Him

Allah mentions the threats that the Fir`awn - may Allah curse him - made to the magicians after they believed Musa, peace be upon him, and the deceit and cunning that Fir`awn showed the people. Fir`awn said,

(Surely, this is a plot which you have plotted in the city to drive out its people,) meaning Fir`awn proclaimed, `Musa's defeating you today was because you plotted with him and agreed to that.' Fir`awn also said,

(He (Musa) is your chief who has taught you magic.) (20:71) However, Fir`awn and all those who had any sense of reason knew for sure that what Fir`awn said was utterly false. As soon as Musa came from Madyan, he called Fir`awn to Allah and demonstrated tremendous miracles and clear proofs for the Truth that he brought. Fir`awn then sent emissaries to various cities of his kingdom and collected magicians who were scattered throughout Egypt. Fir`awn and his people chose from them, summoned them, and Fir`awn promised them great rewards. These magicians were very eager to prevail over Musa in front of Fir`awn, so that they might become closer to him. Musa neither knew any of them nor saw or met them before. Fir`awn knew that, but he claimed otherwise to deceive the ignorant masses of his kingdom, just as Allah described them,

(Thus he (Fir`awn) fooled his people, and they obeyed him.) (43:54) Certainly, a people who believed Fir`awn in his statement,

("I am your lord, most high.") (79:24), are among the most ignorant and misguided creatures of Allah. In his Tafsir, As-Suddi reported that Ibn Mas`ud, Ibn `Abbas, and several other Companions, commented,

("Surely, this is a plot which you have plotted in the city...") "Musa met the leader of the magicians and said to him, `If I defeat you, will you believe in me and bear witness that what I brought is the truth' The magician said, `Tomorrow, I will produce a type of magic that cannot be defeated by another magic. By Allah! If you defeat me, I will believe in you and testify to your truth.' Fir`awn was watching them, and this is why he said what he said." His statement,

("to drive out its people"), means, so that you all cooperate to gain influence and power, replacing the chiefs and masters of this land. In this case, power in the state will be yours,

("but you shall come to know"), what I will do to you. He then explained his threat,

("Surely, I will cut off your hands and your feet from opposite sides.") by cutting the right hand and the left leg or the opposite,

("then I will crucify you all.") just as he said in another Ayah,

Chapter 7: Al-Araf (The Heights), Verses 088-206

("Fi the trunks of date palms") (20:71), Fi in this Ayah means "on". Ibn `Abbas said that Fir`awn was the first to crucify and cut off hands and legs on opposite sides. The magicians said,

("Verily, we are returning to our Lord.") They said, `We are now sure that we will go back to Allah. Certainly, Allah's punishment is more severe than your punishment and His torment for what you are calling us to, this day, and the magic you forced us to practice, is greater than your torment. Therefore, we will observe patience in the face of your punishment today, so that we are saved from Allah's torment.' They continued,

("Our Lord! pour out on us patience"), with your religion and being firm in it,

("and cause us to die as Muslims."), as followers of Your Prophet Musa, peace be upon him. They also said to Fir`awn,

("So decide whatever you desire to decree, for you can only decide for the life of this world. Verily, we have believed in our Lord, that He may forgive us our faults, and the magic to which you did compel us. And Allah is better (to reward) and more lasting (in punishment). Verily, whoever comes to his Lord as a criminal, then surely, for him is Hell, wherein he will neither die nor live. But whoever comes to Him (Allah) as a believer, and has done righteous good deeds, for such are the high ranks (in the Hereafter).) (20:72-75). The magicians started the day as sorcerers and ended as honorable martyrs! Ibn `Abbas, `Ubayd bin `Umayr, Qatadah and Ibn Jurayj commented, "They started the day as sorcerers and ended it as martyrs."

Surah: 7 Ayah: 127, Ayah: 128 & Ayah: 129

﴿ وَقَالَ ٱلْمَلَأُ مِن قَوْمِ فِرْعَوْنَ أَتَذَرُ مُوسَىٰ وَقَوْمَهُۥ لِيُفْسِدُواْ فِى ٱلْأَرْضِ وَيَذَرَكَ وَءَالِهَتَكَ ۚ قَالَ سَنُقَتِّلُ أَبْنَآءَهُمْ وَنَسْتَحْىِۦ نِسَآءَهُمْ وَإِنَّا فَوْقَهُمْ قَٰهِرُونَ ﴿١٢٧﴾

127. The chiefs of Fir'aun's (Pharaoh) people said: "Will you leave Mûsâ (Moses) and his people to spread mischief in the land, and to abandon you and your gods?" He said: "We will kill their sons, and let live their women, and we have indeed irresistible power over them."

﴿ قَالَ مُوسَىٰ لِقَوْمِهِ ٱسْتَعِينُواْ بِٱللَّهِ وَٱصْبِرُوٓاْ إِنَّ ٱلْأَرْضَ لِلَّهِ يُورِثُهَا مَن يَشَآءُ مِنْ عِبَادِهِۦ ۖ وَٱلْعَٰقِبَةُ لِلْمُتَّقِينَ ﴿١٢٨﴾

128. Mûsâ (Moses) said to his people: "Seek help in Allâh and be patient. Verily, the earth is Allâh's. He gives it as a heritage to whom He will of His slaves; and the (blessed) end is for the Muttaqûn (pious - see V.2:2)."

﴿ قَالُوٓاْ أُوذِينَا مِن قَبْلِ أَن تَأْتِيَنَا وَمِنۢ بَعْدِ مَا جِئْتَنَا ۚ قَالَ عَسَىٰ رَبُّكُمْ أَن يُهْلِكَ عَدُوَّكُمْ وَيَسْتَخْلِفَكُمْ فِى ٱلْأَرْضِ فَيَنظُرَ كَيْفَ تَعْمَلُونَ ۝ ﴾

129. They said: "We (Children of Israel) had suffered troubles before you came to us, and since you have come to us." He said: "It may be that your Lord will destroy your enemy and make you successors on the earth, so that He may see how you act?"

Transliteration

127. Waqala almalao min qawmi firAAawna atatharu moosa waqawmahu liyufsidoo fee al-ardi wayatharaka waalihataka qala sanuqattilu abnaahum wanastahyee nisaahum wa-inna fawqahum qahiroona 128. Qala moosa liqawmihi istaAAeenoo biAllahi waisbiroo inna al-arda lillahi yoorithuha man yashao min AAibadihi waalAAaqibatu lilmuttaqeena 129. Qaloo ootheena min qabli an ta/tiyana wamin baAAdi ma ji/tana qala AAasa rabbukum an yuhlika AAaduwwakum wayastakhlifakum fee al-ardi fayanthura kayfa taAAmaloona

Tafsir Ibn Kathir

Fir`awn vows to kill the Children of Israel, Who complain to Musa; Allah promises Them Victory

Allah mentions the conspiracy of Fir`awn and his people, their ill intentions and their hatred for Musa and his people.

(The chiefs of Fir`awn's people said), to Fir`awn,

("Will you leave Musa and his people"), will you let them be free,

("to spread mischief in the land"), spreading unrest among your subjects and calling them to worship their Lord instead of you Amazingly, these people were worried that Musa and his people would cause mischief! Rather, Fir`awn and his people are the mischief-makers, but they did not realize it. They said,

("and to abandon you and your gods") `Your gods', according to Ibn `Abbas, as As-Suddi narrated from him, "Were cows. Whenever they saw a beautiful cow, Fir`awn would command them to worship it. This is why As-Samiri, made the statue of a calf that seemed to moo for the Children of Israel." Fir`awn accepted his people's recommendation, saying,

("We will kill their sons, and let their women live") thus reiterating his previous order concerning the Children of Israel. He had tormented them (killing every newly born male) before Musa was born, so that Musa would not live. However, the opposite of what Fir`awn sought and intended occurred. The same end struck Fir`awn that he intended to subjugate and humiliate the Children of Israel with. Allah gave victory to the Children of Israel, humiliated and disgraced Fir`awn, and caused him to drown along with his soldiers. When Fir`awn insisted on his evil plot against the Children of Israel,

Chapter 7: Al-Araf (The Heights), Verses 088-206 33

(Musa said to his people: "Seek help in Allah and be patient") and promised them that the good end will be theirs and that they will prevail, saying,

("Verily, the earth is Allah's. He gives it as a heritage to whom He wills of His servants; and the (blessed) end is for the pious and righteous persons." They said: "We suffered troubles before you came to us, and since you have come to us.") The Children of Israel replied to Musa, `they (Fir`awn and his people) inflicted humiliation and disgrace on us, some you witnessed, both before and after you came to us, O Musa'! Musa replied, reminding them of their present situation and how it will change in the future,

("It may be that your Lord will destroy your enemy. ..") encouraging them to appreciate Allah when the afflictions are removed and replaced by a bounty.

Surah: 7 Ayah: 130 & Ayah: 131

﴿ وَلَقَدْ أَخَذْنَا ءَالَ فِرْعَوْنَ بِالسِّنِينَ وَنَقْصٍ مِّنَ الثَّمَرَاتِ لَعَلَّهُمْ يَذَّكَّرُونَ ۝ ﴾

130. And indeed We punished the people of Fir'aun (Pharaoh) with years of drought and shortness of fruits (crops), that they might remember (take heed).

﴿ فَإِذَا جَاءَتْهُمُ ٱلْحَسَنَةُ قَالُوا۟ لَنَا هَٰذِهِۦ ۖ وَإِن تُصِبْهُمْ سَيِّئَةٌ يَطَّيَّرُوا۟ بِمُوسَىٰ وَمَن مَّعَهُۥٓ ۗ أَلَآ إِنَّمَا طَٰٓئِرُهُمْ عِندَ ٱللَّهِ وَلَٰكِنَّ أَكْثَرَهُمْ لَا يَعْلَمُونَ ۝ ﴾

131. But whenever good came to them, they said: "Ours is this." And if evil afflicted them, they ascribed it to evil omens connected with Mûsâ (Moses) and those with him. Be informed! Verily, their evil omens are with Allâh but most of them know not.

Transliteration

130. Walaqad akhathna ala firAAawna bialssineena wanaqsin mina aluhthamarati laAAallahum yaththakkaroona 131. Fa-itha jaat-humu alhasanatu qaloo lana hathihi wa-in tusibhum sayyi-atun yattayyaroo bimoosa waman maAAahu ala innama ta-iruhum AAinda Allahi walakinna aktharahum la yaAAlamoona

Tafsir Ibn Kathir

Fir`awn and His People suffer Years of Drought

Allah said,

(And indeed We punished the people of Fir`awn) We tested and tried them,

(with years of drought) of famine due to little produce,

(and lack of fruits), which is less severe, according to Mujahid. Abu Ishaq narrated that Raja' bin Haywah said, "The date tree used to produce only one date!"

(That they might remember (take heed). But whenever good came to them) such as a fertile season and provisions,

(they said, "This is for us."), because we deserve it,

(and if evil afflicted them) drought and famine,

(they considered it an omen Musa and those with him.) saying that this hardship is because of them and what they have done.

(Verily, their omens are with Allah) `Ali bin Abi Talhah reported that Ibn `Abbas commented on the Ayah,

(Verily, their omens are with Allah) "Allah says that their afflictions are with and from Him,

(but most of them know not.)"

Surah: 7 Ayah: 132, Ayah: 133, Ayah: 134 & Ayah: 135

﴿ وَقَالُواْ مَهْمَا تَأْتِنَا بِهِۦ مِنْ ءَايَةٍ لِّتَسْحَرَنَا بِهَا فَمَا نَحْنُ لَكَ بِمُؤْمِنِينَ ۝ ﴾

132. They said (to Mûsâ (Moses)) "Whatever Ayât (proofs, evidences, verses, lessons, signs, revelations, etc.) you may bring to us, to work therewith your sorcery on us, we shall never believe in you."

﴿ فَأَرْسَلْنَا عَلَيْهِمُ ٱلطُّوفَانَ وَٱلْجَرَادَ وَٱلْقُمَّلَ وَٱلضَّفَادِعَ وَٱلدَّمَ ءَايَـٰتٍ مُّفَصَّلَـٰتٍ فَٱسْتَكْبَرُواْ وَكَانُواْ قَوْمًا مُّجْرِمِينَ ۝ ﴾

133. So We sent on them: the flood, the locusts, the lice, the frogs, and the blood (as a succession of) manifest signs, yet they remained arrogant, and they were of those people who were Mujrimûn (criminals, polytheists, sinners).

﴿ وَلَمَّا وَقَعَ عَلَيْهِمُ ٱلرِّجْزُ قَالُواْ يَـٰمُوسَى ٱدْعُ لَنَا رَبَّكَ بِمَا عَهِدَ عِندَكَ لَئِن كَشَفْتَ عَنَّا ٱلرِّجْزَ لَنُؤْمِنَنَّ لَكَ وَلَنُرْسِلَنَّ مَعَكَ بَنِىٓ إِسْرَٰٓءِيلَ ۝ ﴾

134. And when the punishment fell on them they said: "O Mûsâ (Moses)! Invoke your Lord for us because of His Promise to you. If you remove the punishment from us, we indeed shall believe in you, and we shall let the Children of Israel go with you."

﴿ فَلَمَّا كَشَفْنَا عَنْهُمُ ٱلرِّجْزَ إِلَىٰٓ أَجَلٍ هُم بَـٰلِغُوهُ إِذَا هُمْ يَنكُثُونَ ۝ ﴾

135. But when We removed the punishment from them to a fixed term, which they had to reach, behold! They broke their word!

Transliteration

132. Waqaloo mahma ta/tina bihi min ayatin litasharana biha fama nahnu laka bimu/mineena 133. Faarsalna AAalayhimu alttoofana waaljarada waalqummala waalddafadiAAa waalddama ayatin mufassalatin faistakbaroo wakanoo qawman mujrimeena 134. Walamma waqaAAa AAalayhimu alrrijzu qaloo ya moosa odAAu lana rabbaka bima AAahida AAindaka la-in kashafta AAanna alrrijza lanu/minanna laka walanursilanna maAAaka banee isra-eela 135. Falamma kashafna AAanhumu alrrijza ila ajalin hum balighoohu itha hum yankuthoona

Tafsir Ibn Kathir

Allah punishes the People of Fir`awn because of Their Rebellion

Allah describes the rebellion, tyranny, defiance of the truth and insistence on falsehood of the people of Fir`awn, prompting them to proclaim,

("Whatever Ayat you may bring to us, to work therewith your sorcery on us, we shall never believe in you.") They said, `whatever miracle, proof and evidence you bring us, we will neither accept it from you nor believe in you or what you came with.' Allah said,

(So We sent on them the Tufan) Ibn `Abbas commented; "It was a heavy rain that ruined the produce and fruits." He is also reported to have said that Tuwfan refers to mass death. Mujahid said it is water that carries the plague every where. As for the locust, it is the well-known insect, which is permissible to eat. It is recorded in the Two Sahihs, that Abu Ya`fur said that he asked `Abdullah bin Abi Awfa about locust. He said, "We participated in seven battles with the Messenger of Allah , and we used to eat locusts." Ash-Shafi`i, Ahmad bin Hanbal and Ibn Majah recorded from `Abdur-Rahman bin Zayd bin Aslam that his father narrated from Ibn `Umar that the Prophet said,

«أُحِلَّتْ لَنَا مَيْتَتَانِ وَدَمَانِ: الْحُوتُ وَالْجَرَادُ وَالْكَبِدُ وَالطِّحَالُ»

(We were allowed two dead animals and two (kinds of) blood: fish and locust, and kidney and spleen.) Ibn Abi Najih narrated from Mujahid about Allah's statement,

(So We sent on them: the flood, the locusts …) "Eating the nails on their doors and leaving the wood." As for the Qummal, Ibn `Abbas said that it is the grain bug, or, according to another view; small locusts that do not have wings. Similar was reported from Mujahid, `Ikrimah and Qatadah. Al-Hasan and Sa`id bin Jubayr said that `Qummal' are small black insects. Abu Ja`far bin Jarir recorded that Sa`id bin Jubayr said, "When Musa came to Fir`awn, he demanded, `Release the Children of Israel to me.' But, Fir`awn did not comply; and Allah sent the Tuwfan, and that is a rain which continued until they feared that it was a form of torment. They said to Musa, `Invoke your Lord to release us from this rain, and we will believe in you and send the

Children of Israel with you.' Musa invoked his Lord and He removed the affliction from them. However, they did not believe, nor did they send the Children of Israel with him. In that year, Allah allowed (the earth) to grow various types of produce, fruits and grass for them as never before. They said, `This is what we hoped for.' So Allah sent the locusts, and the locusts started to feed on the grass. When they saw the effect the locusts had on the grass, they knew that no vegetation would be saved from devastation. They said, `O Musa! Invoke your Lord so that He will remove the locusts from us, and we will believe in you and release the Children of Israel to you.' Musa invoked his Lord, and He removed the locusts. Still, they did not believe and did not send the Children of Israel with him.

They collected grains and kept them in their homes. They said, `We saved our crops.' However, Allah sent the Qummal, grain bugs, and one of them would take ten bags of grains to the mill, but only reap three small bags of grain. They said, `O Musa! Ask your Lord to remove the Qummal (weevil) from us and we will believe in you and send the Children of Israel with you.' Musa invoked his Lord, and Allah removed the Qummal from them. However, they did not send the Children of Israel with him. Once, when he was with Fir`awn, Musa heard the sound of a frog and said to Fir`awn, `What will you and your people suffer from this (the frogs)' Fir`awn said, `What can frogs do' Yet, by the time that night arrived a person would be sitting in a crowd of frogs that reached up to his chin and could not open his mouth to speak without a frog jumping in it. They said to Musa, `Invoke your Lord to remove these frogs from us, and we will believe in you and send the Children of Israel with you.' Musa invoked his Lord, but they did not believe.

Allah then sent blood that filled the rivers, wells and the water containers they had. They complained to Fir`awn, saying, `We are inflicted with blood and do not have anything to drink.' He said, `Musa has bewitched you.' They said, `How could he do that when whenever we look for water in our containers we found that it has turned into blood' They came to Musa and said, `Invoke your Lord to save us from this blood, and we will believe in you and send the Children of Israel with you.' Musa invoked his Lord and the blood stopped, but they did not believe nor send the Children of Israel with him." A similar account was attributed to Ibn `Abbas, As-Suddi, Qatadah and several others among the Salaf. Muhammad bin Ishaq bin Yasar said, "The enemy of Allah, Fir`awn, went back defeated and humiliated, after the sorcerers believed (in Musa). He insisted on remaining in disbelief and persisted in wickedness. Allah sent down the signs to him, and he (and his people) were first inflicted by famine. Allah then sent the flood, the locusts, the Qummal, the frogs then blood, as consecutive signs. When Allah sent the flood, it filled the surface of the earth with water. But the water level receded, and they could not make use of it to till the land or do anything else. They became hungry. This is when,

(They said: "O Musa! Invoke your Lord for us because of His promise to you. If you remove the punishment from us, we indeed shall believe in you, and we shall let the Children of Israel go with you.") Musa invoked his Lord and He removed the affliction from them, but they did not keep their promises. So Allah sent locusts that ate the trees and consumed the nails on their doors, until the doors fell from their homes and residences. They again said what they said to Musa before, and he called on his Lord and He removed the affliction. Still, they did not keep their promises, and Allah sent the Qummal. Musa, peace be upon him, was commanded to go to a mound and strike it with his staff. So Musa went to a huge mound, struck it with his staff and the Qummal fell out of it in tremendous numbers, until they overwhelmed the houses and food reserves, ultimately depriving them of sleep and rest. When they suffered under this affliction, they said similar to what they said before, and Musa invoked his Lord and He removed the affliction. They did not keep their promise and Allah sent the frogs to them, and they filled the houses, foods and pots. One of them would not pick up a piece of clothing, or uncover some food, without finding frogs in it. When this affliction became hard on them, they made similar promises as before, Musa supplicated to his Lord and Allah removed the affliction. They did not keep any of the promises they made, and Allah sent the blood, and the waters of the people of Fir`awn turned to blood. Any water they collected from a well, a river, or a container, turned to blood."

Surah: 7 Ayah: 136 & Ayah: 137

﴿ فَٱنتَقَمۡنَا مِنۡهُمۡ فَأَغۡرَقۡنَٰهُمۡ فِى ٱلۡيَمِّ بِأَنَّهُمۡ كَذَّبُواْ بِـَٔايَٰتِنَا وَكَانُواْ عَنۡهَا غَٰفِلِينَ ۝ ﴾

136. So We took retribution from them. We drowned them in the sea, because they belied Our Ayât (proofs, evidences, verses, lessons, signs, revelations, etc.) and were heedless about them.

﴿ وَأَوۡرَثۡنَا ٱلۡقَوۡمَ ٱلَّذِينَ كَانُواْ يُسۡتَضۡعَفُونَ مَشَٰرِقَ ٱلۡأَرۡضِ وَمَغَٰرِبَهَا ٱلَّتِى بَٰرَكۡنَا فِيهَاۖ وَتَمَّتۡ كَلِمَتُ رَبِّكَ ٱلۡحُسۡنَىٰ عَلَىٰ بَنِىٓ إِسۡرَٰٓءِيلَ بِمَا صَبَرُواْۖ وَدَمَّرۡنَا مَا كَانَ يَصۡنَعُ فِرۡعَوۡنُ وَقَوۡمُهُۥ وَمَا كَانُواْ يَعۡرِشُونَ ۝ ﴾

137. And We made the people who were considered weak to inherit the eastern parts of the land and the western parts thereof which We have blessed. And the fair Word of your Lord was fulfilled for the Children of Israel, because of their endurance. And We destroyed completely all the great works and buildings which Fir'aun (Pharaoh) and his people erected.

Transliteration

136. Faintaqamna minhum faaghraqnahum fee alyammi bi-annahum kaththaboo bi-ayatina wakanoo AAanha ghafileena   137. Waawrathna alqawma allatheena kanoo yustadAAafoona mashariqa al-ardi wamagharibaha allatee barakna feeha watammat kalimatu rabbika alhusna AAala banee isra-eela bima sabaroo wadammarna ma kana yasnaAAu firAAawnu waqawmuhu wama kanoo yaAArishoona

Tafsir Ibn Kathir

The People of Fir`awn drown in the Sea; the Children of Israel inherit the Holy Land

Allah states that when the people of Fir`awn rebelled and transgressed, even though He inflicted them with consecutive signs, one after another, He took retribution from them by drowning them in the sea that Musa parted by Allah's power, and he and the Children of Israel passed through. In their pursuit, Fir`awn and his soldiers went in the sea chasing Musa and his people. When they all had gone inside the water, the sea closed in on them and they all drowned, because they belied the Ayat of Allah and were heedless of them. Allah said that He has granted the people who were considered weak, the Children of Israel, to inherit the eastern and western parts of the land. Al-Hasan Al-Basri and Qatadah commented that Allah's statement,

(...the eastern parts of the land and the western parts thereof which We have blessed.) refers to the Sham area (Greater Syria). Also, Mujahid and Ibn Jarir said that Allah's statement,

(And the fair Word of your Lord was fulfilled for the Children of Israel, because of their endurance.) is explained by Allah's other statement,

(And We wished to do a favor to those who were weak (and oppressed) in the land, and to make them rulers and to make them the inheritors. And to establish them in the land, and We let Fir`awn and Haman and their hosts receive from them that which they feared) (28:5-6). Further, Allah's statement,

(And We destroyed what Fir`awn and his people produced,) meaning, We destroyed what Fir`awn and his people produced, such as agriculture and buildings.

(and what they erected.) Ibn `Abbas and Mujahid said that

(they erected) means, they built.

Surah: 7 Ayah: 138 & Ayah: 139

﴿ وَجَاوَزْنَا بِبَنِىٓ إِسْرَٰٓءِيلَ ٱلْبَحْرَ فَأَتَوْا۟ عَلَىٰ قَوْمٍ يَعْكُفُونَ عَلَىٰٓ أَصْنَامٍ لَّهُمْ قَالُوا۟ يَـٰمُوسَى ٱجْعَل لَّنَآ إِلَـٰهًا كَمَا لَهُمْ ءَالِهَةٌ قَالَ إِنَّكُمْ قَوْمٌ تَجْهَلُونَ ﴾

138. And We brought the Children of Israel (with safety) across the sea, and they came upon a people devoted to some of their idols (in worship). They said: "O Mûsâ (Moses)! Make for us an ilâh (a god) as they have âliha (gods)." He said: "Verily, you are a people who know not (the Majesty and Greatness of Allâh and what is obligatory upon you, i.e. to worship none but Allâh Alone, the One and the Only God of all that exists)."

﴿ إِنَّ هَـٰٓؤُلَآءِ مُتَبَّرٌ مَّا هُمْ فِيهِ وَبَـٰطِلٌ مَّا كَانُوا۟ يَعْمَلُونَ ﴾

139. (Mûsâ (Moses) added:) "Verily, these people will be destroyed for that which they are engaged in (idols-worship). And all that they are doing is in vain."

Transliteration

138. Wajawazna bibanee isra-eela albahra faataw AAala qawmin yaAAkufoona AAala asnamin lahum qaloo ya moosa ijAAal lana ilahan kama lahum alihatun qala innakum qawmun tajhaloona 139. Inna haola-i mutabbarun ma hum feehi wabatilun ma kanoo yaAAmaloona

Tafsir Ibn Kathir

The Children of Israel safely cross the Sea, but still held on to the Idea of Idol Worshipping

Allah mentions the words that the ignorant ones among the Children of Israel uttered to Musa after they crossed the sea and witnessed Allah's Ayat and great power.

(And they came upon a people devoted to some of their idols (in worship).) Some scholars of Tafsir said that the people mentioned here were from Canaan, or from the tribe of Lakhm. Ibn Jarir commented, "They were worshipping idols that they made in the shape of cows, and this influenced the Children of Israel later when they worshipped the calf. They said here,

("O Musa! Make for us a god as they have gods." He said: "Verily, you are an ignorant people.") Musa replied, you are ignorant of Allah's greatness and majesty and His purity from any partners or anything resembling Him.

("Verily, these people will be destroyed for that which they are engaged in) they will perish,

("and all that they are doing is in vain.") Commenting on this Ayah, Imam Abu Ja`far bin Jarir reported from Abu Waqid Al-Laythi that they (the Companions) went out from Makkah with the Messenger of Allah for (the battle of) Hunayn. Abu Waqid said, "Some of the disbelievers had a lote tree whose vicinity they used to remain in, and upon which they would hang their weapons on. That tree was called `Dhat Al-Anwat'. So when we passed by a huge, green lote tree, we said, `O Messenger of Allah! Appoint for us a Dhat Al-Anwat as they have.' He said,

»قُلْتُمْ وَالَّذِي نَفْسِي بِيَدِهِ كَمَا قَالَ قَوْمُ مُوسَى لِمُوسَى:

(by He in Whose Hand is my soul! You said just as what the people of Musa said to him:

(اجْعَل لَّنَآ إِلَـهًا كَمَا لَهُم ءَالِهَةٌ قَالَ إِنَّكُمْ قَوْمٌ تَجْهَلُونَ)

$$\left(\text{إِنَّ هَٰؤُلَاءِ مُتَبَّرٌ مَّا هُمْ فِيهِ وَبَاطِلٌ مَّا كَانُوا يَعْمَلُونَ} \right)$$

(("Make for us a god as they have gods." He said: "Verily, you are an ignorant people. Verily, these people will be destroyed for that which they are engaged in, and all that they are doing is in vain."))"

Surah: 7 Ayah: 140 & Ayah: 141

$$\left\{ \text{قَالَ أَغَيْرَ اللَّهِ أَبْغِيكُمْ إِلَٰهًا وَهُوَ فَضَّلَكُمْ عَلَى الْعَالَمِينَ} \right\}$$

140. He said: "Shall I seek for you an Ilâh (a God) other than Allâh, while He has given you superiority over the 'Alamîn (mankind and jinn of your time)."

$$\left\{ \text{وَإِذْ أَنجَيْنَاكُم مِّنْ آلِ فِرْعَوْنَ يَسُومُونَكُمْ سُوءَ الْعَذَابِ يُقَتِّلُونَ أَبْنَاءَكُمْ وَيَسْتَحْيُونَ نِسَاءَكُمْ وَفِي ذَٰلِكُم بَلَاءٌ مِّن رَّبِّكُمْ عَظِيمٌ} \right\}$$

141. And (remember) when We rescued you from Fir'aun's (Pharaoh) people, who were afflicting you with the worst torment, killing your sons and letting your women live. And in that was a great trial from your Lord.

Transliteration

140. Qala aghayra Allahi abgheekum ilahan wahuwa faddalakum AAala alAAalameena
141. Wa-ith anjaynakum min ali firAAawna yasoomoonakum soo-a alAAathabi yuqattiloona abnaakum wayastahyoona nisaakum wafee thalikum balaon min rabbikum AAatheemun

Tafsir Ibn Kathir

Reminding the Children of Israel of Allah's Blessings for Them

Musa reminded the Children of Israel of Allah's blessings, such as saving them from Fir`awn, his tyranny and the humiliation and disgrace they suffered. He reminded them of the glory and revenge against their enemy, when they watched them suffering in disgrace, destroyed by drowning and meeting utter demise. We mentioned this subject in the Tafsir of Surat Al-Baqarah.

Surah: 7 Ayah: 142

$$\left\{ \text{وَوَاعَدْنَا مُوسَىٰ ثَلَاثِينَ لَيْلَةً وَأَتْمَمْنَاهَا بِعَشْرٍ فَتَمَّ مِيقَاتُ رَبِّهِ أَرْبَعِينَ لَيْلَةً وَقَالَ مُوسَىٰ لِأَخِيهِ هَارُونَ اخْلُفْنِي فِي قَوْمِي وَأَصْلِحْ وَلَا تَتَّبِعْ سَبِيلَ الْمُفْسِدِينَ} \right\}$$

142. And We appointed for Mûsâ (Moses) thirty nights and added (to the period) ten (more), and he completed the term, appointed by his Lord, of forty nights. And

Mûsâ (Moses) said to his brother Hârûn (Aaron): "Replace me among my people, act in the Right Way (by ordering the people to obey Allâh and to worship Him Alone) and follow not the way of the Mufsidûn (mischief-makers)."

Transliteration

142. WawaAAadna moosa thalatheena laylatan waatmamnaha biAAashrin fatamma meeqatu rabbihi arbaAAeena laylatan waqala moosa li-akheehi haroona okhlufnee fee qawmee waaslih wala tattabiAA sabeela almufsideena

Tafsir Ibn Kathir

Musa fasts and worships Allah for Forty Days

Allah reminds the Children of Israel of the guidance that He sent to them by speaking directly to Musa and revealing the Tawrah to him. In it, was their law and the details of their legislation. Allah stated here that He appointed thirty nights for Musa. The scholars of Tafsir said that Musa fasted this period, and when they ended, Musa cleaned his teeth with a twig. Allah commanded him to complete the term adding ten more days, making the total forty. When the appointed term finished, Musa was about to return to Mount Tur, as Allah said,

(O Children of Israel! We delivered you from your enemy, and We made a covenant with you on the right side of the Mount) (20:80). Musa left his brother Harun with the Children of Israel and commanded him to use wisdom and refrain from mischief. This was only a reminder, for Harun was an honorable and noble Prophet who had grace and exalted standard with Allah, may Allah's peace and blessings be upon him and the rest of the Prophets.

Surah: 7 Ayah: 143

﴿ وَلَمَّا جَآءَ مُوسَىٰ لِمِيقَـٰتِنَا وَكَلَّمَهُ رَبُّهُ قَالَ رَبِّ أَرِنِىٓ أَنظُرْ إِلَيْكَ ۚ قَالَ لَن تَرَىٰنِى وَلَـٰكِنِ ٱنظُرْ إِلَى ٱلْجَبَلِ فَإِنِ ٱسْتَقَرَّ مَكَانَهُۥ فَسَوْفَ تَرَىٰنِى ۚ فَلَمَّا تَجَلَّىٰ رَبُّهُۥ لِلْجَبَلِ جَعَلَهُۥ دَكًّا وَخَرَّ مُوسَىٰ صَعِقًا ۚ فَلَمَّآ أَفَاقَ قَالَ سُبْحَـٰنَكَ تُبْتُ إِلَيْكَ وَأَنَا۠ أَوَّلُ ٱلْمُؤْمِنِينَ ﴾ ۝

143. And when Mûsâ (Moses) came at the time and place appointed by Us, and his Lord spoke to him; he said: "O my Lord! Show me (Yourself), that I may look upon You." Allâh said: "You cannot see Me, but look upon the mountain; if it stands still in its place then you shall see Me." So when his Lord appeared to the mountain, He made it collapse to dust, and Mûsâ (Moses) fell down unconscious. Then when he recovered his senses he said: "Glory be to You, I turn to You in repentance and I am the first of the believers."

Transliteration

143. Walamma jaa moosa limeeqatina wakallamahu rabbuhu qala rabbi arinee anthur ilayka qala lan taranee walakini onthur ila aljabali fa-ini istaqarra makanahu fasawfa taranee falamma tajalla rabbuhu liljabali jaAAalahu dakkan wakharra moosa saAAiqan falamma afaqa qala subhanaka tubtu ilayka waana awwalu almu/mineena

Tafsir Ibn Kathir

Musa asks to see Allah

Allah said that when Musa came for His appointment and spoke to Him directly, he asked to see Him,

("O my Lord! Show me (Yourself), that I may look upon You." Allah said: "You cannot see Me,") `You cannot' (Lan) by no means indicates that seeing Allah will never occur, as (the misguided sect of) Al-Mu`tazilah claimed. The Hadiths of Mutawatir grade narrated from the Messenger of Allah, affirm that the believers will see Allah in the Hereafter. We will mention these Hadiths under the explanation of Allah's statement,

(Some faces that Day shall be radiant. Looking at their Lord.) (75:22-23) In earlier Scriptures, it was reported that Allah said to Musa, "O Musa! No living soul sees Me, but will perish, and no solid but will be demolished." Allah said here,

(So when his Lord appeared to the mountain, He made it collapse to dust, and Musa fell down unconscious.) In his Musnad Imam Ahmad recorded from Anas bin Malik that the Prophet said about Allah's saying;

(فَلَمَّا تَجَلَّى رَبُّهُ لِلْجَبَلِ)

(And when his Lord appeared to the mountain,)

«هكذا»

(Like this) then he held out the tip of his little finger. At-Tirmidhi recorded this in the chapter of Tafsir for this Ayah, then he said; "This Hadith is Hasan Sahih Gharib." This was also recorded by Al-Hakim in his Mustadrak through the route of Hamad bin Salamah, and he said; "This Hadith is Sahih according to the criteria of Muslim and they did not record it." And As-Suddi reported that `Ikrimah reported from Ibn `Abbas about Allah's saying,

(And when his Lord appeared to the mountain,) Only the extent of the little finger appeared from Him,

(He made it collapse) as dust;

(And Musa fell down unconscious) fainting from it. Ibn Jarir recorded these because of the relation to the word Al-Ghashi.

Chapter 7: Al-Araf (The Heights), Verses 088-206

(Then when he (Musa) recovered his senses) after he lost consciousness,

(he said: "Glory be to You,") thus, praising, glorifying and honoring Allah since no living soul could see Him in this life and remain alive. Musa' statement,

("I turn to You in repentance") means, according to Mujahid, that from asking you to look at you,

("and I am the first of the believers."), among the Children of Israel, according to Ibn `Abbas, Mujahid, and Ibn Jarir preferred this view. Or, according to another narration from Ibn `Abbas, the meaning of,

("and I am the first of the believers."), is that `none shall see You (in this life).' Allah said,

(And Musa fell down unconscious.) Abu Sa`id Al-Khudri and Abu Hurayrah narrated a Hadith from the Prophet that is suitable to mention here. As for the Hadith from Abu Sa`id, Al-Bukhari recorded in his Sahih that he said: A Jew came to the Prophet after his face was smacked, and said, "O Muhammad! One of your companions from Al-Ansar smacked me on the face." The Prophet said,

«ادْعُوهُ»

(Summon him) and he was summoned. The Prophet asked him,

«لِمَ لَطَمْتَ وَجْهَهُ؟»

(Why did you smack his face) He said, "O Allah's Messenger! I passed by that Jew and heard him swearing, `No, by He Who has chosen Musa over mankind!' I said, `Over Muhammad too', and I became angry and struck his face." The Prophet said,

«لَا تُخَيِّرُونِي مِنْ بَيْنِ الْأَنْبِيَاءِ فَإِنَّ النَّاسَ يَصْعَقُونَ يَوْمَ الْقِيَامَةِ فَأَكُونُ أَوَّلَ مَنْ يُفِيقُ، فَإِذَا أَنَا بِمُوسَى آخِذٌ بِقَائِمَةٍ مِنْ قَوَائِمِ الْعَرْشِ، فَلَا أَدْرِي أَفَاقَ قَبْلِي أَمْ جُوزِيَ بِصَعْقَةِ الطُّورِ»

(Do not prefer me above the Prophets. Verily, on the Day of Resurrection, people will be struck unconscious, and I (feel that I) am the first to wake up. Thereupon I will find that Musa is holding onto a pillar of the Throne (`Arsh of Allah). I will not know if he woke up before me or he received his due (because of his) unconsciousness on (Mount) At-Tur.) Al-Bukhari recorded this Hadith in many locations of his Sahih, as did Muslim and Abu Dawud. As for the Hadith from Abu Hurayrah, Imam Ahmad and the Two Shaykhs (Al-Bukhari and Muslim) collected his narration.

Surah: 7 Ayah: 144 & Ayah: 145

﴿ قَالَ يَمُوسَىٰٓ إِنِّى ٱصْطَفَيْتُكَ عَلَى ٱلنَّاسِ بِرِسَٰلَٰتِى وَبِكَلَٰمِى فَخُذْ مَآ ءَاتَيْتُكَ وَكُن مِّنَ ٱلشَّٰكِرِينَ ۞ ﴾

144. (Allâh) said: "O Mûsâ (Moses) I have chosen you above men by My Messages, and by My speaking (to you). So hold that which I have given you and be of the grateful."

﴿ وَكَتَبْنَا لَهُۥ فِى ٱلْأَلْوَاحِ مِن كُلِّ شَىْءٍ مَّوْعِظَةً وَتَفْصِيلًا لِّكُلِّ شَىْءٍ فَخُذْهَا بِقُوَّةٍ وَأْمُرْ قَوْمَكَ يَأْخُذُوا۟ بِأَحْسَنِهَا سَأُو۟رِيكُمْ دَارَ ٱلْفَٰسِقِينَ ۞ ﴾

145. And We wrote for him on the Tablets the lesson to be drawn from all things and the explanation of all things (and said): Hold unto these with firmness, and enjoin your people to take the better therein. I shall show you the home of Al-Fâsiqûn (the rebellious, disobedient to Allâh).

Transliteration

144. Qala ya moosa innee istafaytuka AAala alnnasi birisalatee wabikalamee fakhuth ma ataytuka wakun mina alshshakireena   145. Wakatabna lahu fee al-alwahi min kulli shay-in mawAAithatan watafseelan likulli shay-in fakhuthha biquwwatin wa/mur qawmaka ya/khuthoo bi-ahsaniha saoreekum dara alfasiqeena

Tafsir Ibn Kathir

Allah chooses Musa and gives Him the Tablets

Allah states that He spoke to Musa directly and informed him that He has chosen him above the people of his time, by His Message and by speaking to him. Here we should mention that there is no doubt that Muhammad is the chief of all the Children of Adam, the earlier and later ones among them. This is why Allah has chosen him to be the Final and Last Prophet and Messenger, whose Law shall remain dominant and valid until the commencement of the Last Hour. Muhammad's followers are more numerous than the followers of all Prophets and Messengers. After Muhammad , the next in rank of honor and virtue is Ibrahim upon him be peace,, then Musa, son of `Imran, who spoke to the Most Beneficent directly. Allah commanded Musa, saying,

(So hold to that which I have given you), of My Speech and conversation with you,

(and be of the grateful) , for it and do not ask for what is beyond your capacity to bear. Allah stated that He has written lessons and exhortation for all things and explanations for all things on the Tablets. It was said that in the Tablets, Allah wrote advice and the details of the commandments for lawful and prohibited matters. The Tablets contained the Tawrah, that Allah described;

(And indeed We gave Musa -- after We had destroyed the generations of old -- the Scripture as an enlightenment for mankind)(28: 43). It was also said that Allah gave Musa the Tablets before the Tawrah, and Allah knows best. Allah said next,

(Hold unto these with firmness), be firm on the obedience,

(and enjoin your people to take the better therein.) Sufyan bin `Uyaynah said, "Abu Sa`d narrated to us from `Ikrimah from Ibn `Abbas that "Musa, peace be upon him, was commanded to adhere to the toughest of what was ordained on his people." Allah's statement,

(I shall show you the home of the rebellious), means, you will witness the recompense of those who defy My order and deviate from My obedience, the destruction, demise and utter loss they will suffer.

Surah: 7 Ayah: 146 & Ayah: 147

﴿ سَأَصْرِفُ عَنْ ءَايَـٰتِىَ ٱلَّذِينَ يَتَكَبَّرُونَ فِى ٱلْأَرْضِ بِغَيْرِ ٱلْحَقِّ وَإِن يَرَوْاْ كُلَّ ءَايَةٍ لَّا يُؤْمِنُواْ بِهَا وَإِن يَرَوْاْ سَبِيلَ ٱلرُّشْدِ لَا يَتَّخِذُوهُ سَبِيلًا وَإِن يَرَوْاْ سَبِيلَ ٱلْغَىِّ يَتَّخِذُوهُ سَبِيلًا ۚ ذَٰلِكَ بِأَنَّهُمْ كَذَّبُواْ بِـَٔايَـٰتِنَا وَكَانُواْ عَنْهَا غَـٰفِلِينَ ۝

146. I shall turn away from My Ayât (verses of the Qur'ân) those who behave arrogantly on the earth, without a right, and (even) if they see all the Ayât (proofs, evidences, verses, lessons, signs, revelations, etc.), they will not believe in them. And if they see the way of righteousness (monotheism, piety, and good deeds), they will not adopt it as the Way, but if they see the way of error (polytheism, crimes and evil deeds), they will adopt that way, that is because they have rejected Our Ayât (proofs, evidences, verses, lessons, signs, revelations, etc.) and were heedless (to learn a lesson) from them.

﴿ وَٱلَّذِينَ كَذَّبُواْ بِـَٔايَـٰتِنَا وَلِقَآءِ ٱلْأَخِرَةِ حَبِطَتْ أَعْمَـٰلُهُمْ ۚ هَلْ يُجْزَوْنَ إِلَّا مَا كَانُواْ يَعْمَلُونَ ۝

147. Those who deny Our Ayât (proofs, evidences, verses, lessons, signs, revelations, etc.) and the Meeting in the Hereafter (Day of Resurrection,), vain are their deeds. Are they requited with anything except what they used to do?

Transliteration

146. Saasrifu AAan ayatiya allatheena yatakabbaroona fee al-ardi bighayri alhaqqi wa-in yaraw kulla ayatin la yu/minoo biha wa-in yaraw sabeela alrrushdi la yattakhithoohu sabeelan wa-in yaraw sabeela alghayyi yattakhithoohu sabeelan thalika bi-annahum kaththaboo bi-ayatina wakanoo AAanha ghafileena   147. Waallatheena kaththaboo

bi-ayatina waliqa-i al-akhirati habitat aAAmaluhum hal yujzawna illa ma kanoo yaAAmaloona

Tafsir Ibn Kathir

Arrogant People will be deprived of Allah's Ayat

Allah said,

(I shall turn away from My Ayat those who behave arrogantly on the earth, without a right). Allah says, "I shall deprive the hearts of those who are too proud to obey Me, and arrogant with people without right, from understanding the signs and proofs that testify to My Might, Law and Commandments." And just as they acted arrogantly without justification, Allah has disgraced them with ignorance. Allah said in another Ayah,

(And We shall turn their hearts and their eyes away (from guidance), as they refused to believe therein for the first time) (6:110), and,

(So when they turned away (from the path of Allah), Allah turned their hearts away (from the right path).) (61:5) Sufyan bin `Uyaynah commented on this Ayah,

(I shall turn away from My Ayat those who behave arrogantly on the earth, without a right), "(Allah says) I shall snatch away comprehension of the Qur'an from them and turn them away from My Ayat." Ibn Jarir commented on Sufyan's statement that, "This indicates that this part of the Ayah is addressed to this Ummah." This is not necessarily true, for Ibn `Uyaynah actually meant that this occurs in every Ummah and that there is no difference between one Ummah and another Ummah in this regard. Allah knows best. Allah said next,

(and (even) if they see all the Ayat, they will not believe in them). Allah said in a similar Ayah,

(Truly, those, against whom the Word (wrath) of your Lord has been justified, will not believe. Even if every sign should come to them, until they see the painful torment.) (10:96-97) Allah's statement,

(And if they see the way of righteousness, they will not adopt it as the way,) means, even if the way of guidance and safety appears before them, they will not take it, but if the way that leads to destruction and misguidance appears to them, they adopt that way. Allah explains why they do this,

(that is because they have rejected Our Ayat), in their hearts,

(and were heedless of them.), gaining no lessons from the Ayat. Allah's statement,

(Those who deny Our Ayat and the meeting in the Hereafter, vain are their deeds.) indicates that whoever among them does this, remaining on this path until death, then all his deeds will be in vain. Allah said next,

(Are they requited with anything except what they used to do) meaning, `We only recompense them according to the deeds that they performed, good for good and evil for evil. Surely, as you bring forth, you reap the harvest thereof.'

Surah: 7 Ayah: 148 & Ayah: 149

﴿ وَٱتَّخَذَ قَوْمُ مُوسَىٰ مِنۢ بَعْدِهِۦ مِنْ حُلِيِّهِمْ عِجْلًا جَسَدًا لَّهُۥ خُوَارٌ أَلَمْ يَرَوْاْ أَنَّهُۥ لَا يُكَلِّمُهُمْ وَلَا يَهْدِيهِمْ سَبِيلًا ٱتَّخَذُوهُ وَكَانُواْ ظَٰلِمِينَ ۝ ﴾

148. And the people of Mûsâ (Moses) made in his absence, out of their ornaments, the image of a calf (for worship). It had a sound (as if it was mooing). Did they not see that it could neither speak to them nor guide them to the way? They took it for worship and they were Zâlimûn (wrong-doers).

﴿ وَلَمَّا سُقِطَ فِىٓ أَيْدِيهِمْ وَرَأَوْاْ أَنَّهُمْ قَدْ ضَلُّواْ قَالُواْ لَئِن لَّمْ يَرْحَمْنَا رَبُّنَا وَيَغْفِرْ لَنَا لَنَكُونَنَّ مِنَ ٱلْخَٰسِرِينَ ۝ ﴾

149. And when they regretted and saw that they had gone astray, they (repented and) said: "If our Lord have not mercy upon us and forgive us, we shall certainly be of the losers."

Transliteration

148. Waittakhatha qawmu moosa min baAAdihi min huliyyihim AAijlan jasadan lahu khuwarun alam yaraw annahu la yukallimuhum wala yahdeehim sabeelan ittakhathoohu wakanoo thalimeena 149. Walamma suqita fee aydeehim waraaw annahum qad dalloo qaloo la-in lam yarhamna rabbuna wayaghfir lana lanakoonanna mina alkhasireena

Tafsir Ibn Kathir

Story of worshipping the Calf

Allah describes the misguidance of those who worshipped the calf that As-Samiri made for them from the ornaments they borrowed from the Copts. He made the shape of a calf with these ornaments and threw in it a handful of dust from the trace of the horse that the Angel Jibril was riding, and the calf seemed to moo. This occurred after Musa went for the appointed term with his Lord, where Allah told him about what happened when he was on Mount Tur. Allah said about His Honorable Self,

((Allah) said: "Verily, We have tried your people in your absence, and As-Samiri has led them astray") (20:85). The scholars of Tafsir have different views over the calf, whether it actually became alive and mooing, or if it remained made of gold, but the air entering it made it appear to be mooing. These are two opinions. Allah knows best. It was reported that when the statue mooed, the Jews started dancing around it and fell into misguidance because they adored it. They said that this, the calf, is your god and the god of Musa, but Musa forgot it! Allah answered them,

(Did they not see that it could not return them a word (for answer), and that it had neither power to harm them nor to do them good) (20:89). Allah said here,

(Did they not see that it could neither speak to them nor guide them to the way) Allah condemned the Jews for falling into misguidance, worshipping the calf and ignoring the Creator of the heavens and earth, the Lord and King of all things. They worshipped besides Him a statue made in the shape of a calf, that seemed to moo, but it neither spoke to them nor brought them any benefit. Rather, their very sense of reason was blinded because of ignorance and misguidance. Allah's statement,

(And when they regretted), and felt sorrow for their action,

(and saw that they had gone astray, they said: "If our Lord have not mercy upon us and forgive us, we will certainly become among the losers.") or among the destroyed ones. This was their recognition of their sin and their way of seeking salvation from Allah the Most Mighty and Majestic.

Surah: 7 Ayah: 150 & Ayah: 151

﴿ وَلَمَّا رَجَعَ مُوسَىٰ إِلَىٰ قَوْمِهِ غَضْبَٰنَ أَسِفًا قَالَ بِئْسَمَا خَلَفْتُمُونِى مِنۢ بَعْدِىٓ أَعَجِلْتُمْ أَمْرَ رَبِّكُمْ وَأَلْقَى ٱلْأَلْوَاحَ وَأَخَذَ بِرَأْسِ أَخِيهِ يَجُرُّهُۥٓ إِلَيْهِ قَالَ ٱبْنَ أُمَّ إِنَّ ٱلْقَوْمَ ٱسْتَضْعَفُونِى وَكَادُوا۟ يَقْتُلُونَنِى فَلَا تُشْمِتْ بِىَ ٱلْأَعْدَآءَ وَلَا تَجْعَلْنِى مَعَ ٱلْقَوْمِ ٱلظَّٰلِمِينَ ۝ ﴾

150. And when Mûsâ (Moses) returned to his people, angry and grieved, he said: "What an evil thing is that which you have done (i.e. worshipping the calf) during my absence. Did you hasten and go ahead as regards the matter of your Lord (you left His worship)?" And he threw down the Tablets and seized his brother by (the hair of) his head and dragged him towards him. Hârûn (Aaron) said: "O son of my mother! Indeed the people judged me weak and were about to kill me, so make not the enemies rejoice over me, nor put me amongst the people who are Zâlimûn (wrong-doers)."

﴿ قَالَ رَبِّ ٱغْفِرْ لِى وَلِأَخِى وَأَدْخِلْنَا فِى رَحْمَتِكَ وَأَنتَ أَرْحَمُ ٱلرَّٰحِمِينَ ۝ ﴾

151. Mûsâ (Moses) said: "O my Lord! Forgive me and my brother, and admit us into Your Mercy, for you are the Most Merciful of those who show mercy."

Transliteration

150. Walamma rajaAAa moosa ila qawmihi ghadbana asifan qala bi/sama khalaftumoonee min baAAdee aAAajiltum amra rabbikum waalqa al-alwaha waakhatha bira/si akheehi yajurruhu ilayhi qala ibna omma inna alqawma istadAAafoonee wakadoo yaqtuloonanee fala tushmit biya al-aAAdaa wala tajAAalnee maAAa alqawmi alththalimeena 151. Qala rabbi ighfir lee wali-akhee waadkhilna fee rahmatika waanta arhamu alrrahimeena

Tafsir Ibn Kathir

Allah states that when Musa returned to his people after conversation with his Lord, he became angry and full of regret. Abu Ad-Darda' said that Asif, or regret, is the severest type of anger.

(He (Musa) said: "What an evil thing is that which you have done during my absence.") evil it is that which you committed after I departed and left you, by worshiping the calf,

(Did you hasten in the matter of your Lord) Musa said, `You wanted me to rush back to you, even though (being there) this was Allah's decision' Allah said next,

(And he threw down the Tablets and seized his brother by his head and dragged him towards him.) This Ayah demonstrates the meaning of the Hadith,

«لَيْسَ الْخَبَرُ كَالْمُعَايَنَةِ»

(Information is not the same as observation.) It indicates that Musa threw down the Tablets because he was angry at his people, according to the majority of scholars of early and latter times. Allah said,

(and seized his brother by (the hair of) his head and dragged him towards him.) for Musa feared that Harun might have not tried hard enough to forbid them from their evil action. In another Ayah, Allah said,

.(He (Musa) said: "O Harun ! What prevented you when you saw them going astray. That you followed me not (according to my advice to you) Have you then disobeyed my order" He (Harun) said: "O son of my mother! Seize (me) not by my beard, nor by my head! Verily, I feared lest you should say: `You have caused a division among the Children of Israel, and you have not respected (waited or observed) my word!'") (20:92-94). Here, Allah said that Harun said,

("O son of my mother! Indeed the people judged me weak and were about to kill me, so make not the enemies rejoice over me, nor put me among the people who are wrongdoers.") Harun said, `Do not place me on the same level as they are, as if I was one of them.' Further, Harun said, `O son of my mother', so that Musa would feel more mercy and leniency towards him, even though Harun was also the son of Musa's father. When Musa was satisfied that his brother was innocent,

(And Harun indeed had said to them beforehand: "O my people! You are being tried in this, and verily, your Lord is (Allah) the Most Gracious, so follow me and obey my order.") (20:90), this is when,

(he said) Musa,

("O my Lord! Forgive me and my brother, and admit us into Your mercy, for you are the Most Merciful of those who show mercy.") Ibn Abi Hatim recorded that Ibn `Abbas said that the Messenger of Allah said,

«يَرْحَمُ اللهُ مُوسَى لَيْسَ الْمُعَايِنُ كَالْمُخْبِرِ أَخْبَرَهُ رَبُّهُ عَزَّ وَجَلَّ أَنَّ قَوْمَهُ فُتِنُوا بَعْدَهُ فَلَمْ يَلْقِ الْأَلْوَاحَ فَلَمَّا رَآهُمْ وَعَايَنَهُمْ أَلْقَى الْأَلْوَاحَ»

(May Allah grant His mercy to Musa! Surely, he who observes (something) is nothing like he who is informed about it. His Lord, the Exalted and Most Honored, told him that his people were tested after him, but he did not throw the Tablets. When he saw them with his eyes, then he threw the Tablets.)

Surah: 7 Ayah: 152 & Ayah: 153

﴿ إِنَّ ٱلَّذِينَ ٱتَّخَذُواْ ٱلْعِجْلَ سَيَنَالُهُمْ غَضَبٌ مِّن رَّبِّهِمْ وَذِلَّةٌ فِى ٱلْحَيَوٰةِ ٱلدُّنْيَا وَكَذَٰلِكَ نَجْزِى ٱلْمُفْتَرِينَ ﴾

152. Certainly, those who took the calf (for worship), wrath from their Lord and humiliation will come upon them in the life of this world. Thus do We recompense those who invent lies.

﴿ وَٱلَّذِينَ عَمِلُواْ ٱلسَّيِّـَٔاتِ ثُمَّ تَابُواْ مِنۢ بَعْدِهَا وَءَامَنُوٓاْ إِنَّ رَبَّكَ مِنۢ بَعْدِهَا لَغَفُورٌ رَّحِيمٌ ﴾

153. But those who committed evil deeds and then repented afterwards and believed, verily, your Lord after (all) that is indeed Oft-Forgiving, Most Merciful.

Transliteration

152. Inna allatheena ittakhathoo alAAijla sayanaluhum ghadabun min rabbihim wathillatun fee alhayati alddunya wakathalika najzee almuftareena 153. Waallatheena AAamiloo alssayyi-ati thumma taboo min baAAdiha waamanoo inna rabbaka min baAAdiha laghafoorun raheemun

Tafsir Ibn Kathir

The `wrath' mentioned here that struck the Children of Israel because of their worshipping the calf, means, Allah did not accept their repentance until some of them (who did not worship the calf) killed others (who worshipped the calf). We mentioned this story in Surat Al-Baqarah,

(So turn in repentance to your Creator and kill yourselves (the guilty), that will be better for you before your Creator." Then He accepted your repentance. Truly, He is the One Who accepts repentance, the Most Merciful.) (2:54) As for the humiliation mentioned in the Ayah, it pertains to the disgrace and humiliation that the Jews suffered in the life of this world. Allah's statement,

(Thus do We recompense those who invent lies) is for all those who invent an innovation (in religion). Surely, the disgrace resulting from inventing an innovation (in religion) and defying Allah's Message, will be placed in the heart and from there on to the shoulders. Al-Hasan Al-Basri said; "The disgrace of innovation will weigh on their shoulders even if they were to gallop on their mules or trot on their work horses." Ayyub As-Sakhtiyani narrated from Abu Qilabah Al-Jarmi that he commented on this Ayah,

(Thus do We recompense those who invent lies.) "By Allah! This Ayah is for all those who invent a lie, until the Day of Resurrection." Also, Sufyan bin `Uyaynah said, "Every person who invents a Bid`ah (innovation in the religion) will taste disgrace."Allah tells His servants that He accepts repentance from His servants for any sin, even Shirk, Kufr, hypocrisy and disobedience. Allah said:

(But those who committed evil deeds and then repented afterwards and believed, verily, your Lord) O Muhammad, Messenger of Repentance and Prophet of Mercy,

(after that) after committing that evil action,

(is indeed Oft-Forgiving, Most Merciful.) Ibn Abi Hatim reported that `Abdullah bin Mas`ud was asked about a man committing fornication with a woman and then marrying her, and Ibn Mas`ud recited this Ayah,

(But those who committed evil deeds and then repented afterwards and believed, verily, your Lord after (all) that is indeed Oft-Forgiving, Most Merciful.) `Abdullah recited this Ayah ten times, neither allowing nor disallowing it.

Surah: 7 Ayah: 154

﴿ وَلَمَّا سَكَتَ عَن مُّوسَى ٱلْغَضَبُ أَخَذَ ٱلْأَلْوَاحَ وَفِي نُسْخَتِهَا هُدًى وَرَحْمَةٌ لِّلَّذِينَ هُمْ لِرَبِّهِمْ يَرْهَبُونَ ﴾

154. And when the anger of Mûsâ (Moses) was calmed down, he took up the Tablets; and in their inscription was guidance and mercy for those who fear their Lord.

Transliteration

154. Walamma sakata AAan moosa alghadabu akhatha al-alwaha wafee nuskhatiha hudan warahmatun lillatheena hum lirabbihim yarhaboona

Tafsir Ibn Kathir

Musa picked up the Tablets when His Anger subsided

Allah said next,

(And when calmed) and subsided,

(the anger of Musa) with his people,

(he took up the Tablets), which he had thrown out of jealousy for Allah and anger for His sake, because of his people worshipping the calf,

(and in their inscription was guidance and mercy for those who fear their Lord.) Several scholars of Tafsir said that when Musa threw the Tablets on the ground they were shattered and he collected the pieces afterwards. Musa found in its inscription guidance and mercy, but the specific details of the Law was lost, so they said. They also claimed that the shattered pieces of the Tablets still remained in the treasury safes of some Israelite kings until the Islamic State came into existence. Only Allah knows if these statements are true.

Surah: 7 Ayah: 155 & Ayah: 156

﴿ وَٱخْتَارَ مُوسَىٰ قَوْمَهُۥ سَبْعِينَ رَجُلًا لِّمِيقَـٰتِنَا ۖ فَلَمَّآ أَخَذَتْهُمُ ٱلرَّجْفَةُ قَالَ رَبِّ لَوْ شِئْتَ أَهْلَكْتَهُم مِّن قَبْلُ وَإِيَّـٰىَ ۖ أَتُهْلِكُنَا بِمَا فَعَلَ ٱلسُّفَهَآءُ مِنَّآ ۖ إِنْ هِىَ إِلَّا فِتْنَتُكَ تُضِلُّ بِهَا مَن تَشَآءُ وَتَهْدِى مَن تَشَآءُ ۖ أَنتَ وَلِيُّنَا فَٱغْفِرْ لَنَا وَٱرْحَمْنَا ۖ وَأَنتَ خَيْرُ ٱلْغَـٰفِرِينَ ۞ ﴾

155. And Mûsâ (Moses) chose out of his people seventy (of the best) men for Our appointed time and place of meeting, and when they were seized with a violent earthquake, he said: "O my Lord, if it had been Your Will, You could have destroyed them and me before; would You destroy us for the deeds of the foolish ones among us? It is only Your Trial by which You lead astray whom You will, and keep guided whom You will. You are our Walî (Protector), so forgive us and have Mercy on us: for You are the Best of those who forgive.

﴿ ۞ وَٱكْتُبْ لَنَا فِى هَـٰذِهِ ٱلدُّنْيَا حَسَنَةً وَفِى ٱلْـَٔاخِرَةِ إِنَّا هُدْنَآ إِلَيْكَ ۚ قَالَ عَذَابِىٓ أُصِيبُ بِهِۦ مَنْ أَشَآءُ ۖ وَرَحْمَتِى وَسِعَتْ كُلَّ شَىْءٍ ۚ فَسَأَكْتُبُهَا لِلَّذِينَ يَتَّقُونَ وَيُؤْتُونَ ٱلزَّكَوٰةَ وَٱلَّذِينَ هُم بِـَٔايَـٰتِنَا يُؤْمِنُونَ ۞ ﴾

156. And ordain for us good in this world, and in the Hereafter. Certainly we have turned unto You." He said: (As to) My Punishment I afflict therewith whom I will and My Mercy embraces all things. That (Mercy) I shall ordain for those who are

the Muttaqûn (pious - see V.2:2), and give Zakât; and those who believe in Our Ayât (proofs, evidences, verses, lessons, signs and revelations, etc.);

Transliteration

155. Waikhtara moosa qawmahu sabAAeena rajulan limeeqatina falamma akhathathumu alrrajfatu qala rabbi law shi/ta ahlaktahum min qablu wa-iyyaya atuhlikuna bima faAAala alssufahao minna in hiya illa fitnatuka tudillu biha man tashao watahdee man tashao anta waliyyuna faighfir lana wairhamna waanta khayru alghafireena 156. Waoktub lana fee hathihi alddunya hasanatan wafee al-akhirati inna hudna ilayka qala AAathabee oseebu bihi man ashao warahmatee wasiAAat kulla shay-in fasaaktubuha lillatheena yattaqoona wayu/toona alzzakata waallatheena hum bi-ayatina yu/minoona

Tafsir Ibn Kathir

Seventy Men from the Children of Israel go for the appointed Meeting Place that Allah designated, Allah later on destroys Them

`Ali bin Abi Talhah reported that Ibn `Abbas commented; "Allah commanded Musa to choose seventy men. So he chose them and proceeded with them in order that they supplicate to their Lord. Their supplication included asking Allah, `O Allah! Give us what you have never given anyone before us and will never give anyone after us!' Allah disliked this supplication and they were seized with a violent earthquake, Musa said:

("O my Lord, if it had been Your will, You could have destroyed them and me before.)'" As-Suddi said, "Allah commanded Musa to come with thirty men from the Children of Israel, apologizing for worshipping the calf; and He gave them an appointed time and place.

(And Musa chose out of his people seventy (of the best) men.) He chose these men and went along with them so that they could apologize. When they reached the appointed place, they said,

(We shall never believe in you), (2:55) `O Musa,

(until we see Allah plainly,) for you spoke to Him,' they said, `therefore, show Him to us,'

(but they were struck with a bolt of lightning) (4:153) and they died. Musa stood up crying, invoking Allah, `O Lord! What should I tell the Children of Israel, when I go back to them after You destroyed their best men'

("O my Lord, if it had been Your will, You could have destroyed them and me before").'" Muhammad bin Ishaq said, "Musa chose seventy of the best men from the Children of Israel. He said to them, `Go to the meeting with Allah and repent for what you committed. Beg His forgiveness for those of your people whom you left behind. Fast, purify yourselves and clean your clothes.' So, he went with them to Mount Tur in Sinai for the meeting place and time designated by his Lord. He went there only with the leave and knowledge of Allah. According to what has been mentioned to me, when the seventy did what he ordered them to do, and went with him to the meeting of Musa with his Lord, they said, `Request that we may also hear the words of our Lord.' So he replied, `I shall.' When Musa approached the mountain it became completely covered with columns of clouds, Musa approached it and entered in them. He said to the people, `Approach.' But when Allah spoke to Musa, his cloak was surrounded by a brilliant light which no human could bear to look at, so below him a barrier was placed and the people approached. When they entered the cloud they fell prostrate and they heard Him while he was speaking to Musa, commanding him and forbidding him, saying what to do and what not to do. When He completed commanding him, and removed the cloud from Musa, he faced the people and they said, `O Musa! We will not believe in you unless we see Allah directly.' So the thunder shook them, their souls were captured and they all died. Musa stood up invoking, begging and supplicating to his Lord,

("O my Lord, if it had been Your will, You could have destroyed them and me before.")' meaning, `They were foolish. Would You destroy anyone who comes after me from the Children of Israel' Ibn `Abbas, Qatadah, Mujahid and Ibn Jarir At-Tabari said, "They were seized by the tremor or lightning, because they neither shunned nor forbade their people who worshipped the calf." This is supported by Musa's statement,

("would You destroy us for the deeds of the fools among us") He said next,

("It is only Your Fitnah") affliction, test and trial, according to Ibn `Abbas, Sa`id bin Jubayr, Abu Al-`Aliyah, Ar-Rabi` bin Anas and several among the Salaf and latter scholars. This is the only plausible meaning, in which Musa says, "The decision is Yours (O Allah), and the judgment, and whatever You will occurs. You misguide whom You will, guide whom You will, and none can guide whom You misguide or misguide whom You guide. There is none who can give what You deprive or avert what You give. The sovereignty is all Yours, and Yours is the judgment, the creation and the decision." The Ayah,

("You are our protector, so forgive us and have mercy on us: for You are the best of those who forgive."), pertains to (Allah's) covering the mistake and not punishing for the sin. Whenever mercy is mentioned along with forgiveness (such as in Musa's supplication to Allah), it includes the hope that Allah does not permit one to fall into that act again.

("for You are the best of those who forgive,") for none except You can forgive the sin.

("And ordain for us good in this world, and in the Hereafter.") The first part of Musa's supplication was to fend off what should be avoided, while this part is a request for what is sought. The meaning of,

("And ordain for us good in this world, and in the Hereafter. ") is, `ordain for us and grant us all that is good in both lives. We mentioned the meaning of `good' before in Surat Al-Baqarah.

("We have Hudna unto You") 'we repent, go back and return unto You,' according to the meaning of, `Hudna', given by Ibn `Abbas, Sa`id bin Jubayr, Mujahid, Abu Al-`Aliyah, Ad-Dahhak, Ibrahim At-Taymi, As-Suddi, Qatadah and several others.

(He said: (As to) My punishment I afflict therewith whom I will and My mercy embraces all things. That (mercy) I shall ordain for those who have Taqwa, and give Zakah; and those who believe in Our Ayat.) (7:156)

Allah's Mercy is for Those Who have Taqwa and believe in Allah's Ayat and His Messenger

Allah answers the statement,

("It is only Your trial...") (7:155), by saying,

((As to) My punishment I afflict therewith whom I will and My mercy embraces all things.) Allah says here, `I do what I will, decide what I will and I have wisdom and justice in all matters.' Certainly, there is no deity worthy of worship except Allah. Allah's statement,

(and My mercy embraces all things) testifies to His encompassing mercy. Allah said that the angels who carry His Throne and those around the Throne supplicate,

("Our Lord! You comprehend all things in mercy and knowledge.") (40:7) Imam Ahmad recorded that Jundub bin `Abdullah Al-Bajali said, "A bedouin man came, he made his camel kneel and he tied it. Then he prayed behind the Messenger of Allah . When the Messenger of Allah finished the prayer, that man untied his camel mounted it and supplicated aloud, `O Allah! Grant Your mercy to me and to Muhammad, and do not give a share in it to anyone else.' The Messenger of Allah commented (to his Companions),

»أَتَقُولُونَ هَذَا أَضَلُّ أَمْ بَعِيرُهُ أَلَمْ تَسْمَعُوا مَا قَالَ؟«

(Do you think that this man is more misguided or his camel Did you not hear what this man has said) They said, `Yes.' He said,

»لَقَدْ حَظَّرْتَ رَحْمَةً وَاسِعَةً إِنَّ اللهَ عَزَّ وَجَلَّ خَلَقَ مِائَةَ رَحْمَةٍ فَأَنْزَلَ رَحْمَةً يَتَعَاطَفُ بِهَا الْخَلْقُ جِنُّهَا وَإِنْسُهَا وَبَهَائِمُهَا وَأَخَّرَ عِنْدَهُ تِسْعًا وَتِسْعِينَ رَحْمَةً أَتَقُولُونَ هُوَ أَضَلُّ أَمْ بَعِيرُهُ؟«

(You (the bedouin man) have restricted a vast mercy! Allah, the Exalted, the most Honored has created a hundred mercies and sent down one of them by which the creation, men, Jinn and animals, show mercy to each other. He left with Him ninety-nine mercies, so do you say that this man is more misguided or his camel) Ahmad and

Abu Dawud collected this Hadith. Imam Ahmad recorded that Salman narrated that the Prophet said,

﴿إِنَّ للهِ عَزَّ وَجَلَّ مِائَةَ رَحْمَةٍ فَمِنْهَا رَحْمَةٌ يَتَرَاحَمُ بِهَا الْخَلْقُ وَبِهَا تَعْطِفُ الْوُحُوشُ عَلَى أَوْلَادِهَا وَأَخَّرَ تِسْعَةً وَتِسْعِينَ إِلَى يَوْمِ الْقِيَامَة﴾

(Allah, the Exalted and Most Honored, has a hundred mercies. With one of them, the creations show mercy to each other, and even the beasts show kindness to their offspring. He has kept ninety-nine mercies with Him for the Day of Resurrection.) Muslim recorded it. Allah said next,

(That (mercy) I shall ordain for those who have Taqwa,) meaning, I will ordain My mercy for them, as a favor and kindness from Me to them. Allah said in a similar Ayah,

(He has prescribed mercy for Himself) (6:12) Allah's statement,

(for those who have Taqwa), means, `I will ordain My mercy for those who possess these qualities, and they are the Ummah of Muhammad,'

(for those who have Taqwa), who avoid Shirk and major sins,

(and give the Zakah), purify themselves, according to one opinion. It was also said that, `the Zakah', here pertains to wealth. It is possible that both meanings are included here, for this Ayah was revealed in Makkah (before Zakah in fixed shares was ordained),

(and those who believe in Our Ayat.), those who have faith in them.

Surah: 7 Ayah: 157

﴿ٱلَّذِينَ يَتَّبِعُونَ ٱلرَّسُولَ ٱلنَّبِىَّ ٱلْأُمِّىَّ ٱلَّذِى يَجِدُونَهُۥ مَكْتُوبًا عِندَهُمْ فِى ٱلتَّوْرَىٰةِ وَٱلْإِنجِيلِ يَأْمُرُهُم بِٱلْمَعْرُوفِ وَيَنْهَىٰهُمْ عَنِ ٱلْمُنكَرِ وَيُحِلُّ لَهُمُ ٱلطَّيِّبَٰتِ وَيُحَرِّمُ عَلَيْهِمُ ٱلْخَبَٰٓئِثَ وَيَضَعُ عَنْهُمْ إِصْرَهُمْ وَٱلْأَغْلَٰلَ ٱلَّتِى كَانَتْ عَلَيْهِمْ ۚ فَٱلَّذِينَ ءَامَنُوا۟ بِهِۦ وَعَزَّرُوهُ وَنَصَرُوهُ وَٱتَّبَعُوا۟ ٱلنُّورَ ٱلَّذِىٓ أُنزِلَ مَعَهُۥٓ ۙ أُو۟لَٰٓئِكَ هُمُ ٱلْمُفْلِحُونَ﴾

157. Those who follow the Messenger, the Prophet who can neither read nor write (i.e. Muhammad (peace be upon him)) whom they find written with them in the Taurât (Torah) (Deut, xviii, 15) and the Injeel (Gospel) (John xiv, 16), - he commands them for Al-Ma'rûf (i.e. Islâmic Monotheism and all that Islâm has ordained); and forbids them from Al-Munkar (i.e. disbelief, polytheism of all

kinds, and all that Islâm has forbidden); he allows them as lawful At-Taiyibât ((i.e. all good and lawful) as regards things, deeds, beliefs, persons, foods), and prohibits them as unlawful Al-Khabâ'ith (i.e. all evil and unlawful as regards things, deeds, beliefs, persons, foods), he releases them from their heavy burdens (of Allâh's Covenant), and from the fetters (bindings) that were upon them. So those who believe in him (Muhammad (peace be upon him)) honor him, help him, and follow the light (the Qur'ân) which has been sent down with him, it is they who will be successful.

Transliteration

157. Allatheena yattabiAAoona alrrasoola alnnabiyya al-ommiyya allathee yajidoonahu maktooban AAindahum fee alttawrati waal-injeeli ya/muruhum bialmaAAroofi wayanhahum AAani almunkari wayuhillu lahumu alttayyibati wayuharrimu AAalayhimu alkhaba-itha wayadaAAu AAanhum israhum waal-aghlala allatee kanat AAalayhim faallatheena amanoo bihi waAAazzaroohu wanasaroohu waittabaAAoo alnnoora allathee onzila maAAahu ola-ika humu almuflihoona

Tafsir Ibn Kathir

The Description of that Messenger

(Those who follow the Messenger, the Prophet who can neither read nor write whom they find written with them in the Tawrah and the Injil,) This is the description of the Prophet Muhammad in the Books of the Prophets. They delivered the good news of his advent to their nations and commanded them to follow him. His descriptions were still apparent in their Books, as the rabbis and the priests well know. Imam Ahmad recorded that Abu Sakhr Al-`Uqayli said that a bedouin man said to him, "I brought a milk-producing camel to Al-Madinah during the life time of Allah's Messenger. After I sold it, I said to myself, `I will meet that man (Muhammad) and hear from him.' So I passed by him while he was walking between Abu Bakr and `Umar, and I followed them until they went by a Jewish man, who was reading from an open copy of the Tawrah. He was mourning a son of his who was dying and who was one of the most handsome boys. The Messenger of Allah asked him (the father),

«أَنْشُدُكَ بِالَّذِي أَنْزَلَ التَّوْرَاةَ هَلْ تَجِدُ فِي كِتَابِكَ هَذَا صِفَتِي وَمُخْرَجِي؟»

(I ask you by He Who has sent down the Tawrah, do you not find the description of me and my advent in your Book) He nodded his head in the negative. His son said, `Rather, yes, by He Who has sent down the Tawrah! We find the description of you and your advent in our Book. I bear witness that there is no deity worthy of worship except Allah and that you are the Messenger of Allah. ' The Prophet said (to the Companions),

«أَقِيمُوا الْيَهُودِيَّ عَنْ أَخِيكُم»

(Stop the Jew (the father) from (taking care of) your brother (in Islam).) The Prophet then personally took care of the son's funeral and led the funeral prayer on him.'" This Hadith is sound and is supported by a similar Hadith in the Sahih narrated from Anas. Ibn Jarir recorded that Al-Muthanna said that `Ata' bin Yasar said, "I met `Abdullah bin `Amr and asked him, `Tell me about the description of Allah's Messenger in the Tawrah.' He said, `Yes, by Allah! He is described in the Tawrah, just as he is described in the Qur'an,

(O Prophet! Verily, We have sent you as a witness, and a bearer of glad tidings, and a warner.) (33:45) as a safe refuge for the unlettered ones. `You are My servant and Messenger. I have called you `Al-Mutawakkil' (who trusts in Allah), not hard or harsh.' Neither uttering foul speech in the markets nor returning evil deed with one in kind. Rather, he forgives and forgoes. Allah will not end his life until He straightens through him the crooked religion, so that they might proclaim, `There is no deity worthy of worship except Allah.' He will open through him sealed hearts, deaf ears and blind eyes.'" `Ata' then said, "I also met Ka`b and asked him the same question, and his answer did not differ from `Abdullah's answer, even concerning one letter. " Al-Bukhari recorded it from `Abdullah bin `Amr. It was also recorded by Al-Bukhari (up to the word) forgoes. And he mentioned the narration of `Abdullah bin `Amr then he said; "It was common in the speech of our Salaf that they describe the Books of the People of the Two Scriptures as the Tawrah, as some Hadiths concur. Allah knows best." Allah's statement,

(He commands them to do good; and forbids them from evil;) This is the description of the Messenger of Allah in previous Books. These were the true qualities of our Messenger , as well, for he only ordained good and forbade evil. We should mention here that `Abdullah bin Mas`ud said, "When you hear Allah's statement,

(O you who believe!), then pay it your full attention, for it is a good that you are being commanded, or an evil that you are being forbidden." And the most important and greatest of these commands and prohibitions, is that Allah has sent the Messenger to order worshipping Him Alone without partners and forbid worshipping others besides Him. This is the Message that Allah has sent all Messengers with before Muhammad , just as Allah said,

(And verily, We have sent among every Ummah a Messenger (proclaiming): "Worship Allah, and avoid the Taghut (false deities)")(16:36). Allah's statement,

(He makes lawful for them the good things, and forbids them from the evil things,) meaning, he makes the Bahirah, Sa'ibah, Wasilah and Ham, etc., lawful. They were prohibitions that they invented which were only hard for themselves. He also forbids them from evil things, such as the flesh of the pig, Riba, and foods that were treated as lawful although Allah the Exalted had forbidden them. `Ali bin Abi Talhah reported this from Ibn `Abbas. Allah's statement,

(He (Muhammad) releases them from their heavy burdens, and from the fetters that were upon them.) indicates that Muhammad came with leniency and an easy religion. As mentioned in the Hadith recorded from many routes that Allah's Messenger said,

Chapter 7: Al-Araf (The Heights), Verses 088-206

«بُعِثْتُ بِالْحَنِيفِيَّةِ السَّمْحَةِ»

(I was sent with the easy way of Hanifiyyah (monotheism)) The Prophet said to the two Commanders he appointed, Mu`adh and Abu Musa Al-Ash`ari, when he sent them to Yemen,

«بَشِّرَا وَلَا تُنَفِّرَا وَيَسِّرَا وَلَا تُعَسِّرَا وَتَطَاوَعَا وَلَا تَخْتَلِفَا»

(Bring glad tidings and do not drive people away, make things easy and do not make them difficult, obey each other and do not differ among yourselves). Abu Barzah Al-Aslami, the Prophet's Companion, said, "I accompanied the Messenger of Allah and saw how easy he was. The nations that were before us had things made difficult for them in their laws. Allah made the law encompassing and easy for this Ummah. Hence the statement of the Messenger of Allah,

«إِنَّ اللهَ تَجَاوَزَ لِأُمَّتِي مَا حَدَّثَتْ بِهِ أَنْفُسُهَا مَا لَمْ تَقُلْ أَوْ تَعْمَلْ»

(Allah has forgiven my Ummah for what occurs in themselves, as long as they do not utter it or act upon it.) The Prophet said,

«رُفِعَ عَنْ أُمَّتِي الْخَطَأُ وَالنِّسْيَانُ وَمَا اسْتُكْرِهُوا عَلَيْهِ»

(My Ummah was forgiven (by Allah) unintentional errors, forgetfulness and what they are forced to do.)" This is why Allah has guided this Ummah to proclaim,

("Our Lord! Punish us not if we forget or fall into error, our Lord! Lay not on us a burden like that which You did lay on those before us (Jews and Christians); our Lord! Put not on us a burden greater than we have strength to bear. Pardon us and grant us forgiveness. Have mercy on us. You are our Mawla (Patron, Supporter and Protector) and give us victory over the disbelieving people.) (2:286) It is recorded in Sahih Muslim that (the Prophet said that) Allah the Exalted said after every one of these supplications, "I shall accept (your supplication)." Allah's statement,

(So those who believe in him, honor him, help him.) refers to respecting and honoring Muhammad ,

(and follow the light which has been sent down with him,) the Qur'an and the revelation (Sunnah) that the Prophet delivered to mankind,

(it is they who will be successful.) in this life and the Hereafter.

Surah: 7 Ayah: 158

﴿قُلْ يَـٰٓأَيُّهَا ٱلنَّاسُ إِنِّى رَسُولُ ٱللَّهِ إِلَيْكُمْ جَمِيعًا ٱلَّذِى لَهُۥ مُلْكُ ٱلسَّمَـٰوَٰتِ وَٱلْأَرْضِ لَآ إِلَـٰهَ إِلَّا هُوَ يُحْىِۦ وَيُمِيتُ فَـَٔامِنُوا۟ بِٱللَّهِ وَرَسُولِهِ ٱلنَّبِىِّ ٱلْأُمِّىِّ ٱلَّذِى يُؤْمِنُ بِٱللَّهِ وَكَلِمَـٰتِهِۦ وَٱتَّبِعُوهُ لَعَلَّكُمْ تَهْتَدُونَ ۝﴾

158. Say (O Muhammad (peace be upon him)) "O mankind! Verily, I am sent to you all as the Messenger of Allâh - to Whom belongs the dominion of the heavens and the earth. Lâ ilâha illa Huwa (none has the right to be worshipped but He). It is He Who gives life and causes death. So believe in Allâh and His Messenger (Muhammad (peace be upon him)) the Prophet who can neither read nor write (i.e. Muhammad (peace be upon him)) who believes in Allâh and His Words ((this Qur'ân), the Taurât (Torah) and the Injeel (Gospel) and also Allâh's Word: "Be!" - and he was, i.e. 'Isâ (Jesus) son of Maryam (Mary), (peace be upon them)) and follow him so that you may be guided."

Transliteration

158. Qul ya ayyuha alnnasu innee rasoolu Allahi ilaykum jameeAAan allathee lahu mulku alssamawati waal-ardi la ilaha illa huwa yuhyee wayumeetu faaminoo biAllahi warasoolihi alnnabiyyi al-ommiyyi allathee yu/minu biAllahi wakalimatihi waittabiAAoohu laAAallakum tahtadoona

Tafsir Ibn Kathir

Muhammad's Message is Universal

Allah says to His Prophet and Messenger Muhammad ,

(Say), O Muhammad,

(O mankind!), this is directed to mankind red and black, and the Arabs and non-Arabs alike,

(I am sent to you all as the Messenger of Allah,) This Ayah mentions the Prophet's honor and greatness, for he is the Final Prophet who was sent to all mankind (and the Jinns). Allah said,

(Say, "Allah is Witness between you and I; this Qur'an has been revealed to me that I may therewith warn you and whomsoever it may reach.") (6:19),

(but those of the sects that reject it, the Fire will be their promised meeting place)(11:17), and,

(And say to those who were given the Scripture and to the illiterates (Arab pagans): "Do you (also) submit yourselves (to Allah in Islam)" If they do, they are rightly guided; but if they turn away, your duty is only to convey the Message.) (3:20) There are many other Ayat and more Hadiths than can be counted on this subject. It is also well-known in our religion that the Messenger of Allah was sent to all mankind (and the Jinns). Al-Bukhari recorded that Abu Ad-Darda' said, "Abu Bakr and `Umar had an argument in which Abu Bakr made `Umar angry. So `Umar went away while angry and Abu Bakr followed him asking him to forgive him, but `Umar refused. `Umar shut his door closed in Abu Bakr's face and Abu Bakr went to the Messenger of Allah while we were with him. The Messenger of Allah said,

﴿أَمَّا صَاحِبُكُمْ هَذَا فَقَدْ غَامَرَ﴾

(This fellow of yours (Abu Bakr) has made someone angry!) `Umar became sorry for what he did, went to the Prophet and greeted him with the Salam and sat next to him, telling him what had happened. The Messenger of Allah became angry (at `Umar), and realizing that, Abu Bakr said, `O Allah's Messenger! It was me who was unjust.' The Messenger of Allah said,

﴿هَلْ أَنْتُمْ تَارِكُو لِي صَاحِبِي؟ إِنِّي قُلْتُ: يَا أَيُّهَا النَّاسُ إِنِّي رَسُولُ اللهِ إِلَيْكُمْ جَمِيعًا فَقُلْتُمْ: كَذَبْتَ وَقَالَ أَبُو بَكْرٍ: صَدَقْتَ﴾

(Will you leave my Companion (Abu Bakr) alone! I said, `O People! I am the Messenger of Allah to you all,' and you said, `You lie,' but Abu Bakr declared, `You said the truth.')" Al-Bukhari recorded it. Imam Ahmad recorded that Ibn `Abbas said that the Messenger of Allah said,

﴿أُعْطِيتُ خَمْسًا لَمْ يُعْطَهُنَّ نَبِيٌّ قَبْلِي وَلَا أَقُولُهُ فَخْرًا بُعِثْتُ إِلَى النَّاسِ كَافَّةً الْأَحْمَرِ وَالْأَسْوَدِ وَنُصِرْتُ بِالرُّعْبِ مَسِيرَةَ شَهْرٍ وَأُحِلَّتْ لِيَ الْغَنَائِمُ وَلَمْ تَحِلَّ لِأَحَدٍ قَبْلِي وَجُعِلَتْ لِيَ الْأَرْضُ مَسْجِدًا وَطَهُورًا وَأُعْطِيتُ الشَّفَاعَةَ فَأَخَّرْتُهَا لِأُمَّتِي يَوْمَ الْقِيَامَةِ فَهِيَ لِمَنْ لَا يُشْرِكُ بِاللهِ شَيْئًا﴾

(I have been given five things which were not given to any Prophet before me, and I do not say it out of pride. I was sent to all mankind (their) black and white alike. Allah made me victorious by fright, (by His frightening my enemies) for a distance of one month's journey. The spoils of war are lawful for me, yet it was not lawful for anyone else before me. The earth has been made for me (and for my followers) a place for praying and a thing to perform purification with. I have been given the Shafa'ah (right of intercession), and I saved it for my Ummah on the Day of Resurrection. Therefore, the Shafa'ah will reach those who associate none with Allah in worship.) This Hadith's chain of narration is suitable, but the Two Sahihs did not record it. Allah's statement, (to Whom belongs the dominion of the heavens and the earth. None has the right to be worshipped but He. It is He Who gives life and causes death.) describes Allah by the words of the Messenger that He Who has sent him is the Creator, Lord and King of all things and in His Hand is the control, life, death and the decision. Just as Allah said

(So believe in Allah and His Messenger, the Prophet who can neither read nor write,) Allah proclaims here that Muhammad is His Messenger and reiterates this fact by commanding that he be believed in and followed. Allah said,

(The Prophet who can neither read nor write) who you were promised and given the good news of in previous revealed books. Certainly, Muhammad was amply described in the previous books, including his description as being the unlettered Prophet. Allah's statement,

(who believes in Allah and His Words), means, his actions conform with his words and he believes in what he was given from his Lord.

(And follow him), embrace his path and guidance,

(so that you may be guided) to the Straight Path.

Surah: 7 Ayah: 159

﴿ وَمِن قَوْمِ مُوسَىٰٓ أُمَّةٌ يَهْدُونَ بِٱلْحَقِّ وَبِهِۦ يَعْدِلُونَ ۝ ﴾

159. And of the people of Mûsa (Moses) there is a community who lead (the men) with truth and establish justice therewith (i.e. judge men with truth and justice).

Transliteration

159. Wamin qawmi moosa ommatun yahdoona bialhaqqi wabihi yaAAdiloona

Tafsir Ibn Kathir

Allah stated that of the Children of Israel there are some who follow the truth and judge by it, just as He said in another Ayah,

(A party of the people of the Scripture stand for the right, they recite the verses of Allah during the hours of the night, prostrating themselves in prayer) (3:113),

(And there are, certainly, among the People of the Scripture, those who believe in Allah and in that which has been revealed to you, and in that which has been revealed to them, humbling themselves before Allah. They do not sell the verses of Allah for a small price, for them is a reward with their Lord. Surely, Allah is Swift in account.) (3:199)

(Those to whom We gave the Scripture before it, they believe in it (the Qur'an). And when it is recited to them, they say: "We believe in it. Verily, it is the truth from our Lord. Indeed even before it we have been from those who submit themselves. These will be given their reward twice over, because they are patient.)(28:52-54), and,

(Verily, those who were given knowledge before it, when it (this Qur'an) is recited to them, fall down on their faces in humble prostration. And they say: "Glory be to our Lord! Truly, the promise of our Lord must be fulfilled." And they fall down on their faces weeping and it increases their humility.)(17:107-109)

Surah: 7 Ayah: 160, Ayah: 161 & Ayah: 162

﴿ وَقَطَّعْنَاهُمُ ٱثْنَتَىْ عَشْرَةَ أَسْبَاطًا أُمَمًا ۚ وَأَوْحَيْنَا إِلَىٰ مُوسَىٰٓ إِذِ ٱسْتَسْقَىٰهُ قَوْمُهُۥٓ أَنِ ٱضْرِب بِّعَصَاكَ ٱلْحَجَرَ ۖ فَٱنۢبَجَسَتْ مِنْهُ ٱثْنَتَا عَشْرَةَ عَيْنًا ۖ قَدْ عَلِمَ كُلُّ أُنَاسٍ مَّشْرَبَهُمْ ۚ وَظَلَّلْنَا عَلَيْهِمُ ٱلْغَمَٰمَ وَأَنزَلْنَا عَلَيْهِمُ ٱلْمَنَّ وَٱلسَّلْوَىٰ ۖ كُلُوا۟ مِن طَيِّبَٰتِ مَا رَزَقْنَٰكُمْ ۚ وَمَا ظَلَمُونَا وَلَٰكِن كَانُوٓا۟ أَنفُسَهُمْ يَظْلِمُونَ ﴾

160. And We divided them into twelve tribes (as distinct) nations. We revealed to Mûsâ (Moses) when his people asked him for water, (saying): "Strike the stone with your stick", and there gushed forth out of it twelve springs, each group knew its own place for water. We shaded them with the clouds and sent down upon them Al-Manna and the quails (saying): "Eat of the good things with which We have provided you." They harmed Us not but they used to harm themselves.

﴿ وَإِذْ قِيلَ لَهُمُ ٱسْكُنُوا۟ هَٰذِهِ ٱلْقَرْيَةَ وَكُلُوا۟ مِنْهَا حَيْثُ شِئْتُمْ وَقُولُوا۟ حِطَّةٌ وَٱدْخُلُوا۟ ٱلْبَابَ سُجَّدًا نَّغْفِرْ لَكُمْ خَطِيٓـَٰٔتِكُمْ ۚ سَنَزِيدُ ٱلْمُحْسِنِينَ ﴾

161. And (remember) when it was said to them: "Dwell in this town (Jerusalem) and eat therefrom wherever you wish, and say, '(O Allâh) forgive our sins'; and enter the gate prostrate (bowing with humility). We shall forgive you your wrong-doings. We shall increase (the reward) for the good-doers."

﴿ فَبَدَّلَ ٱلَّذِينَ ظَلَمُوا۟ مِنْهُمْ قَوْلًا غَيْرَ ٱلَّذِى قِيلَ لَهُمْ فَأَرْسَلْنَا عَلَيْهِمْ رِجْزًا مِّنَ ٱلسَّمَآءِ بِمَا كَانُوا۟ يَظْلِمُونَ ﴾

162. But those among them who did wrong changed the word that had been told to them. So We sent on them a torment from the heaven in return for their wrong-doings.

Transliteration

160. WaqattaAAnahumu ithnatay AAashrata asbatan omaman waawhayna ila moosa ithi istasqahu qawmuhu ani idrib biAAasaka alhajara fainbajasat minhu ithnata AAashrata AAaynan qad AAalima kullu onasin mashrabahum wathallalna AAalayhimu alghamama waanzalna AAalayhimu almanna waalssalwa kuloo min tayyibati ma razaqnakum wama thalamoona walakin kanoo anfusahum yathlimoona 161. Wa-ith

qeela lahumu oskunoo hathihi alqaryata wakuloo minha haythu shi/tum waqooloo hittatun waodkhuloo albaba sujjadan naghfir lakum khatee-atikum sanazeedu almuhsineena 162. Fabaddala allatheena thalamoo minhum qawlan ghayra allathee qeela lahum faarsalna AAalayhim rijzan mina alssama-i bima kanoo yathlimoona

Tafsir Ibn Kathir

We discussed these Ayat in Surat Al-Baqarah, which was revealed in Al-Madinah, while these Ayat were revealed in Makkah. We also mentioned the difference between the two narrations, and thus we do not need to repeat it here, all thanks are due to Allah and all the favors are from Him.

Surah: 7 Ayah: 163

﴿ وَسْئَلْهُمْ عَنِ ٱلْقَرْيَةِ ٱلَّتِى كَانَتْ حَاضِرَةَ ٱلْبَحْرِ إِذْ يَعْدُونَ فِى ٱلسَّبْتِ إِذْ تَأْتِيهِمْ حِيتَانُهُمْ يَوْمَ سَبْتِهِمْ شُرَّعًا وَيَوْمَ لَا يَسْبِتُونَ ۙ لَا تَأْتِيهِمْ ۚ كَذَٰلِكَ نَبْلُوهُم بِمَا كَانُوا۟ يَفْسُقُونَ ﴾

163. And ask them (O Muhammad (peace be upon him)) about the town that was by the sea; when they transgressed in the matter of the Sabbath (i.e. Saturday): when their fish came to them openly on the Sabbath day, and did not come to them on the day they had no Sabbath. Thus We made a trial of them for they used to rebel against Allah's Command (disobey Allah) (see the Qur'ân: V.4:154).

Transliteration

163. Wais-alhum AAani alqaryati allatee kanat hadirata albahri ith yaAAdoona fee alssabti ith ta/teehim heetanuhum yawma sabtihim shurraAAan wayawma la yasbitoona la ta/teehim kathalika nabloohum bima kanoo yafsuqoona

Tafsir Ibn Kathir

The Jews transgress the Sanctity of the Sabbath

This Ayah explains Allah's statement,

(And indeed you knew those among you who transgressed in the matter of the Sabbath..) (2:65) Allah says to His Prophet here,

(And ask them) ask the Jews who are with you, about the story of their fellow Jews who defied Allah's command, so that His punishment overtook them all of a sudden for their evil actions, transgression and defiance by way of deceit. Also, warn the Jews (O Muhammad) against hiding your description that they find in their books, so that they do not suffer what their forefathers suffered. The village mentioned here is Aylah, on the shore of the Qulzum (Red) Sea. Muhammad bin Ishaq recorded from Dawud bin Al-Husayn from `Ikrimah that Ibn `Abbas commented on Allah's statement,

(And ask them about the town that was by the sea...) "A village called Aylah between Madyan and At-Tur (which is in Sinai). `Ikrimah, Mujahid, Qatadah and As-Suddi said similarly. Allah's statement,

(when they transgressed in the matter of the Sabbath;) means, they transgressed in the Sabbath and defied Allah's command to them to keep it sanctified,

(when their fish came to them openly on the Sabbath day,) visible on top of the water, according to Ad-Dahhak who reported it from Ibn `Abbas. Ibn Jarir said, "Allah's statement,

(and did not come to them on the day they had no Sabbath. Thus We made a trial of them,) means, this is how We tested them by making the fish swim close to the surface of the water , on the day which they were prohibited to fish. The fish would be hidden from them on the day when they were allowed to fish,

(Thus We made a trial for them,) so that We test them,

(for they used to rebel against Allah's command) by defying His obedience and rebelling against it." Therefore, these were a people who used a trick to violate Allah's prohibitions, taking an action that seemed legal on the surface. However, in reality, this action was meant to transgress the prohibition. Imam and scholar Abu `Abdullah Ibn Battah reported that Abu Hurayrah said that the Messenger of Allah said,

«لَا تَرْتَكِبُوا مَا ارْتَكَبَتِ الْيَهُودُ فَتَسْتَحِلُّوا مَحَارِمَ اللهِ بِأَدْنَى الْحِيَلِ»

(Do not repeat what the Jews committed, and violate Allah's prohibitions using deceitful tricks.) This Hadith has a reasonable chain.

Surah: 7 Ayah: 164, Ayah: 165 & Ayah: 166

﴿ وَإِذْ قَالَتْ أُمَّةٌ مِّنْهُمْ لِمَ تَعِظُونَ قَوْمًا ٱللَّهُ مُهْلِكُهُمْ أَوْ مُعَذِّبُهُمْ عَذَابًا شَدِيدًا قَالُوا۟ مَعْذِرَةً إِلَىٰ رَبِّكُمْ وَلَعَلَّهُمْ يَتَّقُونَ ﴾

164. And when a community among them said: "Why do you preach to a people whom Allâh is about to destroy or to punish with a severe torment?" (The preachers) said: "In order to be free from guilt before your Lord (Allâh), and perhaps they may fear Allâh."

﴿ فَلَمَّا نَسُوا۟ مَا ذُكِّرُوا۟ بِهِۦ أَنجَيْنَا ٱلَّذِينَ يَنْهَوْنَ عَنِ ٱلسُّوٓءِ وَأَخَذْنَا ٱلَّذِينَ ظَلَمُوا۟ بِعَذَابٍۭ بَـِٔيسٍۭ بِمَا كَانُوا۟ يَفْسُقُونَ ﴾

165. So when they forgot the reminders that had been given to them, We rescued those who forbade evil, but We seized those who did wrong with a severe torment because they used to rebel against Allah's Command (disobey Allâh).

﴿ فَلَمَّا عَتَوْا۟ عَن مَّا نُهُوا۟ عَنْهُ قُلْنَا لَهُمْ كُونُوا۟ قِرَدَةً خَٰسِـِٔينَ ۝ ﴾

166. So when they exceeded the limits of what they were prohibited, We said to them: "Be you monkeys, despised and rejected."

Transliteration

164. Wa-ith qalat ommatun minhum lima taAAithoona qawman Allahu muhlikuhum aw muAAaththibuhum AAathaban shadeedan qaloo maAAthiratan ila rabbikum walaAAallahum yattaqoona   165. Falamma nasoo ma thukkiroo bihi anjayna allatheena yanhawna AAani alssoo-i waakhathna allatheena thalamoo biAAathabin ba-eesin bima kanoo yafsuqoona   166. Falamma AAataw AAan ma nuhoo AAanhu qulna lahum koonoo qiradatan khasi-eena

Tafsir Ibn Kathir

Those Who breached the Sabbath were turned into Monkeys, but Those Who prohibited Their Actions were saved

Allah said that the people of this village were divided into three groups, a group that committed the prohibition, catching fish on the Sabbath, as we described in the Tafsir of Surat Al-Baqarah. Another group prohibited them from transgression and avoided them. A third group neither prohibited them, nor participated in their action. The third group said to the preachers,

("Why do you preach to a people whom Allah is about to destroy or to punish with a severe torment"). They said, `why do you forbid these people from evil, when you know that they are destroyed and have earned Allah's punishment' Therefore, they said, there is no benefit in forbidding them. The preachers replied,

("In order to be free from guilt before your Lord (Allah),") `for we were commanded to enjoin righteousness and forbid evil,' r

("and perhaps they may fear Allah") for on account of our advice, they might stop this evil and repent to Allah. Certainly, if they repent to Allah, Allah will accept their repentance and grant them His mercy.' Allah said,

(So when they forgot the reminder that had been given to them,) when the evil doers refused the advice,

(We rescued those who forbade evil, but We seized who did wrong,) who committed the transgression,

(with a severe torment). Allah stated that those who enjoined good were saved, while those who committed the transgression were destroyed, but He did not mention the end of those who were passive (the third group), for the compensation is comparable to the deed. This type did not do what would warrant praise, nor commit wrong so that they are admonished. `Ikrimah said, "Ibn `Abbas said about the Ayah: `I do not know whether or not the people were saved who said;

("Why do you preach to a people whom Allah is about to destroy...") So I continued discussing it with him until I convinced him that they were. Then he gave me (the gift of) a garment." Allah said,

(and We seized those who did wrong with a Ba'is torment) indicating that those who remained were saved. As for `Ba'is', it means `severe', according to Mujahid, or `painful', according to Qatadah. These meanings are synonymous, and Allah knows best. Allah said next,

(despised), humiliated, disgraced and rejected.

Surah: 7 Ayah: 167

﴿ وَإِذْ تَأَذَّنَ رَبُّكَ لَيَبْعَثَنَّ عَلَيْهِمْ إِلَىٰ يَوْمِ ٱلْقِيَـٰمَةِ مَن يَسُومُهُمْ سُوٓءَ ٱلْعَذَابِ ۗ إِنَّ رَبَّكَ لَسَرِيعُ ٱلْعِقَابِ ۖ وَإِنَّهُۥ لَغَفُورٌ رَّحِيمٌ ﴿١٦٧﴾ ﴾

167. And (remember) when your Lord declared that He would certainly keep on sending against them (i.e. the Jews), till the Day of Resurrection, those who would afflict them with a humiliating torment. Verily, your Lord is Quick in Retribution (for the disobedient, wicked) and certainly He is Oft-Forgiving, Most Merciful (for the obedient and those who beg Allâh's Forgiveness).

Transliteration

167. Wa-ith taaththana rabbuka layabAAathanna AAalayhim ila yawmi alqiyamati man yasoomuhum soo-a alAAathabi inna rabbaka lasareeAAu alAAiqabi wa-innahu laghafoorun raheemun

Tafsir Ibn Kathir

Eternal Humiliation placed on the Jews

(Ta'dhdhana) means `declared', according to Mujahid, or `ordained', according to others. This part of the Ayah indicates a vow,

(that He will keep on sending against them) against the Jews,

(till the Day of Resurrection, those who would afflict them with a humiliating torment.) on account of their disobedience, defying Allah's orders and Law and using tricks to transgress the prohibitions. It was reported that Musa required the Jews to pay the production tax for seven or thirteen years, and he was the first to do so. Also, the Jews fell under the humiliating rule of the Greek Kushdanin, Chaldeans and later on the Christians, who subjugated and disgraced them, and required them to pay the Jizyah (tribute tax). When Islam came and Muhammad was sent, they became under his power and had to pay the Jizyah, as well. Therefore, the humiliating torment mentioned here includes disgrace and paying the Jizyah, as Al-`Awfi narrated from Ibn `Abbas. In the future, the Jews will support the Dajjal (False Messiah); and the Muslims, along with `Isa, son of Mary, will kill the Jews. This will occur just before the end of this world. Allah said next,

(Verily, your Lord is quick in retribution), with those who disobey Him and defy His Law,

(and certainly He is Oft-Forgiving, Most Merciful.) for those who repent and go back to Him. This Ayah mentions both the mercy, as well as, the punishment, so that no despair is felt. Allah often mentions encouragement and warning together, so that hearts always have a sense of hope and fear.

Surah: 7 Ayah: 168, Ayah: 169 & Ayah: 170

﴿ وَقَطَّعْنَـٰهُمْ فِى ٱلْأَرْضِ أُمَمًا مِّنْهُمُ ٱلصَّـٰلِحُونَ وَمِنْهُمْ دُونَ ذَٰلِكَ وَبَلَوْنَـٰهُم بِٱلْحَسَنَـٰتِ وَٱلسَّيِّـَٔاتِ لَعَلَّهُمْ يَرْجِعُونَ ۝ ﴾

168. And We have broken them (i.e. the Jews) up into various separate groups on the earth: some of them are righteous and some are away from that. And We tried them with good (blessings) and evil (calamities) in order that they might turn (to Allâh's Obedience).

﴿ فَخَلَفَ مِنۢ بَعْدِهِمْ خَلْفٌ وَرِثُوا۟ ٱلْكِتَـٰبَ يَأْخُذُونَ عَرَضَ هَـٰذَا ٱلْأَدْنَىٰ وَيَقُولُونَ سَيُغْفَرُ لَنَا وَإِن يَأْتِهِمْ عَرَضٌ مِّثْلُهُ يَأْخُذُوهُ أَلَمْ يُؤْخَذْ عَلَيْهِم مِّيثَـٰقُ ٱلْكِتَـٰبِ أَن لَّا يَقُولُوا۟ عَلَى ٱللَّهِ إِلَّا ٱلْحَقَّ وَدَرَسُوا۟ مَا فِيهِ وَٱلدَّارُ ٱلْـَٔاخِرَةُ خَيْرٌ لِّلَّذِينَ يَتَّقُونَ أَفَلَا تَعْقِلُونَ ۝ ﴾

169. Then after them succeeded an (evil) generation, which inherited the Book, but they chose (for themselves) the goods of this low life (evil pleasures of this world) saying (as an excuse): "(Everything) will be forgiven to us." And if (again) the offer of the like (evil pleasures of this world) came their way, they would (again) seize them (would commit those sins). Was not the covenant of the Book taken from them that they would not say about Allâh anything but the truth? And they have studied what is in it (the Book). And the home of the Hereafter is better for those who are Al-Muttaqûn (the pious - see V.2:2). Do not you then understand?

﴿ وَٱلَّذِينَ يُمَسِّكُونَ بِٱلْكِتَـٰبِ وَأَقَامُوا۟ ٱلصَّلَوٰةَ إِنَّا لَا نُضِيعُ أَجْرَ ٱلْمُصْلِحِينَ ۝ ﴾

170. And as to those who hold fast to the Book (i.e. act on its teachings) and perform As-Salât (Iqâmat-as-Salât), certainly We shall never waste the reward of those who do righteous deeds.

Transliteration

168. WaqattaAAnahum fee al-ardi omaman minhumu alssalihoona waminhum doona thalika wabalawnahum bialhasanati waalssayyi-ati laAAallahum yarjiAAoona 169. Fakhalafa min baAAdihim khalfun warithoo alkitaba ya/khuthoona AAarada hatha al-adna wayaqooloona sayughfaru lana wa-in ya/tihim AAaradun mithluhu ya/khuthoohu alam yu/khath AAalayhim meethaqu alkitabi an la yaqooloo AAala Allahi illa alhaqqa wadarasoo ma feehi waalddaru al-akhiratu khayrun lillatheena yattaqoona afala taAAqiloona 170. Waallatheena yumassikoona bialkitabi waaqamoo alssalata inna la nudeeAAu ajra almusliheena

Tafsir Ibn Kathir

The Children of Israel scatter throughout the Land

Allah states that He divided the Jews into various nations, sects and groups,

(And We said to the Children of Israel after him (after Musa died): "Dwell in the land, then, when the final and the last promise comes near, We shall bring you altogether as a mixed crowd (gathered out of various nations).")(17:104)

(some of them are righteous and some are away from that), some of them are led aright and some are not righteous, just as the Jinns declared,

("There are among us some that are righteous, and some the contrary; we are groups having different ways (religious sects).") (72:11) Allah said here,

(And We tried them), and tested them,

(with good and evil), with times of ease, difficulty, eagerness, fear, well-being and affliction,

(in order that they might turn (to Allah)) Allah said next,

(Then after them succeeded an (evil) generation, which inherited the Book, but they chose (for themselves) the goods of this low life) This Ayah means, after the generation made up of righteous and unrighteous people, another generation came that did not have goodness in them, and they inherited the Tawrah and studied it. Mujahid commented on Allah's statement,

(They chose (for themselves) the goods of this low life) "They will consume anything they can consume in this life, whether legally or illegally. Yet, they wish for forgiveness,

(Saying: "(Everything) will be forgiven for us." And if (again) the offer of the like came their way, they would (again) seize them.)" Qatadah commented on Allah's statement,

(they chose (for themselves) the goods of this low life) "This, by Allah, is an evil generation, (which inherited the Book) after their Prophets and Messengers, for they were entrusted with this job by Allah's command to them. Allah said in another Ayah,

(Then, there has succeeded them a posterity who neglect the Salah (the prayers).) (19:59) Allah said next,

(They chose the goods of this low life saying: "(Everything) will be forgiven to us.") They wish and hope from Allah, while deceiving themselves,

(And if (again) the offer of the like came their way, they would (again) seize them.) Nothing stops them from this behavior, for whenever they are given an opportunity in this life, they will consume regardless of it being allowed or not." As-Suddi said about Allah's statement,

(Then after them succeeded an (evil) generation) until,

(and they have studied what is in it (the Book).) "Every time the Children of Israel appointed a judge, he used to take bribes. The best ones among them held a counsel and took covenants from each that they would not take bribes. However, when one of them would take bribes in return for judgment and was asked, `What is the matter with you; you take a bribe to grant judgment', he replied, `I will be forgiven.' So the rest of his people would admonish him for what he did. But when he died, or was replaced, the one who replaced him would take bribes too. Therefore, Allah says, if the others (who admonished him) would have a chance to loot this world, they will take it.'" Allah said,

(Was not the covenant of the Book taken from them that they would not say about Allah anything but the truth) thus, admonishing them for this behavior. Allah took a pledge from them that they would declare the truth to people and not hide it. Allah said in another Ayah,

((And remember) when Allah took a covenant from those who were given the Scripture to make it known and clear to mankind, and not to hide it, but they threw it away behind their backs, and purchased with it some miserable gain! And indeed worst is that which they bought) (3:187). Ibn Jurayj said that Ibn `Abbas said about the Ayah,

(Was not the covenant of the Book taken from them that they would not say about Allah anything but the truth), "Their claim that Allah will forgive the sins they keep committing without repenting from them." Allah said,

(And the home in the Hereafter is better for those who have Taqwa Do not you then understand) Encouraging them to seek Allah's tremendous reward and warning them against His severe torment. Allah says here, `My reward and what I have are better for those who avoid prohibitions, abandon lusts and become active in the obedience of their Lord.'

(Do not you then understand) Allah says' Do not these people, who preferred this life instead of what is with Me, have any sense to prohibit them from their foolish and extravagant ways' Allah then praises those who adhere to His Book, which directs them to follow His Messenger Muhammad ,

(And as to those who hold fast to the Book) adhere to it, implement its commands and refrain from its prohibitions,

(and perform the Salah, certainly We shall never waste the reward of those who do righteous deeds.)

Surah: 7 Ayah: 171

﴿ ۞ وَإِذْ نَتَقْنَا ٱلْجَبَلَ فَوْقَهُمْ كَأَنَّهُ ظُلَّةٌ وَظَنُّوٓاْ أَنَّهُ وَاقِعٌۢ بِهِمْ خُذُواْ مَآ ءَاتَيْنَٰكُم بِقُوَّةٍ وَٱذْكُرُواْ مَا فِيهِ لَعَلَّكُمْ تَتَّقُونَ ﴾

171. And (remember) when We raised the mountain over them as if it had been a canopy, and they thought that it was going to fall on them. (We said): "Hold firmly to what We have given you (i.e. the Taurât (Torah)) and remember that which is therein (act on its commandments), so that you may fear Allâh and obey Him."

Transliteration

171. Wa-ith nataqna aljabala fawqahum kaannahu thullatun wathannoo annahu waqiAAun bihim khuthoo ma ataynakum biquwwatin waothkuroo ma feehi laAAallakum tattaqoona

Tafsir Ibn Kathir

Raising Mount Tur over the Jews, because of Their Rebellion

`Ali bin Abi Talhah reported that Ibn `Abbas commented on the Ayah,

(And (remember) when We Nataqna the mountain over them), "We raised the mountain, as Allah's other statement testifies,

(And for their covenant, We raised over them the mountain) (4:154)." Also, Sufyan Ath-Thawri narrated that Al-A`mash said that, Sa`id bin Jubayr said that Ibn `Abbas said, "The angels raised the Mount over their heads, as reiterated by Allah's statement,

(We raised over them the mountain) (4:154)." Al-Qasim bin Abi Ayyub narrated that Sa`id bin Jubayr said that Ibn `Abbas said, "Musa later on proceeded with them to the Sacred Land. He took along the Tablets, after his anger subsided, and commanded them to adhere to the orders that Allah ordained to be delivered to them. But these orders became heavy on them and they did not want to implement them until Allah raised the mountain over them,

(as if it had been a canopy), that is, when the angels raised the mountain over their heads." An-Nasa'i collected it.

Surah: 7 Ayah: 172, Ayah: 173 & Ayah: 174

﴿ وَإِذْ أَخَذَ رَبُّكَ مِنْ بَنِى ءَادَمَ مِن ظُهُورِهِمْ ذُرِّيَّتَهُمْ وَأَشْهَدَهُمْ عَلَىٰ أَنفُسِهِمْ أَلَسْتُ بِرَبِّكُمْ قَالُوا۟ بَلَىٰ شَهِدْنَا أَن تَقُولُوا۟ يَوْمَ ٱلْقِيَـٰمَةِ إِنَّا كُنَّا عَنْ هَـٰذَا غَـٰفِلِينَ ۝ ﴾

172. And (remember) when your Lord brought forth from the Children of Adam, from their loins, their seed (or from Adam's loin his offspring) and made them testify as to themselves (saying): "Am I not your Lord?" They said: "Yes! We testify," lest you should say on the Day of Resurrection: "Verily, we have been unaware of this."

﴿ أَوْ تَقُولُوٓا۟ إِنَّمَآ أَشْرَكَ ءَابَآؤُنَا مِن قَبْلُ وَكُنَّا ذُرِّيَّةً مِّنۢ بَعْدِهِمْ أَفَتُهْلِكُنَا بِمَا فَعَلَ ٱلْمُبْطِلُونَ ۝ ﴾

173. Or lest you should say: "It was only our fathers aforetime who took others as partners in worship along with Allâh, and we were (merely their) descendants after them; will You then destroy us because of the deeds of men who practiced Al-Bâtil (i.e. polytheism and committing crimes and sins, invoking and worshipping others besides Allâh)?" (Tafsir At-Tabarî).

﴿ وَكَذَٰلِكَ نُفَصِّلُ ٱلْـَٔايَـٰتِ وَلَعَلَّهُمْ يَرْجِعُونَ ۝ ﴾

174. Thus do We explain the Ayât (proofs, evidences, verses, lessons, signs, revelations, etc.) in detail, so that they may turn (unto the truth).

Transliteration

172. Wa-ith akhatha rabbuka min banee adama min thuhoorihim thurriyyatahum waashhadahum AAala anfusihim alastu birabbikum qaloo bala shahidna an taqooloo yawma alqiyamati inna kunna AAan hatha ghafileena   173. Aw taqooloo innama ashraka abaona min qablu wakunna thurriyyatan min baAAdihim afatuhlikuna bima faAAala almubtiloona 174. Wakathalika nufassilu al-ayati walaAAallahum yarjiAAoona

Tafsir Ibn Kathir

The Covenant taken from the Descendants of Adam

Allah stated that He brought the descendants of Adam out of their fathers' loins, and they testified against themselves that Allah is their Lord and King and that there is no deity worthy of worship except Him. Allah created them on this Fitrah, or way, just as He said,

(So set you (O Muhammad) your face truly towards the religion, Hanifan. Allah's Fitrah with which He has created mankind. No change let there be in Khalqillah.)

Chapter 7: Al-Araf (The Heights), Verses 088-206

(30:30) And it is recorded in the Two Sahihs from Abu Hurayrah who said that the Messenger of Allah said,

«كُلُّ مَوْلُودٍ يُولَدُ عَلَى الْفِطْرَةِ، فَأَبَوَاهُ يُهَوِّدَانِهِ وَيُنَصِّرَانِهِ وَيُمَجِّسَانِهِ كَمَا تُولَدُ بَهِيمَةً جَمْعَاءَ هَلْ تُحِسُّونَ فِيهَا مِنْ جَدْعَاءَ»

(Every child is born upon the Fitrah, it is only his parents who turn him into a Jew, a Christian or a Zoroastrian. Just as animals are born having full bodies, do you see any of them having a cutoff nose (when they are born)) . Muslim recorded that `Iyad bin `Himar said that the Messenger of Allah said;

«يَقُولُ اللهُ: إِنِّي خَلَقْتُ عِبَادِي حُنَفَاءَ فَجَاءَتْهُمُ الشَّيَاطِينُ فَاجْتَالَتْهُمْ عَنْ دِينِهِمْ وَحَرَّمَتْ عَلَيْهِمْ مَا أَحْلَلْتُ لَهُم»

(Allah said, `I created My servants Hunafa' (monotheists), but the devils came to them and deviated them from their religion, prohibiting what I allowed.) There are Hadiths that mention that Allah took Adam's offspring from his loins and divided them into those on the right and those on the left. Imam Ahmad recorded that Anas bin Malik said that the Prophet said,

«يُقَالُ لِلرَّجُلِ مِنْ أَهْلِ النَّارِ يَوْمَ الْقِيَامَةِ أَرَأَيْتَ لَوْ كَانَ لَكَ مَا عَلَى الْأَرْضِ مِنْ شَيْءٍ أَكُنْتَ مُفْتَدِيًا بِهِ قَالَ: فَيَقُولُ: نَعَمْ فَيَقُولُ: قَدْ أَرَدْتُ مِنْكَ أَهْوَنَ مِنْ ذَلِكَ قَدْ أَخَذْتُ عَلَيْكَ فِي ظَهْرِ آدَمَ أَنْ لَا تُشْرِكَ بِي شَيْئًا فَأَبَيْتَ إِلَّا أَنْ تُشْرِكَ بِي»

(It will be said to a man from the people of the Fire on the Day of Resurrection, `If you owned all that is on the earth, would you pay it as ransom' He will reply, `Yes.' Allah will say, `I ordered you with what is less than that, when you were still in Adam's loins, that is, associate none with Me (in worship). You insisted that you associate with Me (in worship).') This was recorded in the Two Sahihs Commenting on this Ayah (7:172), At-Tirmidhi recorded that Abu Hurayrah said that the Messenger of Allah said,

«لَمَّا خَلَقَ اللهُ آدَمَ مَسَحَ ظَهْرَهُ فَسَقَطَ مِنْ ظَهْرِهِ كُلُّ نَسَمَةٍ هُوَ خَالِقُهَا مِنْ ذُرِّيَّتِهِ إِلَى يَوْمِ الْقِيَامَةِ وَجَعَلَ بَيْنَ عَيْنَيْ كُلِّ إِنْسَانٍ مِنْهُمْ وَبِيصًا مِنْ نُورٍ ثُمَّ عَرَضَهُمْ عَلَى آدَمَ فَقَالَ: أَيْ رَبِّ مَنْ هَؤُلَاءِ؟ قَالَ: هَؤُلَاءِ ذُرِّيَّتُكَ فَرَأَى رَجُلًا مِنْهُمْ فَأَعْجَبَهُ وَبِيصُ مَا بَيْنَ عَيْنَيْهِ قَالَ: أَيْ رَبِّ مَنْ هَذَا؟ قَالَ: هَذَا رَجُلٌ مِنْ آخِرِ الْأُمَمِ مِنْ ذُرِّيَّتِكَ يُقَالُ لَهُ دَاوُدُ قَالَ: رَبِّ وَكَمْ جَعَلْتَ عُمْرَهُ؟ قَالَ: سِتِّينَ سَنَةً، قَالَ: أَيْ رَبِّ وَقَدْ وَهَبْتُ لَهُ مِنْ عُمْرِي أَرْبَعِينَ سَنَةً فَلَمَّا انْقَضَى عُمُرُ آدَمَ جَاءَهُ مَلَكُ الْمَوْتِ قَالَ: أَوَ لَمْ يَبْقَ مِنْ عُمْرِي أَرْبَعُونَ سَنَةً قَالَ: أَوَ لَمْ تُعْطِهَا ابْنَكَ دَاوُدَ؟ قَالَ: فَجَحَدَ آدَمُ فَجَحَدَتْ ذُرِّيَّتُهُ وَنَسِيَ آدَمُ فَنَسِيَتْ ذُرِّيَّتُهُ وَخَطِىءَ آدَمُ فَخَطِئَتْ ذُرِّيَّتُهُ»

(When Allah created Adam, He wiped Adam's back and every person that He will create from him until the Day of Resurrection fell out from his back. Allah placed a glimmering light between the eyes of each one of them. Allah showed them to Adam and Adam asked, `O Lord! Who are they' Allah said, `These are your offspring.' Adam saw a man from among them whose light he liked. He asked, `O Lord! Who is this man' Allah said, `This is a man from the latter generations of your offspring. His name is Dawud.' Adam said, `O Lord! How many years would he live' Allah said, `Sixty years.' Adam said, `O Lord! I have forfeited forty years from my life for him.' When Adam's life came to an end, the angel of death came to him (to take his soul). Adam said, `I still have forty years from my life term, don't I' He said, `Have you not given it to your son Dawud' So Adam denied that and his offspring followed suit (denying Allah's covenant), Adam forgot and his offspring forgot, Adam made a mistake and his offspring made mistakes.) At-Tirmidhi said, "This Hadith is Hasan Sahih, and it was reported from various chains of narration through Abu Hurayrah from the Prophet ". Al-Hakim also recorded it in his Mustadrak, and said; "Sahih according to the criteria of Muslim, and they did not record it." These and similar Hadiths testify that Allah, the Exalted and Most Honored, brought forth Adam's offspring from his loins and separated between the inhabitants of Paradise and those of the Fire. Allah then said,

(and made them testify as to themselves (saying): "Am I not your Lord" They said: "Yes!") Therefore, Allah made them testify with themselves by circumstance and words. Testimony is sometimes given in words, such as,

(They will say: "We bear witness against ourselves.") (6:130) At other times, testimony is given by the people themselves, such as Allah's statement,

(It is not for the Mushrikin, (polytheists) to maintain the mosques of Allah, while they testify against their own selves of disbelief.) (9:17) This Ayah means that their disbelief testifies against them, not that they actually testify against themselves here. Another Ayah of this type is Allah's statement,

(And to that he bears witness (by his deeds).) (100:7) The same is the case with asking, sometimes takes the form of words and sometimes a situation or circumstance. For instance, Allah said,

(And He gave you of all that you asked for.) (14:34) Allah said here,

(lest you should say), on the Day of Resurrection

(we were of this) of Tawhid

(unaware. Or lest you should say: "It was only our fathers aforetime who took others as partners in worship along with Allah,") (7:172-173)

Surah: 7 Ayah: 175, Ayah: 176 & Ayah: 177

﴿ وَٱتْلُ عَلَيْهِمْ نَبَأَ ٱلَّذِى ءَاتَيْنَـٰهُ ءَايَـٰتِنَا فَٱنسَلَخَ مِنْهَا فَأَتْبَعَهُ ٱلشَّيْطَـٰنُ فَكَانَ مِنَ ٱلْغَاوِينَ ۝ ﴾

175. And recite (O Muhammad (peace be upon him)) to them the story of him to whom We gave Our Ayât (proofs, evidences, verses, lessons, signs, revelations, etc.), but he threw them away; so Shaitân (Satan) followed him up, and he became of those who went astray.

﴿ وَلَوْ شِئْنَا لَرَفَعْنَـٰهُ بِهَا وَلَـٰكِنَّهُۥٓ أَخْلَدَ إِلَى ٱلْأَرْضِ وَٱتَّبَعَ هَوَىٰهُ ۚ فَمَثَلُهُۥ كَمَثَلِ ٱلْكَلْبِ إِن تَحْمِلْ عَلَيْهِ يَلْهَثْ أَوْ تَتْرُكْهُ يَلْهَث ۚ ذَّٰلِكَ مَثَلُ ٱلْقَوْمِ ٱلَّذِينَ كَذَّبُوا۟ بِـَٔايَـٰتِنَا ۚ فَٱقْصُصِ ٱلْقَصَصَ لَعَلَّهُمْ يَتَفَكَّرُونَ ۝ ﴾

176. And had We willed, We would surely have elevated him therewith but he clung to the earth and followed his own vain desire. So his parable is the parable of a dog: if you drive him away, he lolls his tongue out, or if you leave him alone, he (still) lolls his tongue out. Such is the parable of the people who reject Our Ayât (proofs, evidences, verses, lessons, signs, revelations, etc.). So relate the stories, perhaps they may reflect.

﴿ سَآءَ مَثَلًا ٱلْقَوْمُ ٱلَّذِينَ كَذَّبُوا۟ بِـَٔايَـٰتِنَا وَأَنفُسَهُمْ كَانُوا۟ يَظْلِمُونَ ۝ ﴾

177. Evil is the parable of the people who reject Our Ayât (proofs, evidences, verses and signs, etc.), and used to wrong their own selves.

Transliteration

175. Waotlu AAalayhim nabaa allathee ataynahu ayatina fainsalakha minha faatbaAAahu alshshaytanu fakana mina alghaweena 176. Walaw shi/na larafaAAnahu biha walakinnahu akhlada ila al-ardi waittabaAAa hawahu famathaluhu kamathali alkalbi in tahmil AAalayhi yalhath aw tatruk-hu yalhath thalika mathalu alqawmi allatheena kaththaboo bi-ayatina faoqsusi alqasasa laAAallahum yatafakkaroona 177. Saa mathalan alqawmu allatheena kaththaboo bi-ayatina waanfusahum kanoo yathlimoona

Tafsir Ibn Kathir

Story Bal`am bin Ba`ura

`Abdur-Razzaq recorded that `Abdullah bin Mas`ud said that Allah's statement,

(And recite to them the story of him to whom We gave Our Ayat, but he threw them away) "Is about Bal`am bin Ba`ura' a man from the Children of Israel." Shu`bah and several other narrators narrated this statement from Mansur who got it from Ibn Mas`ud. Sa`id bin Abi `Arubah narrated that Qatadah said that Ibn `Abbas said, "He is Sayfi, son of Ar-Rahib." Qatadah commented that Ka`b said, "He was a man from Al-Balqla' (a province of Jordan) who knew Allah's Greatest Name. He used to live in Bayt Al-Maqdis with the tyrants." Al-`Awfi reported that Ibn `Abbas said, "He is Bal`am bin Ba`ura', a man from Yemen whom Allah had given the knowledge of His Ayat, but he abandoned them." Malik bin Dinar said, "He was one of the scholars of the Children of Israel whose supplication was acceptable. They used to seek his lead in suplication in times of difficulty. Allah's Prophet Musa sent him to the King of Madyan to call him to Allah. That king appeased him and gave him land and gifts, and he reverted from the religion of Musa and followed the king's religion." `Imran bin `Uyaynah narrated that `Husayn said that `Imran bin Al-Harith said that Ibn `Abbas said, "He is Bal`am son of Ba`ura'." Similar was said by Mujahid and `Ikrimah. Therefore, it is well-known that this honorable Ayah was revealed about a man from the Children of Israel in ancient times, according to Ibn Mas`ud and several others among the Salaf. `Ali bin Abi Talhah reported that Ibn `Abbas said, "He is a man from the city of the tyrants (Jerusalem) whose name was Bal`am and who knew Allah's Greatest Name." `Ali bin Abi Talhah also reported that Ibn `Abbas that he said, "When Musa and those with him went to the city of the tyrants (Jerusalem), the cousins of Bal`am and his people came to him and said, `Musa is a strong man, and he has many soldiers. If he gains the upper hand over us, we will be destroyed. Therefore, supplicate to Allah that He prevents Musa and those with him from prevailing over us.' Bal`am said, `If I supplicate to Allah that He turns back Musa and those with him, I will lose in this life and the Hereafter.' They kept luring him until he supplicated against Musa and his people, and Allah took away what he bestowed on him (of knowledge). Hence Allah's statement,

(but he threw them away; so Shaytan followed him up).'" Allah said next,

(And had We willed, We would surely have elevated him therewith but he clung to the earth and followed his own vain desires.) Allah said,

Chapter 7: Al-Araf (The Heights), Verses 088-206

(And had We willed, We would surely have elevated him therewith) from the filth of this earthly life through the Ayat that We gave him knowledge of,

(but he clung to the earth), he became interested in the adornment of this life and its delights. He indulged in the lusts of life and its joys and was deceived by it, just as life deceived others like him, without sound comprehension or a good mind. Muhammad bin Ishaq bin Yasar narrated from Salim, from Abu An-Nadr that when Musa entered the land of Bani Canaan in the area of Ash-Sham (Greater Syria), the people of Bal`am came to him, saying, "This is Musa, son of `Imran with the Children of Israel. He wants to drive us out from our land, kill us and replace us with the Children of Israel. We are your people and have no other dwelling area. You are a person whose supplication is acceptable (to Allah), so go out and supplicate to Allah against them." He said, "Woe to you! Here is Allah's Prophet (Musa) with whom the angels and believers are! How can I supplicate against them when I know from Allah what I know" They said, "We have no other dwelling area." So they kept luring and begging him until he was tempted by the trial and went on his donkey towards Mount Husban, which was behind the Israelite military barracks. When he proceeded on the Mount for a while, the donkey sat down and refused to proceed. He got off the donkey and struck it until it stood up again and he rode it. The donkey did the same after a little while, and he struck it again until it stood up... So he proceeded and tried to supplicate against Musa and his people. However, Allah made his tongue mention his people with evil and the Children of Israel with good instead of his people, who protested, "O Bal`am! What are you doing You are supplicating for them and against us!" He said, "It is against my will. This is a matter that Allah has decided." He then said to them, as his tongue was made to loll out of his mouth, "Now I have lost this life and the Hereafter." This Ayah was revealed about the story of Bal`am son of Ba`ura'

(And recite to them the story of him to whom We gave Our Ayat, but he threw them away.), until,

(perhaps they may reflect.) Allah said next,

(So his parable is the parable of a dog: if you drive him away, he pants, or if you leave him alone, he (still) pants.) Scholars of Tafsir have conflicting opinions regarding the meaning of this Ayah. Some scholars said that it refers to the end of Bal`am's tongue which flickered out of his mouth, as in the story narrated from Ibn Ishaq, from Salim, from Abu An-Nadr. Therefore, his example is the example of the dog, its tongue pants regardless of whether it is driven away or not. It was also said that the meaning here is a parable of this man -- and his like -- concerning their misguidance, persisting the wrong path and not being able to benefit from faith or comprehend what they are being called to. So his example is that of a dog which pants whether it was driven away or left alone. The person described here does not benefit from the advice or the call to faith, just as if the advice and call never occurred. Allah said in another Ayah, k

(It is the same to them (disbelievers) whether you warn them or do not warn them, they will not believe.)(2:6) and,

(Whether you ask forgiveness for them (hypocrites) or ask not forgiveness for them -- (and even) if you ask seventy times for their forgiveness -- Allah will not forgive them.) (9:80) and similar Ayat. It was also said that the meaning here, is that the heart of the disbeliever, the hypocrite and the wicked is weak and devoid of guidance. Therefore, it keeps faltering. Similar was narrated from Al-Hasan Al-Basri.

(So relate the stories, perhaps they may reflect) Allah said next to His Prophet Muhammad ,

(So relate the stories, perhaps they may) the Children of Israel, who have knowledge of the story of Bal`am and what happened to him when Allah allowed him to stray and expelled him from His mercy. Allah favored him by teaching him His Greatest Name, by which, if He is asked, He will grant, and if He is called upon, He answers. But Bal`am used it in disobedience to Allah and invoked Him against His own party of the people of faith, followers of His servant and Messenger during that time, Musa, the son of `Imran, peace be upon him, whom Allah spoke to directly,

(perhaps they may reflect.) and avoid Bal`am's behavior, for Allah has given the Jews knowledge and made them superior to the bedouins surrounding them. He gave them the description of Muhammad which would allow them to recognize him, as they recognize their own children. They, among people, have the most right to follow, aid and support Muhammad , in obedience to their Prophets who informed them of him and commanded them to follow him. Therefore, whoever among them defies the knowledge in their Books or hides it from the servants, Allah will place disgrace on him in this life, followed by humiliation in the Hereafter. Allah said,

(Evil is the parable of the people who rejected Our Ayat.) Allah says, evil is the example of the people who deny Our Ayat in that they are equated with dogs that have no interest but to collect food and satisfy lusts.' Therefore, whoever goes out of the area of knowledge and guidance, and seeks satisfaction for his lusts and vain desires, is just like a dog; what an evil example. The Sahih recorded that the Messenger of Allah said,

«لَيْسَ لَنَا مَثَلُ السَّوْءِ، الْعَائِدُ فِي هِبَتِهِ كَالْكَلْبِ يَعُودُ فِي قَيْئِهِ»

(The evil example is not suitable for us: he who goes back on his gift is just like the dog that eats its vomit.) Allah's statement,

(and they used to wrong themselves.) means, Allah did not wrong them, but they wronged themselves by rejecting guidance, not obeying the Lord, being content with this life that will soon end, all the while seeking to fulfill desires and obey lusts.

Surah: 7 Ayah: 178

﴿مَن يَهْدِ ٱللَّهُ فَهُوَ ٱلْمُهْتَدِى وَمَن يُضْلِلْ فَأُوْلَٰٓئِكَ هُمُ ٱلْخَٰسِرُونَ﴾

178. Whomsoever Allâh guides, he is the guided one, and whomsoever He sends astray,- then those! They are the losers.

Transliteration

178. Man yahdi Allahu fahuwa almuhtadee waman yudlil faola-ika humu alkhasiroona

Tafsir Ibn Kathir

Allah says, whomever He leads aright, then none can lead him to misguidance, and whomever He leads astray, will have acquired failure, loss and sure misguidance. Verily, whatever Allah wills occurs; and whatever He does not will, does not occur. A Hadith narrated from `Abdullah bin Mas`ud reads,

»إِنَّ الْحَمْدَ لِلَّهِ نَحْمَدُهُ وَنَسْتَعِينُهُ وَنَسْتَهْدِيهِ وَنَسْتَغْفِرُهُ وَنَعُوذُ بِاللَّهِ مِنْ شُرُورِ أَنْفُسِنَا وَمِنْ سَيِّئَاتِ أَعْمَالِنَا، مَنْ يَهْدِ اللَّهُ فَلَا مُضِلَّ لَهُ وَمَنْ يُضْلِلِ اللَّهُ فَلَا هَادِيَ لَهُ، وَأَشْهَدُ أَنْ لَا إِلَهَ إِلَّا اللَّهُ وَحْدَهُ لَا شَرِيكَ لَهُ وَأَشْهَدُ أَنَّ مُحَمَّدًا عَبْدُهُ وَرَسُولُهُ«

(All praise is due to Allah, Whom we praise and seek help, guidance and forgiveness from. We seek refuge with Allah from the evils within ourselves and from the burden of our evil deeds. He whom Allah guides, will never be misled; and he whom He misguides, will never have one who will guide him. I bear witness that there is no deity worthy of worship except Allah without partners and that Muhammad is His servant and Messenger.) The complete Hadith was collected by Imam Ahmad and the collectors of Sunan and others.

Surah: 7 Ayah: 179

﴿وَلَقَدْ ذَرَأْنَا لِجَهَنَّمَ كَثِيرًا مِّنَ ٱلْجِنِّ وَٱلْإِنسِ ۖ لَهُمْ قُلُوبٌ لَّا يَفْقَهُونَ بِهَا وَلَهُمْ أَعْيُنٌ لَّا يُبْصِرُونَ بِهَا وَلَهُمْ ءَاذَانٌ لَّا يَسْمَعُونَ بِهَآ ۚ أُو۟لَـٰٓئِكَ كَٱلْأَنْعَـٰمِ بَلْ هُمْ أَضَلُّ ۚ أُو۟لَـٰٓئِكَ هُمُ ٱلْغَـٰفِلُونَ﴾

179. And surely, We have created many of the jinn and mankind for Hell. They have hearts wherewith they understand not, and they have eyes wherewith they see not, and they have ears wherewith they hear not (the truth). They are like cattle, nay even more astray; those! They are the heedless ones.

Transliteration

179. Walaqad thara/na lijahannama katheeran mina aljinni waal-insi lahum quloobun la yafqahoona biha walahum aAAyunun la yubsiroona biha walahum athanun la yasmaAAoona biha ola-ika kaal-anAAami bal hum adallu ola-ika humu alghafiloona

Tafsir Ibn Kathir

Disbelief and the Divine Decree

Allah said,

(And surely, We have created for Hell) We made a share in the Fire for,

(many of the Jinn and mankind) We prepared them for it by their performance of the deeds of its people. When Allah intended to create the creation, He knew what their work will be before they existed. He wrote all this in a Book, kept with Him, fifty thousand years before He created the heavens and earth. Muslim recorded that `Abdullah bin `Amr narrated that the Messenger of Allah said,

«إِنَّ اللهَ قَدَّرَ مَقَادِيرَ الْخَلْقِ قَبْلَ أَنْ يَخْلُقَ السَّمَوَاتِ وَالْأَرْضَ بِخَمْسِينَ أَلْفَ سَنَةٍ وَكَانَ عَرْشُهُ عَلَى الْمَاءِ»

(Verily, Allah decided the destination and due measurement of the creation fifty thousand years before He created the heavens and earth, and His Throne was over the water.) There are many Hadiths on this subject, and certainly, the matter of Al-Qadar is of utmost importance, yet this is not where we should discuss it. Allah said,

(They have hearts wherewith they understand not, and they have eyes wherewith they see not, and they have ears wherewith they hear not.) meaning, they do not benefit from these senses that Allah made for them as a means of gaining guidance. Similarly, Allah said,

(And We had assigned them the (faculties of) hearing, seeing, and hearts; but their hearing, seeing, and their hearts availed them nothing since they used to deny the Ayat.) (46:26). Allah also said about the hypocrites,

((They are) deaf, dumb, and blind, so they return not (to the right path)) (2:18), and about the disbelievers,

((They are) deaf, dumb and blind. So they do not understand.) (2:171) However, they are not deaf, dumb or blind, except in relation to the guidance. Allah said;

(Had Allah known of any good in them, He would indeed have made them listen; and even if He had made them listen, they would but have turned away with aversion (to the truth).) (8:23),

(Verily, it is not the eyes that grow blind, but it is the hearts which are in the breasts that grow blind.) (22:46), and,

(And whosoever turns away blindly from the remembrance of the Most Gracious (Allah), We appoint for him Shaytan to be an intimate companion to him. And verily, they hinder them from the path, but they think that they are guided aright!)(43:36-37) Allah's statement,

(They are like cattle), means, those who neither hear the truth, nor understand it, nor see the guidance, are just like grazing cattle that do not benefit from these senses, except for what sustains their life in this world. Allah said in a similar Ayah,

(And the example of those who disbelieve is as that of one who shouts to those who hear nothing but calls and cries.) (2:171) meaning, their example, when they are called to the faith, is the example of cattle that hear only the voice of their shepherd, but cannot understand what he is saying. Allah further described them

(nay even more astray), than cattle, because cattle still respond to the call of their shepherd, even though they do not understand what he is saying. As for the people described here, they are unlike cattle, which fulfill the purpose and service they were created for. The disbeliever was created to worship Allah alone in Tawhid, but he disbelieved in Allah and associated others in His worship. Therefore, those people who obey Allah are more honorable than some angels, while cattle are better than those who disbelieve in Him. So Allah said;

(They are like cattle, nay even more astray; those! They are the heedless ones.)

Surah: 7 Ayah: 180

﴿ وَلِلَّهِ ٱلْأَسْمَآءُ ٱلْحُسْنَىٰ فَٱدْعُوهُ بِهَا ۖ وَذَرُوا۟ ٱلَّذِينَ يُلْحِدُونَ فِىٓ أَسْمَـٰٓئِهِۦ ۚ سَيُجْزَوْنَ مَا كَانُوا۟ يَعْمَلُونَ ﴾

180. And (all) the Most Beautiful Names belong to Allâh, so call on Him by them, and leave the company of those who belie or deny (or utter impious speech against) His Names. They will be requited for what they used to do.

Transliteration

180. Walillahi al-asmao alhusna faodAAoohu biha watharoo allatheena yulhidoona fee asma-ihi sayujzawna ma kanoo yaAAmaloona

Tafsir Ibn Kathir

Allah's Most Beautiful Names

Abu Hurayrah narrated that the Messenger of Allah said,

«إِنَّ لِلَّهِ تِسْعًا وَتِسْعِينَ اسْمًا مِائَةً إِلَّا وَاحِدًا، مَنْ أَحْصَاهَا دَخَلَ الْجَنَّةَ وَهُوَ وِتْرٌ يُحِبُّ الْوِتْرَ»

(Verily, Allah has ninety-nine Names, a hundred less one; whoever counts (and preserves) them, will enter Paradise. Allah is Witr (One) and loves Al-Witr (the odd numbered things),) The Two Sahihs collected this Hadith. We should state that Allah's

Names are not restricted to only ninety-nine. For instance, in his Musnad, Imam Ahmad recorded that `Abdullah bin Mas`ud said that the Messenger of Allah said,

«مَا أَصَابَ أَحَدًا قَطُّ هَمٌّ وَلَا حَزَنٌ فَقَالَ: اللَّهُمَّ إِنِّي عَبْدُكَ، ابْنُ أَمَتِكَ، نَاصِيَتِي بِيَدِكَ مَاضٍ فِيَّ حُكْمُكَ، عَدْلٌ فِيَّ قَضَاؤُكَ، أَسْأَلُكَ بِكُلِّ اسْمٍ هُوَ لَكَ سَمَّيْتَ بِهِ نَفْسَكَ أَوْ أَنْزَلْتَهُ فِي كِتَابِكَ أَوْ عَلَّمْتَهُ أَحَدًا مِنْ خَلْقِكَ أَوِ اسْتَأْثَرْتَ بِهِ فِي عِلْمِ الْغَيْبِ عِنْدَكَ أَنْ تَجْعَلَ الْقُرْآنَ الْعَظِيمَ رَبِيعَ قَلْبِي، وَنُورَ صَدْرِي، وَجَلَاءَ حُزْنِي، وَذَهَابَ هَمِّي، إِلَّا أَذْهَبَ اللهُ حُزْنَهُ وَهَمَّهُ وَأَبْدَلَ مَكَانَهُ فَرَحًا»

(Any person who is overcome by sadness or grief and supplicates, `O Allah! I am Your servant, son of Your female servant. My forelock is in Your Hand. Your decision concerning me shall certainly come to pass. Just is Your Judgement about me. I invoke You by every Name that You have and that You called Yourself by, sent down in Your Book, taught to any of Your creatures, or kept with You in the knowledge of the Unseen that is with You. Make the Glorious Qur'an the spring of my heart, the light of my chest, the remover of my grief and the dissipater of my concern.' Surely, Allah will remove his grief and sadness and exchange them for delight.) The Prophet was asked "O Messenger of Allah! Should we learn these words" He said,

«بَلَى يَنْبَغِي لِكُلِّ مَنْ سَمِعَهَا أَنْ يَتَعَلَّمَهَا»

(Yes. It is an obligation on all those who hear this supplication to learn it.) Al-`Awfi said that Ibn `Abbas said about Allah's statement,

(and leave the company of those who belie His Names) "To belie Allah's Names includes saying that Al-Lat (an idol) derived from Allah's Name." Ibn Jurayj narrated from Mujahid that he commented,

(and leave the company of those who belie His Names) "They derived Al-Lat (an idol's name) from Allah, and Al-`Uzza (another idol) from Al-`Aziz (the All-Mighty)." Qatadah stated that Ilhad refers to associating others with Allah in His Names (such as calling an idol Al-`Uzza). The word Ilhad (used in the Ayah in another from) means deviation, wickedness, injustice and straying. The hole in the grave is called Lahd, because it is a hole within a hole, that is turned towards the Qiblah (the direction of the prayer).

Surah: 7 Ayah: 181

﴿ وَمِمَّنْ خَلَقْنَآ أُمَّةٌ يَهْدُونَ بِٱلْحَقِّ وَبِهِۦ يَعْدِلُونَ ۞ ﴾

181. And of those whom We have created, there is a community who guides (others) with the truth, and establishes justice therewith.

Transliteration

181. Wamimman khalaqna ommatun yahdoona bialhaqqi wabihi yaAAdiloona

Tafsir Ibn Kathir

Allah said,

(And of those whom We have created), in reference to some nations,

(a community), that stands in truth, in words and action,

(who guides (others) with the truth), they proclaim it and call to it,

(and establishes justice therewith), adhere to it themselves and judge by it. It was reported that this Ayah refers to the Ummah of Muhammad . In the Two Sahihs, it is recorded that Mu`awiyah bin Abi Sufyan said that the Messenger of Allah said,

«لَا تَزَالُ طَائِفَةٌ مِنْ أُمَّتِي ظَاهِرِينَ عَلَى الْحَقِّ لَا يَضُرُّهُمْ مَنْ خَذَلَهُمْ وَلَا مَنْ خَالَفَهُمْ حَتَّى تَقُومَ السَّاعَة»

(There will always be a group of my Ummah who are apparent on the Truth, unabated by those who fail or oppose them, until the (Last) Hour commences.) rIn another narration, the Messenger said,

«حَتَّى يَأْتِيَ أَمْرُ اللهِ وَهُمْ عَلَى ذَلِك»

(Until Allah's command (the Last Hour) comes while they are still like this.) and in yet another narration,

«وَهُمْ بِالشَّام»

(And they will dwell in Ash-Sham (Greater Syria).)

Surah: 7 Ayah: 182 & Ayah: 183

﴿ وَٱلَّذِينَ كَذَّبُوا۟ بِـَٔايَٰتِنَا سَنَسْتَدْرِجُهُم مِّنْ حَيْثُ لَا يَعْلَمُونَ ﴾

182. Those who reject Our Ayât (proofs, evidences, verses, lessons, signs, revelations, etc.), We shall gradually seize them with punishment in ways they perceive not.

﴿ وَأُمْلِى لَهُمْ إِنَّ كَيْدِى مَتِينٌ ﴾

183. And I respite them; certainly My Plan is strong.

Transliteration

182. Waallatheena kaththaboo bi-ayatina sanastadrijuhum min haythu la yaAAlamoona 183. Waomlee lahum inna kaydee mateenun

Tafsir Ibn Kathir

Allah said,

(Those who reject Our Ayat, We shall gradually seize them in ways they perceive not) meaning, the doors of provisions will be opened for them and also the means of livelihood, in this life. They will be deceived by all this and think that they are on the correct path. Allah said in another instance,

(So, when they forgot (the warning) with which they had been reminded, We opened for them the gates of every (pleasant) thing, until in the midst of their enjoyment in that which they were given, all of a sudden, We took them (in punishment), and lo! They were plunged into destruction with deep regrets and sorrow. So the root of the people who did wrong was cut off. And all the praises and thanks are to Allah, the Lord of all that exists.)(6:44-45). Allah said here,

(And I respite them) prolong what they are in,

(certainly My plan is strong) and perfect.

Surah: 7 Ayah: 184

﴿ أَوَلَمْ يَتَفَكَّرُواْ مَا بِصَاحِبِهِم مِّن جِنَّةٍ إِنْ هُوَ إِلَّا نَذِيرٌ مُّبِينٌ ﴾

184. Do they not reflect? There is no madness in their companion (Muhammad (peace be upon him)) He is but a plain warner.

Transliteration

184. Awa lam yatafakkaroo ma bisahibihim min jinnatin in huwa illa natheerun mubeenun

Tafsir Ibn Kathir

Allah said,

(Do they not reflect) `those who deny Our Ayat,'

(there is not in their companion), Muhammad ,

(madness) Muhammad is not mad, rather, he is truly the Messenger of Allah, calling to Truth,

(but he is a plain warner), and this is clear for those who have a mind and a heart by which they understand and comprehend. Allah said in another Ayah,

(And (O people) your companion is not a madman.)(81:22) Allah also said,

(Say: "I exhort you to one (thing) only, that you stand up for Allah's sake in pairs and singly, and reflect, there is no madness in your companion. He is only a warner to you in face of a severe torment.") (34:46) meaning, `I ask you to stand for Allah in sincerity without stubbornness or bias,'

(in pairs and singly) (34:46) individuals and in groups,

(and reflect) (34:46), about this man who brought the Message from Allah, is he mad If you do this, it will become clear to you that he is the Messenger of Allah in truth and justice. Qatadah bin Di'amah said, "We were informed that the Prophet of Allah once was on (Mount) As-Safa and called the Quraysh, subtribe by subtribe, proclaiming,

«يَا بَنِي فُلَانٍ، يَا بَنِي فُلَانٍ فَحَذَّرَهُمْ بَأْسَ اللهِ وَوَقَائِعَ اللهِ»

(O Children of so-and-so, O Children of so-and-so! He warned them against Allah's might and what He has done (such as revenge from His enemies).) Some of them commented, `This companion of yours (Prophet Muhammad) is mad; he kept shouting until the morning' Allah sent down this Ayah,

(Do they not reflect There is no madness in their companion. He is but a plain warner) (7:184).'"

Surah: 7 Ayah: 185

﴿ أَوَلَمْ يَنظُرُوا۟ فِى مَلَكُوتِ ٱلسَّمَـٰوَٰتِ وَٱلْأَرْضِ وَمَا خَلَقَ ٱللَّهُ مِن شَىْءٍ وَأَنْ عَسَىٰٓ أَن يَكُونَ قَدِ ٱقْتَرَبَ أَجَلُهُمْ ۖ فَبِأَىِّ حَدِيثٍۭ بَعْدَهُۥ يُؤْمِنُونَ ﴾

185. Do they not look in the dominion of the heavens and the earth and all things that Allâh has created; and that it may be that the end of their lives is near. In what message after this will they then believe?

Transliteration

185. Awalam yanthuroo fee malakooti alssamawati waal-ardi wama khalaqa Allahu min shay-in waan AAasa an yakoona qadi iqtaraba ajaluhum fabi-ayyi hadeethin baAAdahu yu/minoona

Tafsir Ibn Kathir

Allah asks, those who denied faith, did they not contemplate about Our Ayat in the kingdom of the heavens and earth and what was created in them Do they not contemplate about all this and learn lessons from it, so that they are certain that He Who has all this, has no equal or rival All this was made by He Who Alone deserves the worship and sincere religion, so that they might have faith in Him and believe in His Messenger, all the while turning to Allah's obedience, rejecting any rivals to Him, and rejecting idols. They should be warned that their lifes may have reached their end, and they, thus, face their demise while disbelievers, ending up in Allah's torment and severe punishment. Allah said,

(In what message after this will they then believe) Allah says, what more warnings, and discouragements should compel them to believe, if the warnings and threats that Muhammad brought them from Allah in His Book do not compel them to do so Allah said next,

Surah: 7 Ayah: 186

﴿ مَن يُضْلِلِ ٱللَّهُ فَلَا هَادِيَ لَهُۥ ۚ وَيَذَرُهُمْ فِي طُغْيَـٰنِهِمْ يَعْمَهُونَ ۝ ﴾

186. Whomsoever Allâh sends astray, none can guide him; and He lets them wander blindly in their transgressions.

Transliteration

186. Man yudlili Allahu fala hadiya lahu wayatharuhum fee tughyanihim yaAAmahoona

Tafsir Ibn Kathir

Allah says, those who were destined to be misguided, then none can lead them to guidance, and even if they try their best effort to gain such guidance, this will not avail them,

(And whomsoever Allah wants to put in Fitnah (error, because of his rejecting of Faith, or trial), you can do nothing for him against Allah) (5:41), and,

(Say: "Behold all that is in the heavens and the earth," but neither Ayat nor warners benefit those who believe not) (10:101).

Surah: 7 Ayah: 187

﴿ يَسْـَٔلُونَكَ عَنِ ٱلسَّاعَةِ أَيَّانَ مُرْسَىٰهَا ۖ قُلْ إِنَّمَا عِلْمُهَا عِندَ رَبِّى ۖ لَا يُجَلِّيهَا لِوَقْتِهَآ إِلَّا هُوَ ۚ ثَقُلَتْ فِى ٱلسَّمَـٰوَٰتِ وَٱلْأَرْضِ ۚ لَا تَأْتِيكُمْ إِلَّا بَغْتَةً ۗ يَسْـَٔلُونَكَ كَأَنَّكَ حَفِىٌّ عَنْهَا ۖ قُلْ إِنَّمَا عِلْمُهَا عِندَ ٱللَّهِ وَلَـٰكِنَّ أَكْثَرَ ٱلنَّاسِ لَا يَعْلَمُونَ ۝ ﴾

187. They ask you about the Hour (Day of Resurrection): "When will be its appointed time?" Say: "The knowledge thereof is with my Lord (Alone). None can reveal its

time but He. Heavy is its burden through the heavens and the earth. It shall not come upon you except all of a sudden." They ask you as if you have a good knowledge of it. Say: "The knowledge thereof is with Allâh (Alone) but most of mankind know not."

Transliteration

187. Yas-aloonaka AAani alssaAAati ayyana mursaha qul innama AAilmuha AAinda rabbee la yujalleeha liwaqtiha illa huwa thaqulat fee alssamawati waal-ardi la ta/teekum illa baghtatan yas-aloonaka kaannaka hafiyyun AAanha qul innama AAilmuha AAinda Allahi walakinna akthara alnnasi la yaAAlamoona

Tafsir Ibn Kathir

The Last Hour and its Portents

Allah said here,

(They ask you about the Hour), just as He said in another Ayah,

(People ask you concerning the Hour) (33:63). It was said that this Ayah was revealed about the Quraysh or the Jews, although it appears that it was about the Quraysh, because this Ayah was revealed in Makkah. The Quraysh used to ask about the Last Hour, because they used to deny it and discount its coming. For instance, Allah said in another Ayah,

(And they say: "When will be this promise (the torment or the Day of Resurrection), if you speak the truth") (10:48), and,

(Those who believe not therein seek to hasten it, while those who believe are fearful of it, and know that it is the very truth. Verily, those who dispute concerning the Hour are certainly in error far away) (42:18). Allah said here (that the Quraysh asked),

("When will be its appointed time") in reference to its commencement, according to `Ali bin Abi Talhah who reported this from Ibn `Abbas. They asked about the Hour's appointed term and when the end of this world will begin;

(Say: "The knowledge thereof is with my Lord (Alone). None can reveal its time but He.") Allah commanded His Messenger that when asked about the appointed term of the Last Hour, he referred its knowledge to Allah, the Exalted. Only Allah knows the Last Hour's appointed term and when it will certainly occur, and none besides Him has this knowledge,

(Heavy is its burden through the heavens and the earth) `Abdur-Razzaq narrated that Ma`mar said that Qatadah commented on this Ayah,

(Heavy is its burden through the heavens and the earth) "Its knowledge is heavy on the residents of the heavens and earth, they do not have knowledge in it." Also, Ma`mar said that Al-Hasan commented on this Ayah, "When the Last Hour comes, it will be heavy on the residents of the heavens and earth." Ad-Dahhak said that Ibn `Abbas explained this Ayah,

(Heavy is its burden through the heavens and the earth,) saying, "All creatures will suffer its heaviness on the Day of Resurrection." Ibn Jurayj also said about this Ayah,

(Heavy is its burden through the heavens and the earth.) "When it commences, the heavens will be torn, the stars will scatter all over, the sun will be wound round (thus losing its light), the mountains will be made to pass away and all of which Allah spoke of will occur. This is the meaning of its burden being heavy." As-Suddi said that,

(Heavy is its burden through the heavens and the earth) means, its knowledge is hidden in the heavens and earth, and none, not even a close angel or a sent Messenger has knowledge of its appointed time.

(It shall not come upon you except all of a sudden) indicating that the Hour will start all of a sudden, while they are unaware. Qatadah said, "Allah has decided that,

(It shall not come upon you except all of a sudden.) He then said, "We were informed that Allah's Prophet said,

«إِنَّ السَّاعَةَ تَهِيجُ بِالنَّاسِ، وَالرَّجُلُ يُصْلِحُ حَوْضَهُ وَالرَّجُلُ يَسْقِي مَاشِيَتَهُ، وَالرَّجُلُ يُقِمْ سِلْعَتَهُ فِي السُّوقِ وَيَخْفِضُ مِيزَانَهُ وَيَرْفَعُهُ»

The Hour will start (suddenly) for the people while one is mending his watering hole, giving water to his cattle, setting his goods in the market or lowering his scale and raising it (selling and buying).'" Al-Bukhari recorded that Abu Hurayrah said that the Messenger of Allah said,

«لَا تَقُومُ السَّاعَةُ حَتَّى تَطْلُعَ الشَّمْسُ مِنْ مَغْرِبِهَا، فَإِذَا طَلَعَتْ فَرَآهَا النَّاسُ آمَنُوا أَجْمَعُونَ، فَذَلِكَ حِينَ لَا يَنْفَعُ نَفْسًا إِيمَانُهَا لَمْ تَكُنْ آمَنَتْ مِنْ قَبْلُ أَوْ كَسَبَتْ فِي إِيمَانِهَا خَيْرًا، وَلَتَقُومَنَّ السَّاعَةُ وَقَدْ نَشَرَ الرَّجُلَانِ ثَوْبَهُمَا بَيْنَهُمَا، فَلَا يَتَبَايَعَانِهِ وَلَا يَطْوِيَانِهِ. وَلَتَقُومَنَّ السَّاعَةُ وَقَدِ انْصَرَفَ الرَّجُلُ بِلَبَنِ لِقْحَتِهِ فَلَا يَطْعَمُهُ، وَلَتَقُومَنَّ السَّاعَةُ وَهُوَ يَلِيطُ حَوْضَهُ فَلَا يَسْقِي فِيهِ، وَلَتَقُومَنَّ السَّاعَةُ وَالرَّجُلُ قَدْ رَفَعَ أَكْلَتَهُ إِلَى فِيهِ فَلَا يَطْعَمُهَا»

(The Hour will not commence until the sun rises from the west. When it rises (from the west) and the people see it, then, all people will believe. However, this is when faith does not benefit a soul that did not believe beforehand nor earned good in faith. The Hour will (all of a sudden) commence while two men have spread a garment between them, and they will neither have time to conclude the transaction nor to fold the garment. The Hour will commence after a man milked his animal, but he will not have time to drink it. The Hour will start when a man is making his watering hole (for his animals), but will not have time to make use of the pool. And the Hour will commence while a man has raised his hand with a bite to his mouth, but will not eat it.) Al-`Awfi said that Ibn `Abbas commented on the Ayah,

(They ask you as if you have good knowledge of it.) "As if you have good relations and friendship with them!" Ibn `Abbas said, "When the people (pagans of Quraysh) asked the Prophet about the Last Hour, they did so in a way as if Muhammad was their friend! Allah revealed to him that its knowledge is with Him Alone and He did not inform a close angel or Messenger of it." The correct explanation for this Ayah is, as narrated from Mujahid, through Ibn Abi Najih,

(They ask you as if you have Hafi of it.) means, `as if you had asked about its time and so its knowledge is with you.' Allah said,

(Say: "The knowledge thereof is with Allah (Alone), but most of mankind know not.") When Jibril came in the shape of a bedouin man to teach the people matters of their religion, he sat next to the Messenger of Allah asking him as if to learn. Jibril asked the Messenger about Islam, then about Iman (faith) then about Ihsan (Excellence in the religion). He asked next, "When will the Hour start" Allah's Messenger said,

«مَا الْمَسْؤُولُ عَنْهَا بِأَعْلَمَ مِنَ السَّائِلِ»

(He who is asked about it has no more knowledge of it than the questioner.) Therefore, the Prophet was saying, `I have no more knowledge in it than you (O Jibril), nor does anyone have more knowledge in it than anyone else.' The Prophet then recited the Ayah,

(Verily, Allah, with Him (Alone) is the knowledge of the Hour.) (31:34) In another narration, Jibril asked the Prophet about the portents of the Hour, and the Prophet mentioned them. The Prophet also said in this narration,

«فِي خَمْسٍ لَا يَعْلَمُهُنَّ إِلَّا اللهُ»

(Five, their knowledge is only with Allah) then recited this Ayah (31:34). In response to the Prophet's answers after each question, Jibril would say, "You have said the truth." This made the Companions wonder about this questioner who would ask a question and attest to every answer he was given. When Jibril went away, the Messenger of Allah said to the Companions,

«هَذَا جِبْرِيلُ أَتَاكُمْ يُعَلِّمُكُمْ دِينَكُم»

(This is Jibril, he came to teach you matters of your religion.) In yet another narration, the Prophet commented,

«وَمَا أَتَانِي فِي صُورَةٍ إِلَّا عَرَفْتُهُ فِيهَا إِلَّا صُورَتُهُ هَذِهِ»

(I recognized him (Jibril) in every shape he came to me in, except this one.) Muslim recorded that `Aishah, may Allah be pleased with her, said; "When the bedouins used to come to the Prophet , they used to ask him about the Hour. The Prophet would answer them, while pointing at the youngest person among them,

«إِنْ يَعِشْ هَذَا لَمْ يُدْرِكْهُ الْهَرَمُ حَتَّى قَامَتْ عَلَيْكُمْ سَاعَتُكُمْ»

(If this (young man) lives, he will not become old before your Hour starts.) The Prophet meant the end of their life that introduces them to the life in Barzakh, which is between this life and the Hereafter. Muslim recorded that Anas said that a man asked Allah's Messenger about the Hour, and the Messenger answered,

«إِنْ يَعِشْ هَذَا الْغُلَامُ فَعَسَى أَنْ لَا يُدْرِكَهُ الْهَرَمُ حَتَّى تَقُومَ السَّاعَةُ»

(If this young boy lives, it might be that he will not become old before the Hour starts.) Only Muslim collected this Hadith. Jabir bin `Abdullah said, "I heard the Messenger of Allah saying, one month before he died,

«تَسْأَلُونِي عَنِ السَّاعَةِ، وَإِنَّمَا عِلْمُهَا عِنْدَ اللهِ، وَأُقْسِمُ بِاللهِ مَا عَلَى ظَهْرِ الْأَرْضِ الْيَوْمَ مِنْ نَفْسٍ مَنْفُوسَةٍ تَأْتِي عَلَيْهَا مِائَةُ سَنَةٍ»

(You keep asking me about the Hour, when its knowledge is with Allah. I swear by Allah that there is no living soul on the face of the earth now will be alive a hundred years from now.) Muslim collected this Hadith. A similar Hadith is recorded in Two Sahihs from Ibn `Umar, but he commented, "The Messenger of Allah meant that his generation will be finished by that time reach its appointed term." Imam Ahmad recorded that Ibn Mas`ud said that the Prophet said,

«لَقِيتُ لَيْلَةَ أُسْرِيَ بِي إِبْرَاهِيمَ وَمُوسَى وَعِيسَى، فَتَذَاكَرُوا أَمْرَ السَّاعَةِ قَالَ فَرَدُّوا أَمْرَهُمْ إِلَى إِبْرَاهِيمَ عَلَيْهِ السَّلَامُ، فَقَالَ: لَا عِلْمَ لِي بِهَا، فَرَدُّوا أَمْرَهُمْ إِلَى مُوسَى فَقَالَ: لَا عِلْمَ لِي بِهَا، فَرَدُّوا أَمْرَهُمْ إِلَى عِيسَى فَقَالَ عِيسَى: أَمَّا

وَجْبَتُهَا فَلَا يَعْلَمُ بِهَا أَحَدٌ إِلَّا اللَّهُ عَزَّ وَجَلَّ، وَفِيمَا عَهِدَ إِلَيَّ رَبِّي عَزَّ وَجَلَّ أَنَّ الدَّجَّالَ خَارِجٌ قَالَ وَمَعِي قَضِيبَانِ، فَإِذَا رَآنِي ذَابَ كَمَا يَذُوبُ الرَّصَاصُ، قَالَ: فَيُهْلِكُهُ اللَّهُ عَزَّ وَجَلَّ إِذَا رَآنِي حَتَّى إِنَّ الشَّجَرَ وَالْحَجَرَ يَقُولُ: يَا مُسْلِمُ إِنَّ تَحْتِي كَافِرًا فَتَعَالَ فَاقْتُلْهُ، قَالَ: فَيُهْلِكُهُمُ اللَّهُ عَزَّ وَجَلَّ ثُمَّ يَرْجِعُ النَّاسُ إِلَى بِلَادِهِمْ وَأَوْطَانِهِمْ،قَالَ: فَعِنْدَ ذَلِكَ يَخْرُجُ يَأْجُوجُ وَمَأْجُوجُ وَهُمْ مِنْ كُلِّ حَدَبٍ يَنْسِلُونَ، فَيَطَأُونَ بِلَادَهُمْ لَا يَأْتُونَ عَلَى شَيْءٍ إِلَّا أَهْلَكُوهُ وَلَا يَمُرُّونَ عَلَى مَاءٍ إِلَّا شَرِبُوهُ، قَالَ: ثُمَّ يَرْجِعُ النَّاسُ إِلَيَّ فَيَشْكُونَهُمْ فَأَدْعُو اللَّهَ عَزَّ وَجَلَّ عَلَيْهِمْ فَيُهْلِكُهُمْ وَيُمِيتُهُمْ حَتَّى تَجْوَى الْأَرْضُ مِنْ نَتْنِ رِيحِهِمْ أَيْ تُنْتِنُ، قَالَ: فَيُنْزِلُ اللَّهُ عَزَّ وَجَلَّ الْمَطَرَ فَيَجْتَرِفُ أَجْسَادَهُمْ حَتَّى يَقْذِفَهُمْ فِي الْبَحْرِ. قال يزيد بن هارون: ثُمَّ تُنْسَفُ الْجِبَالُ وَتُمَدُّ الْأَرْضُ مَدَّ الْأَدِيمِ، ثُمَّ رَجَعَ إِلَى حَدِيثِ هُشَيْمٍ، قَالَ: فَفِيمَا عَهِدَ إِلَيَّ رَبِّي عَزَّ وَجَلَّ أَنَّ ذَلِكَ إِذَا كَانَ كَذَلِكَ، فَإِنَّ السَّاعَةَ كَالْحَامِلِ الْمُتِمِّ لَا يَدْرِي أَهْلُهَا مَتَى تُفَاجِئُهُمْ بِوِلَادَتِهَا لَيْلًا أَوْ نَهَارًا»

(During the night of Isra', I met Ibrahim, Musa and `Isa. They mentioned the matter of the Last Hour, and they asked Ibrahim about it, who said, `I do not have knowledge of it.' They asked Musa about it and he said, `I have no knowledge of it.' They then asked `Isa about it, and he said, `As for when it will occur, only Allah, the Exalted and Most Honored, knows that. My Lord has conveyed to me that the Dajjal (False Messiah) will appear, and I will have two staffs (spears) with me. When he sees me, he will dissolve just as lead is dissolved. Allah will destroy him when he sees me, and the tree and the stone will say, `O Muslim! There is a disbeliever under (behind) me, so come and kill him.' Allah will destroy them (the Dajjal and his army), and the people will safely go back to their lands and areas. Thereafter, Gog and Magog will appear, and they will be swarming from every mound, sweeping over the earth and destroying everything they pass by. They will drink every water source they pass. The people will come to me complaining about Gog and Magog and will invoke Allah, the Exalted and Most Honored, against them, and Allah will bring death to all of them until the earth rots with their stinking odor. Allah will send down rain on them and the rain will carry their corpses, until it throws them in the sea... My Lord, the Exalted and Most Honored has conveyed to me that when this occurs, the Hour will be just like the pregnant women when the term of pregnancy is full, her family does not know when she will surprise them and give birth, whether by night or by day.) Ibn Majah also collected a similar Hadith Therefore these are the greatest of the Messengers but they did not have knowledge of the appointed term of the Hour. They asked `Isa about it and he spoke about its Signs, since he will descend in the last generations of this Ummah, implementing the Law of Allah's Messenger , killing the Dajjal and destroying Gog and Magog people by the blessing of his supplication. `Isa merely informed them of the knowledge Allah gave him on this subject. Imam Ahmad recorded that Hudhayfah said, "The Messenger of Allah was asked about the Hour and he said,

«عِلْمُهَا عِنْدَ رَبِّي عَزَّ وَجَلَّ لَا يُجَلِّيهَا لِوَقْتِهَا إِلَّا هُوَ، وَلَكِنْ سَأُخْبِرُكُمْ بِمَشَارِيطِهَا وَمَا يَكُونُ بَيْنَ يَدَيْهَا، إِنَّ بَيْنَ يَدَيْهَا فِتْنَةً وَهَرَجًا»

(Its knowledge is with my Lord, the Exalted and Most Honored, none can reveal its time except Him. However, I will tell you about its portents and the signs that precede it. Before it commences, there will be Fitnah (trials) and Harj.) They asked, `O Allah's Messenger! We know the meaning of the Fitnah, so what is the Harj' He said,

«بِلِسَانِ الْحَبَشَةِ الْقَتْل»

(It means killing, in the Language of the Ethiopians.) He then said,

«وَيُلْقَى بَيْنَ النَّاسِ التَّنَاكُرُ، فَلَا يَكَادُ أَحَدٌ يَعْرِفُ أَحَدًا»

(Isolation and loneliness will be common between people, and therefore, almost no one will be able to recognize any other.)" None among the collectors of the six Sunan collected this Hadith using this chain of narration. Tariq bin Shihab said that the Messenger of Allah kept mentioning the Last Hour (for people kept asking about it), until this Ayah was revealed,

(They ask you about the Hour (Day of Resurrection): "When will be its appointed time"). An-Nasa'i collected this Hadith, which has a strong chain. Therefore, this unlettered Prophet , the chief of the Messengers and their Seal, Muhammad, may Allah's peace and blessings be on him, Muhammad, the Prophet of mercy, repentance, Al-Malhmah (great demise of the disbelievers), Al-`Aqib (who came after many Prophets), Al-Muqaffi (the last of a succession) and Al-Hashir (below whom will all people be gathered (on the Day of Gathering)) Muhammad who said, as collected in the Sahih from Anas and Sahl bin Sa`d,

«بُعِثْتُ أَنَا وَالسَّاعَةَ كَهَاتَيْنِ»

(My sending and the Hour are like this,) and he joined his index and middle fingers. Yet, he was commanded to defer knowledge of the Last Hour to Allah if he was asked about it,

(Say: "The knowledge thereof is with Allah (alone), but most of mankind know not.")

Surah: 7 Ayah: 188

﴿ قُل لَّآ أَمْلِكُ لِنَفْسِى نَفْعًا وَلَا ضَرًّا إِلَّا مَا شَآءَ ٱللَّهُ ۚ وَلَوْ كُنتُ أَعْلَمُ ٱلْغَيْبَ لَٱسْتَكْثَرْتُ مِنَ ٱلْخَيْرِ وَمَا مَسَّنِىَ ٱلسُّوٓءُ ۚ إِنْ أَنَا۠ إِلَّا نَذِيرٌ وَبَشِيرٌ لِّقَوْمٍ يُؤْمِنُونَ ﴾

188. Say (O Muhammad (peace be upon him)) "I possess no power of benefit or hurt to myself except as Allâh wills. If I had the knowledge of the Ghaib (Unseen), I should have secured for myself an abundance of wealth, and no evil should have touched me. I am but a warner, and a bringer of glad tidings unto people who believe."

Transliteration

188. Qul la amliku linafsee nafAAan wala darran illa ma shaa Allahu walaw kuntu aAAlamu alghayba laistakthartu mina alkhayri wama massaniya alssoo-o in ana illa natheerun wabasheerun liqawmin yu/minoona

Tafsir Ibn Kathir

The Messenger does not know the Unseen, and He cannot bring Benefit or Harm even to Himself

Allah commanded His Prophet to entrust all matters to Him and to inform, about himself, that he does not know the unseen future, but he knows of it only what Allah informs him. Allah said in another Ayah,

((He Alone is) the All-Knower of the Ghayb (Unseen), and He reveals to none His Ghayb.) (72:26) Ad-Dahhak reported that Ibn `Abbas said that,

(If I had the knowledge of the Ghayb (Unseen), I should have secured for myself an abundance of wealth.) refers to money. In another narration, Ibn `Abbas commented, "I would have knowledge of how much profit I would make with what I buy, and I would always sell what I would make profit from,

("and no evil should have touched me.") and poverty would never touch me." Ibn Jarir said, "And others said, `This means that if I know the Unseen then I would prepare for the years of famine during the prosperous years, and in the time of high cost, I would have prepared for it.'" `Abdur-Rahman bin Zayd bin Aslam also commented on this Ayah;

("and no evil should have touched me."), "I would have avoided and saved myself from any type of harm before it comes." Allah then stated that the Prophet is a warner and bearer of good news. He warns against the torment and brings good news of Paradise for the believers,

(So We have made this (the Qur'an) easy on your tongue, only that you may give glad tidings to the pious, and warn with it the most quarrelsome of people.) (19:97)

Surah: 7 Ayah: 189 & Ayah: 190

﴿ ۞ هُوَ ٱلَّذِى خَلَقَكُم مِّن نَّفْسٍ وَٰحِدَةٍ وَجَعَلَ مِنْهَا زَوْجَهَا لِيَسْكُنَ إِلَيْهَا ۖ فَلَمَّا تَغَشَّىٰهَا حَمَلَتْ حَمْلًا خَفِيفًا فَمَرَّتْ بِهِۦ ۖ فَلَمَّآ أَثْقَلَت دَّعَوَا ٱللَّهَ رَبَّهُمَا لَئِنْ ءَاتَيْتَنَا صَٰلِحًا لَّنَكُونَنَّ مِنَ ٱلشَّٰكِرِينَ ﴾

189. It is He Who has created you from a single person (Adam), and (then) He has created from him his wife (Hawwâ' (Eve)) in order that he might enjoy the pleasure of living with her. When he had sexual relation with her, she became pregnant and she carried it about lightly. Then when it became heavy, they both invoked Allâh, their Lord (saying): "If You give us a Sâlih (good in every aspect) child, we shall indeed be among the grateful."

﴿ فَلَمَّآ ءَاتَىٰهُمَا صَٰلِحًا جَعَلَا لَهُۥ شُرَكَآءَ فِيمَآ ءَاتَىٰهُمَا ۚ فَتَعَٰلَى ٱللَّهُ عَمَّا يُشْرِكُونَ ﴾

190. But when He gave them a Sâlih (good in every aspect) child, they ascribed partners to Him (Allâh) in that which He has given to them. High is Allâh, Exalted above all that they ascribe as partners to Him. (Tafsir At-Tabarî).

Transliteration

189. Huwa allathee khalaqakum min nafsin wahidatin wajaAAala minha zawjaha liyaskuna ilayha falamma taghashshaha hamalat hamlan khafeefan famarrat bihi falamma athqalat daAAawa Allaha rabbahuma la-in ataytana salihan lanakoonanna mina alshshakireena 190. Falamma atahuma salihan jaAAala lahu shurakaa feema atahuma fataAAala Allahu AAamma yushrikoona

Tafsir Ibn Kathir

All Mankind are the Offspring of Adam

Allah states that He has created all mankind from Adam, peace be upon him, and from Adam, He created his wife, Hawwa' and from them, people started to spread. Allah said in another Ayah,

(O mankind! We have created you from a male and a female, and made you into nations and tribes, that you may know one another. Verily, the most honorable of you with Allah is that (believer) who has Taqwa) (49:13), and,

(O mankind! Have Taqwa of your Lord, Who created you from a single person, and from him He created his wife.)(4:1) In this honorable Ayah, Allah said;

(And (then) He has created from him his wife, in order that he might enjoy the pleasure of living with her.) so that he is intimate and compassionate with her. Allah said in another Ayah,

(And among His Signs is this, that He created for you wives (spouses) from among yourselves, that you may find repose in them, and He has put between you affection and mercy.) (30:21) Indeed, there is no intimacy between two souls like that between the spouses. This is why Allah mentioned that the sorcerer might be able with his trick to separate between a man and his wife (thus indicating the difficulty of separating them in normal circumstances). Allah said next,

(When he covered her) meaning had sexual intercourses with her.

(she became pregnant and she carried it about lightly) in reference to the first stage of pregnancy when the woman does not feel pain, for at that time, the fetus will be just a Nutfah (the mixture of the male and female discharge), then becomes an `Alaqah (a piece of thick coagulated blood) and then a Mudghah (a small lump of flesh). Allah said next,

(and she carried it about), she continued the pregnancy, according to Mujahid. It was reported that Al-Hasan, Ibrahim An-Nakha`i and As-Suddi said similarly. Maymun bin Mahran reported that his father said, "She found the pregnancy unnoticeable." Ayyub said, "I asked Al-Hasan about the Ayah,

(and she carried it about) and he said, `Had you been an Arab, you would know what it means! It means that she continued the pregnancy (through its various stages).'" Qatadah said,

(and she carried it about (lightly).), means, it became clear that she was pregnant. Ibn Jarir commented, "This Ayah means that the liquid remained, whether she stood up or sat down." Al-`Awfi recorded that Ibn `Abbas said, "The semen remained in, but she was unsure if she became pregnant or not,

(Then when it became heavy), she became heavier with the fetus", As-Suddi said, "The fetus grew in her womb."

(they both invoked Allah, their Lord (saying): "If You give us a Salih child,) if he is born human in every respect. Ad-Dahhak said that Ibn `Abbas commented, "They feared that their child might be born in the shape of an animal!" while Abu Al-Bakhtri and Abu Malik commented, "They feared that their newborn might not be human." Al-Hasan Al-Basri also commented, "If You (Allah) give us a boy."

(we shall indeed be among the grateful. But when He gave them a Salih child, they ascribed partners to Him (Allah) in that which He has given to them. High be Allah, Exalted above all that they ascribe as partners to Him.) (7:189-190) Ibn Jarir recorded that Al-Hasan commented on this part of the Ayah, (they ascribed partners to Him (Allah) in that which He has given to them) "This occurred by followers of some religion, not from Adam (or Hawwa')." Al-Hasan also said, "This Ayah refers to those among the offspring of Adam who fell into Shirk,

(they ascribed partners to Him (Allah) in that which He has given to them.)" Qatadah said, "Al-Hasan used to say that it refers to the Jews and Christians. Allah gave them children, and they turned them into Jews and Christians." The explanations from Al-Hasan have authentic chains of narration leading to him, and certainly, it is one of the best interpretations. This Ayah should therefore be understood this way, for it is apparent that it does not refer to Adam and Hawa', but about the idolators among their offspring. Allah mentioned the person first (Adam and Hawwa') and then continued to mention the species (mankind, many of whom committed Shirk). There are similar cases in the Qur'an. For cases, Allah said

(And indeed We have adorned the nearest heaven with lamps) It is well-known that the stars that were made as lamps in the sky are not the same as the shooting missiles that are thrown at the devils (mentioned later in the Ayah). There are similar instances in the Qur'an. Allah knows best.

Surah: 7 Ayah: 191, Ayah: 192, Ayah: 193, Ayah: 194, Ayah: 195, Ayah: 196, Ayah: 197 & Ayah: 198

﴿ أَيُشْرِكُونَ مَا لَا يَخْلُقُ شَيْئًا وَهُمْ يُخْلَقُونَ ﴾

191. Do they attribute as partners to Allâh those who created nothing but they themselves are created?

﴿ وَلَا يَسْتَطِيعُونَ لَهُمْ نَصْرًا وَلَآ أَنفُسَهُمْ يَنصُرُونَ ﴾

192. No help can they give them, nor can they help themselves.

﴿ وَإِن تَدْعُوهُمْ إِلَى ٱلْهُدَىٰ لَا يَتَّبِعُوكُمْ سَوَآءٌ عَلَيْكُمْ أَدَعَوْتُمُوهُمْ أَمْ أَنتُمْ صَـٰمِتُونَ ﴾

193. And if you call them to guidance, they follow you not. It is the same for you whether you call them or you keep silent.

﴿ إِنَّ ٱلَّذِينَ تَدْعُونَ مِن دُونِ ٱللَّهِ عِبَادٌ أَمْثَالُكُمْ فَٱدْعُوهُمْ فَلْيَسْتَجِيبُوا۟ لَكُمْ إِن كُنتُمْ صَـٰدِقِينَ ﴾

194. Verily, those whom you call upon besides Allâh are slaves like you. So call upon them and let them answer you if you are truthful.

﴿ أَلَهُمْ أَرْجُلٌ يَمْشُونَ بِهَآ أَمْ لَهُمْ أَيْدٍ يَبْطِشُونَ بِهَآ أَمْ لَهُمْ أَعْيُنٌ يُبْصِرُونَ بِهَآ أَمْ لَهُمْ ءَاذَانٌ يَسْمَعُونَ بِهَا ۗ قُلِ ٱدْعُوا۟ شُرَكَآءَكُمْ ثُمَّ كِيدُونِ فَلَا تُنظِرُونِ ۞ ﴾

195. Have they feet wherewith they walk? Or have they hands wherewith they hold? Or have they eyes wherewith they see? Or have they ears wherewith they hear? Say (O Muhammad (peace be upon him)) "Call your (so-called) partners (of Allâh) and then plot against me, and give me no respite!

﴿ إِنَّ وَلِـِّۧىَ ٱللَّهُ ٱلَّذِى نَزَّلَ ٱلْكِتَـٰبَ ۖ وَهُوَ يَتَوَلَّى ٱلصَّـٰلِحِينَ ۞ ﴾

196. "Verily, my Walî (Protector, Supporter, and Helper) is Allâh Who has revealed the Book (the Qur'ân), and He protects (supports and helps) the righteous.

﴿ وَٱلَّذِينَ تَدْعُونَ مِن دُونِهِۦ لَا يَسْتَطِيعُونَ نَصْرَكُمْ وَلَآ أَنفُسَهُمْ يَنصُرُونَ ۞ ﴾

197. "And those whom you call upon besides Him (Allâh) cannot help you nor can they help themselves."

﴿ وَإِن تَدْعُوهُمْ إِلَى ٱلْهُدَىٰ لَا يَسْمَعُوا۟ ۖ وَتَرَىٰهُمْ يَنظُرُونَ إِلَيْكَ وَهُمْ لَا يُبْصِرُونَ ۞ ﴾

198. And if you call them to guidance, they hear not and you will see them looking at you, yet they see not.

Transliteration

191. Ayushrikoona ma la yakhluqu shay-an wahum yukhlaqoona 192. No help can they give them, nor can they help themselves. 193. Wa-in tadAAoohum ila alhuda la yattabiAAookum sawaon AAalaykum adaAAawtumoohum am antum samitoona 194. Inna allatheena tadAAoona min dooni Allahi AAibadun amthalukum faodAAoohum falyastajeeboo lakum in kuntum sadiqeena 195. Alahum arjulun yamshoona biha am lahum aydin yabtishoona biha am lahum aAAyunun yubsiroona biha am lahum athanun yasmaAAoona biha quli odAAoo shurakaakum thumma keedooni fala tunthiroona 196. Inna waliyyiya Allahu allathee nazzala alkitaba wahuwa yatawalla alssaliheena 197. Waallatheena tadAAoona min doonihi la yastateeAAoona nasrakum wala anfusahum yansuroona   198. Wa-in tadAAoohum ila alhuda la yasmaAAoo watarahum yanthuroona ilayka wahum la yubsiroona

Tafsir Ibn Kathir

Idols do not create, help, or have Power over Anything

Allah admonishes the idolators who worshipped idols, rivals and images besides Him, although these objects were created by Allah, and neither own anything nor can they bring harm or benefit. These objects do not see or give aid to those who worship them. They are inanimate objects that neither move, hear, or see. Those who worship these objects are better than they are, for they hear see and have strength of their own. Allah said,

(Do they attribute as partners to Allah those who created nothing but they themselves are created) meaning, `Do you associate with Allah others that neither create, nor have power to create anything' Allah said in another Ayah,

(O mankind! A similitude has been coined, so listen to it (carefully): Verily, those on whom you call besides Allah, cannot create (even) a fly, even though they combine together for the purpose. And if the fly snatches away a thing from them, they will have no power to release it from the fly. So weak are (both) the seeker and the sought. They have not estimated Allah His rightful estimate. Verily, Allah is All-Strong, Almighty) (22:73-74). Allah states that if all false gods of the disbelievers gather their strength, they would not be able to create a fly. Rather, if the fly steals anything from them, no matter how insignificant, and flew away, they would not be able to retrieve it. Therefore, if an object is this weak, how can it be worshipped and invoked for provisions and aid This is why Allah said,

(... who created nothing but they themselves are created) these worshipped objects themselves were created and made. Prophet Ibrahim Al-Khalil proclaimed,

("Worship you that which you (yourselves) carve") (37:95) Allah said next,

(No help can they give them) those who worship them,

(nor can they help themselves) nor are they able to aid themselves against those who seek to harm them. For instance, Allah's Khalil, peace be upon him, broke and disgraced the idols of his people, just as Allah said he did,

(Then he turned upon them, striking (them) with (his) right hand,) (37:93) and,

(So he broke them to pieces, (all) except the biggest of them, that they might turn to it.) (21:58) Mu`adh bin `Amr ibn Al-Jamuh and Mu`adh bin Jabal, may Allah be pleased with both of them, were still young when they embraced Islam after the Messenger of Allah came to Al-Madinah. So they were attacking the idols of the idolators at night, breaking, disfiguring them and using them as fuel for needy widows. They sought to give a lesson to their people to make them aware of their error. `Amr bin Al-Jamuh, who was one of the chiefs of his people, had an idol that he used to worship and perfume. The two Mu`adhs used to go to that idol, turn it on its head and tarnish it with animal waste. When `Amr bin Al-Jamuh would see what happened to his idol, he would clean it, perfume it and leave a sword next to it, saying, "Defend yourself." However, the two young men would repeat their actions, and he would do the same as before. Once, they took the idol, tied it to a dead dog and threw it in a well while tied to a rope! When `Amr bin Al-Jamuh saw this, he knew that his religion was false and said, "By Allah! Had you been a god who has might, you would not end up tied to a dog on a rope!" `Amr bin Al-Jamuh embraced Islam, and he was strong in his Islam. He was later martyred during the battle of

Uhud, may Allah be pleased with him, give him pleasure. and grant him Paradise as his dwelling. Allah said,

(And if you call them to guidance, they follow you not.) Allah says, these idols do not hear the calls of those who worship them. Therefore, the result is the same, whether calling the idols or shunning them. Ibrahim, peace be upon said,

("O my father! Why do you worship that which hears not, sees not and cannot avail you in anything") (19:42) Next, Allah states that the idols were created, just as those who worship them. Rather, the people are better than the idols, because they are able to hear, see and exert harm. The idols, on the other hand, have no such powers. Allah said next,

(Say: "Call your (so-called) partners (of Allah)) invoke the idols for aid against me and do not give me respite, even for an instant, and give it your best effort,

(Verily, my protector is Allah Who has revealed the Book (the Qur'an), and He protects the righteous.) Allah's support is sufficient and He will suffice for me, He is My supporter, I trust in Him and take refuge with Him. He is my protector, in this life and the Hereafter, and the protector of every righteous believer after me. Similarly, the people of Hud said,

("All that we say is that some of our gods have seized you with evil (madness). " Hud replied: "I call Allah to witness, and bear you witness that I am free from that which you ascribe (as partners in worship, with Him (Allah)). So plot against me, all of you, and give me no respite. I put my trust in Allah, my Lord and your Lord! There is not a moving (living) creature but He has the grasp of its forelock. Verily, my Lord is on a path that is straight) (11:54-56). Ibrahim Al-Khalil proclaimed (to his people),

(Do you observe that which you have been wershipping, You and your ancient fathers. Verily, they are enemies to me, save the Lord of all that exists. Who has created me, and it is He Who guides me.") (26:75-78) He also said to his father and his people,

("Verily, I am innocent of what you warship. Except Him Who did create me; and verily, He will guide me." And he made it a legacy lasting among his offspring, that they may turn back (to Allah).) (43:26-28) Allah said here,

(Verily, those whom you call upon besides Allah) until the end of the Ayah, reiterating what has been said earlier, but He uses direct speech this time,

(cannot help you nor can they help themselves.) The Ayah,

(And if you call them to guidance, they hear not and you will see them looking at you, yet they see not.) is similar to another Ayah,

(If you invoke (or call upon) them, they hear not your call.) (35:14). Allah said next,

(and you will see them looking at you, yet they see not.) meaning, they have eyes that stare as if they see, although they are solid. Therefore, the Ayah treated them as if they had a mind (saying, Tarahum, instead of Taraha), since they are made in the shape of humans with eyes drawn on them.

Surah: 7 Ayah: 199 & Ayah: 200

$$\textit{﴿ خُذِ ٱلْعَفْوَ وَأْمُرْ بِٱلْعُرْفِ وَأَعْرِضْ عَنِ ٱلْجَٰهِلِينَ ۝ ﴾}$$

199. Show forgiveness, enjoin what is good, and turn away from the foolish (i.e. don't punish them).

$$\textit{﴿ وَإِمَّا يَنزَغَنَّكَ مِنَ ٱلشَّيْطَٰنِ نَزْغٌ فَٱسْتَعِذْ بِٱللَّهِ إِنَّهُ سَمِيعٌ عَلِيمٌ ۝ ﴾}$$

200. And if an evil whisper comes to you from Shaitân (Satan) then seek refuge with Allâh. Verily, He is All-Hearer, All-Knower.

Transliteration

199. Khuthi alAAafwa wa/mur bialAAurfi waaAArid AAani aljahileena 200. Wa-imma yanzaghannaka mina alshshaytani nazghun faistaAAith biAllahi innahu sameeAAun AAaleemun

Tafsir Ibn Kathir

Showing Forgiveness

`Abdur-Rahman bin Zayd bin Aslam commented on Allah's statement,

(Show forgiveness) "Allah commanded (Prophet Muhammad) to show forgiveness and turn away from the idolators for ten years. Afterwards Allah ordered him to be harsh with them." And more than one narration from Mujahid says, "From the (bad) behavior and actions of the people, of those who have not committed espionage." And Hashim bin `Urwah said that his father said, "Allah ordered Allah's Messenger to pardon the people for their behavior." And in one narration, "pardon what I have allowed you of their behavior. In Sahih Al-Bukhari it is recorded that Hisham reported from his father `Urwah from his brother `Abdullah bin Az-Zubayr who said; "(The Ayah);

(Show forgiveness) was only revealed about the peoples (bad) character." There is a narration from Mughirah from Hisham from his father from Ibn `Umar; and another from Hisham from his father from `A'ishah, both of whom said similarly. And Allah knows best. Ibn Jarir and Ibn Abi Hatim recorded that Yunus said that Sufyan bin `Uyaynah narrated that Umay said, "When Allah, the Exalted and Most Honored, revealed this Ayah,

(Show forgiveness, enjoin Al-`Urf (what is good), and turn away from the foolish) to His Prophet, the Messenger of Allah asked,

$$\textit{«مَا هَذَا يَا جِبْرِيل»}$$

(`What does it mean, O Jibril) Jibril said, `Allah commands you to forgive those who wronged you, give to those who deprived you, and keep relations with those who cut theirs with you.'" Al-Bukhari said, "Allah said,

(Show forgiveness, enjoin Al-`Urf and turn away from the ignorant). `Al-`Urf', means, righteousness." Al-Bukhari next recorded from Ibn `Abbas that he said, "`Uyaynah bin Hisn bin Hudhayfah stayed with his nephew Al-Hur bin Qays, who was among the people whom `Umar used to have near him, for `Umar used to like to have the reciters of the Qur'an (who memorized it) near him and would listen to their opinion, regardless of whether they were old or young men. `Uyaynah said to his nephew, `O my nephew! You are close to this chief (`Umar), so ask for permission for me to see him.' Al-Hur said `I will ask him for you,' and he asked `Umar for permission for `Uyaynah to meet him, and `Umar gave him permission. When `Uyaynah entered on `Umar, he said, `O Ibn Al-Khattab! You neither give to us sufficiently nor rule with justice between us.' `Umar became so angry that he almost punished `Uyaynah. However, Al-Hur said, `O Chief of he Faithful! Allah, the Exalted, said to His Prophet,

(Show forgiveness, enjoin Al-`Urf, and turn away from the foolish) Verily this man (`Uyaynah) is one of the fools!' By Allah, `Umar did not do anything after he heard that Ayah being recited, and indeed, he was one who adhered to the Book of Allah, the Exalted and Most Honored." Al-Bukhari recorded this Hadith. Some scholars said that people are of two kinds, a good-doer, so accept his good doing and neither ask him more than he can bear nor what causes him hardship. The other kind is the one who falls in shortcomings, so enjoin righteousness on him. If he still insists on evil, becomes difficult and continues in his ignorance, then turn away from him, so that your ignoring him might avert his evilness. Allah said in other instances,

(Repel evil with that which is better. We are best-acquainted with the things they utter. And say: "My Lord! I seek refuge with You from the whisperings (suggestions) of the Shayatin (devils). And I seek refuge with You, My Lord! lest they should come near me.")(23:96-98) and,

(The good deed and the evil deed cannot be equal. Repel (the evil) with one which is better, then verily he, between whom and you there was enmity, (will become) as though he was a close friend. But none is granted it (the above quality) except those who are patient -- and none is granted it except the owner of the great portion in this world.) (41:34-35) in reference to the advice contained in these Ayat,

(And if an evil whisper from Shaytan tries to turn you away (from doing good), then seek refuge in Allah. Verily, He is the All-Hearer, the All-Knower) (41:36). Allah said in this honorable Suah,

(And if an evil whisper comes to you from Shaytan, then seek refuge with Allah. Verily, He is All-Hearer, All-Knower.) (7:200) These three instances in the Qur'an, in Surahs Al-A`raf, Al-Mu'minun and As-Sajdah, are uinque in the Qur'an. Allah encourages lenient treatment of evil doers, for this might deter them from persistence in their evil, Allah willing, (then verily he, between whom and you there was enmity, (will become) as though he was a close friend) (41:34). Allah also encourages seeking refuge with Him from the devils of the Jinns. The devil will not be deterred if one is lenient with him, because he seeks your destruction and total demise. The devil to you, O mankind, is an open enemy, just as he was for your father before you. Ibn Jarir said, while explaining Allah's statement,

(And if an evil whisper comes to you from Shaytan), "If the devil lures you to get angry, thus directing you away from forgiving the ignorant and towards punishing him

(then seek refuge with Allah.) Allah commands here to seek refuge with Him from the devil's whispers,

(Verily, He is All-Hearer, All-Knower.) Allah hears the ignorance that the fools subject you to, your seeking refuge with Him from the devil's whispers, and the rest of the speech of His creation; none of it escapes His knowledge. He knows what drives the lures of the devil away from you, as well as, the rest of what His creatures do." We mentioned the Hadiths concerning Isti`adhah (seeking refuge with Allah) in the beginning of this Tafsir, so we do not need to repeat them here.

Surah: 7 Ayah: 201 & Ayah: 202

﴿ إِنَّ ٱلَّذِينَ ٱتَّقَوْاْ إِذَا مَسَّهُمْ طَٰٓئِفٌ مِّنَ ٱلشَّيْطَٰنِ تَذَكَّرُواْ فَإِذَا هُم مُّبْصِرُونَ ۝ ﴾

201. Verily, those who are Al-Muttaqûn (the pious - see V.2:2), when an evil thought comes to them from Shaitân (Satan), they remember (Allâh), and (indeed) they then see (aright).

﴿ وَإِخْوَٰنُهُمْ يَمُدُّونَهُمْ فِى ٱلْغَىِّ ثُمَّ لَا يُقْصِرُونَ ۝ ﴾

202. But (as for) their brothers (the devils) they (i.e. the devils) plunge them deeper into error, and they never stop short.

Transliteration

201. Inna allatheena ittaqaw itha massahum ta-ifun mina alshshaytani tathakkaroo fa-itha hum mubsiroona 202. Wa-ikhwanuhum yamuddoonahum fee alghayyi thumma la yuqsiroona

Tafsir Ibn Kathir

The Whispering of Shaytan and the People of Taqwa

Allah mentions His servants who have Taqwa, obeying His orders, and avoid what He forbade:

(when comes to them) an evil thought, or anger, or the whispers of Shaytan cross their mind, or intend to err, or commit an error, (they remember) Allah's punishment, as well as, His tremendous reward. They remember Allah's promises and threats, then repent, go back to Him, seek refuge with Him and ask for forgiveness before death,

(and (indeed) they then see (aright)) they become aright and aware of the error of their ways.

A Brethren of Devils among Mankind lure to Falsehood

Allah said next,

(But (as for) their brothers they plunge them deeper) in reference to the devils' brothers among mankind. Allah said in another Ayah,

(Verily, the spendthrifts are brothers of the Shayatin) (17:27) for they are followers of the Shayatin, who listen to them and obey their orders.

(They plunge them deeper into error) the devils help them commit sins, making this path easy and appealing to them

(and they never stop short) for the devils never cease inciting mankind to commit errors. `Ali bin Abi Talhah reported that Ibn `Abbas commented on Allah's statement,

(But (as for) their brothers they plunge them deeper into error, and they never stop short.) "Neither mankind stop short of the evil that they are doing nor the devils stop short of luring them. " Therefore,

(they never stop short) refers to the devils getting tired or stopping their whispering. Allah said in another Ayah,

(See you not that We have sent Shayatin against the disbelievers to push them to do evil) (19:83) persistently luring the disbelievers to commit evil, according to Ibn `Abbas and others.

Surah: 7 Ayah: 203

﴿ وَإِذَا لَمْ تَأْتِهِم بِآيَةٍ قَالُواْ لَوْلَا ٱجْتَبَيْتَهَا ۚ قُلْ إِنَّمَا أَتَّبِعُ مَا يُوحَىٰ إِلَيَّ مِن رَّبِّى ۚ هَـٰذَا بَصَآئِرُ مِن رَّبِّكُمْ وَهُدًى وَرَحْمَةٌ لِّقَوْمٍ يُؤْمِنُونَ ۝ ﴾

203. And if you do not bring them a miracle (according to their (i.e. Quraish-pagans') proposal), they say: "Why have you not brought it?" Say: "I but follow what is revealed to me from my Lord. This (the Qur'ân) is nothing but evidences from your Lord, and a guidance and a mercy for a people who believe."

Transliteration

203. Wa-itha lam ta/tihim bi-ayatin qaloo lawla ijtabaytaha qul innama attabiAAu ma yooha ilayya min rabbee hatha basa-iru min rabbikum wahudan warahmatun liqawmin yu/minoona

Tafsir Ibn Kathir

Idolators ask to witness Miracles

`Ali bin Abi Talhah reported that Ibn `Abbas commented on Allah's statement,

(they say, "Why have you not brought it") "They say, `Why have you not received a miracle'", or, "Why have you not initiated or made it" Ibn Jarir reported that, `Abdullah bin Kathir said that Mujahid said about Allah's statement,

(And if you do not bring them a miracle, they say: "Why have you not brought it") "They say, `Produce a miracle of your own.'" Qatadah, As-Suddi, `Abdur-Rahman bin Zayd bin Aslam and Ibn Jarir agreed with this. Allah said next,

(And if you do not bring them an Ayah) a miracle or a sign. Similarly, Allah said,

(If We will, We could send down to them from the heaven a sign, to which they would bend their necks in humility.) (26:4) The pagans asked the Prophet, why did you not strive hard to bring us an Ayah (miracle) from Allah so that we witness it and believe in it. Allah said to him,

(Say: "I but follow what is revealed to me from my Lord.") I do not ask such things of my Lord. I only follow what He reveals and commands me. Therefore, if Allah sends a miracle, I will accept it. Otherwise, I will not ask for it unless He allows me. Certainly, Allah is Most Wise, the All-Knower. Allah next directs the servants to the fact that this Qur'an is the most powerful miracle, clearest evidence and most true proof and explanation, saying,

(This (the Qur'an) is nothing but evidences from your Lord, and a guidance and a mercy for a people who believe.)

Surah: 7 Ayah: 204

﴿ وَإِذَا قُرِئَ ٱلْقُرْءَانُ فَٱسْتَمِعُوا۟ لَهُۥ وَأَنصِتُوا۟ لَعَلَّكُمْ تُرْحَمُونَ ﴾

204. So, when the Qur'ân is recited, listen to it, and be silent that you may receive mercy. (i.e. during the compulsory congregational prayers when the Imâm (of a mosque) is leading the prayer (except Sûrat Al-Fâtiha), and also when he is delivering the Friday-prayer Khutbah). (Tafsir At-Tabari)

Transliteration

204. Wa-itha quri-a alqur-anu faistamiAAoo lahu waansitoo laAAallakum turhamoona

Tafsir Ibn Kathir

The Order to listen to the Qur'an

After Allah mentioned that this Qur'an is a clear evidence, guidance and mercy for mankind, He commanded that one listen to the Qur'an when it is recited, in respect and honor of the Qur'an. This is to the contrary of the practice of the pagans of Quraysh, who said,

("Listen not to this Qur'an, and make noise in the midst of its (recitation)") (41:26). Ibn Jarir reported that Ibn Mas`ud said; "We would give Salams to each other during Salah. So the Ayah of Qur'an was revealed;

(When the Qur'an is recited, then listen to it.)

Surah: 7 Ayah: 205 & Ayah: 206

﴿ وَاذْكُر رَّبَّكَ فِى نَفْسِكَ تَضَرُّعًا وَخِيفَةً وَدُونَ ٱلْجَهْرِ مِنَ ٱلْقَوْلِ بِٱلْغُدُوِّ وَٱلْأَصَالِ وَلَا تَكُن مِّنَ ٱلْغَٰفِلِينَ ﴾ ﴿٢٠٥﴾

205. And remember your Lord within yourself, humbly and with fear without loudness in words in the mornings, and in the afternoons and be not of those who are neglectful.

﴿ إِنَّ ٱلَّذِينَ عِندَ رَبِّكَ لَا يَسْتَكْبِرُونَ عَنْ عِبَادَتِهِۦ وَيُسَبِّحُونَهُۥ وَلَهُۥ يَسْجُدُونَ ﴾ ﴿٢٠٦﴾

206. Surely, those who are with your Lord (angels) are never too proud to perform acts of worship to Him, but they glorify His Praise and prostrate themselves before Him.

Transliteration

205. Waothkur rabbaka fee nafsika tadarruAAan wakheefatan wadoona aljahri mina alqawli bialghuduwwi waal-asali wala takun mina alghafileena 206. Inna allatheena AAinda rabbika la yastakbiroona AAan AAibadatihi wayusabbihoonahu walahu yasjudoona

Tafsir Ibn Kathir

Remembering Allah in the Mornings and Afternoons

Allah ordains that He be remembered more often in the mornings and the afternoons. Just as He ordered that He be worshipped during these two times when He said,

(And glorify the praises of your Lord, before the rising of the sun and before (its) setting.) (50:39) Before the night of Isra', when the five daily prayers were ordained, this Ayah was revealed in Makkah ordering that Allah be worshipped at these times, Allah said next,

(humbly and with fear) meaning, remember your Lord in secret, not loudly, with eagerness and fear. This is why Allah said next,

(and without loudness in words). Therefore, it is recommended that remembering Allah in Dhikr is not performed in a loud voice. When the Companions asked the Messenger of Allah, "Is our Lord close, so that we call Him in secret, or far, so that we raise our voices" Allah sent down the verse, h(And when My servants ask you concerning Me, then (answer them), I am indeed near (to them by My knowledge). I respond to the invocations of the supplicant when he calls on Me (without any mediator or intercessor).) (2:186) In the Two Sahihs, it is recorded that Abu Musa Al-Ash`ari said, "The people raised their voices with Du`a' (invoking Allah) while travelling. The Prophet said to them,

»يَا أَيُّهَا النَّاسُ ارْبَعُوا عَلَى أَنْفُسِكُمْ، فَإِنَّكُمْ لَا تَدْعُونَ أَصَمَّ وَلَا غَائِبًا إِنَّ الَّذِي تَدْعُونَهُ سَمِيعٌ قَرِيبٌ أَقْرَبُ إِلَى أَحَدِكُمْ مِنْ عُنُقِ رَاحِلتِه«

(O people! Take it easy on yourselves, for He Whom you are calling is not deaf or absent. Verily, He Whom you are calling is the All-Hearer, close (by His knowledge), closer to one of you than the neck of his animal.)" These texts encourage the servants to invoke Allah in Dhikr often, especially in the mornings and afternoons, so that they are not among those who neglect remembering Him. This is why Allah praised the angels who praise Him night and day without tiring,

(Surely, those who are with your Lord (i.e., angels) are never too proud to perform acts of worship to Him) Allah reminded the servants of this fact so that they imitate the angels in their tireless worship and obedience of Allah. Prostration, here, upon the mention that the angels prostrate to Allah is legitimate. A Hadith reads;

(Why not you stand in line (for the prayer) like the angels stand in line before their Lord They continue the first then the next lines and they stand close to each other in line.) This is the first place in the Qur'an where it has been legitimized -- according to the agreement of the scholars -- for the readers of the Qur'an, and those listening to its recitation, to perform prostration.

INTRODUCTION TO CHAPTER (SURAH) 8: AL-ANFAL (SPOILS OF WAR, BOOTY)

Ibn Kathir's Introduction

There are seventy-five Ayat in this Surah. The word count of this Surah is one thousand, six hundred and thirty-one words and its letters number five thousand, two hundred and ninety-four.

CHAPTER (SURAH) 8: AL-ANFAL (SPOILS OF WAR, BOOTY), VERSES 001–040

﴿بِسْمِ ٱللَّهِ ٱلرَّحْمَٰنِ ٱلرَّحِيمِ ۞﴾

In the Name of Allah the Most Gracious, the Most Merciful

Surah: 8 Ayah: 1

﴿ يَسْـَٔلُونَكَ عَنِ ٱلْأَنفَالِ ۖ قُلِ ٱلْأَنفَالُ لِلَّهِ وَٱلرَّسُولِ ۖ فَٱتَّقُوا۟ ٱللَّهَ وَأَصْلِحُوا۟ ذَاتَ بَيْنِكُمْ ۖ وَأَطِيعُوا۟ ٱللَّهَ وَرَسُولَهُۥٓ إِن كُنتُم مُّؤْمِنِينَ ۝ ﴾

1. They ask you (O Muhammad (peace be upon him)) about the spoils of war. Say: "The spoils are for Allâh and the Messenger." So fear Allâh and adjust all matters of difference among you, and obey Allâh and His Messenger (Muhammad (peace be upon him)) if you are believers.

Transliteration

1. Yas-aloonaka AAani al-anfali quli al-anfalu lillahi waalrrasooli faittaqoo Allaha waaslihoo thata baynikum waateeAAoo Allaha warasoolahu in kuntum mu/mineena

Tafsir Ibn Kathir

Meaning of Anfal

Al-Bukhari recorded that Ibn `Abbas said, "Al-Anfal are the spoils of war." Al-Bukhari also recorded that Sa`id bin Jubayr said, "I said to Ibn `Abbas, `Surat Al-Anfal' He said, `It was revealed concerning (the battle of) Badr.'" `Ali bin Abi Talhah reported, as Al-Bukhari recorded from Ibn `Abbas without a chain of narration, that Ibn `Abbas said, "Al-Anfal are the spoils of war; they were for the Messenger of Allah, and none had a share in them." Similar was said by Mujahid, `Ikrimah, `Ata', Ad-Dahhak, Qatadah, `Ata' Al-Khurasani, Muqatil bin Hayyan, `Abdur-Rahman bin Zayd bin Aslam and several others. It was also said that the Nafl (singular for Anfal) refers to the portion of the spoils of war that the commander gives to some of the fighters after dividing the bulk of the spoils. It was also said that Anfal refers to the Khumus; one-fifth of the captured goods after four-fifths are divided (between the fighters). It was also said that the Anfal refers to the Fay', the possessions taken from the disbelievers without fighting, and the animals, servants or whatever other possessions escape from the disbelievers to Muslims.

Ibn Jarir recorded that `Ali bin Salih bin Hay said: "It has reached me that,

(They ask you about Al-Anfal) is about the divisions. This refer to what the Imam gives to some squads in addition to what is divided among the rest of the soldiers."

The Reason behind revealing Ayah 8:1

Imam Ahmad recorded that Sa`d bin Malik said, "I said, `O Allah's Messenger, Allah has brought comfort to me today over the idolators, so grant me this sword.' He said,

«إِنَّ هَذَا السَّيْفَ لَا لَكَ وَلَا لِي، ضَعْهُ»

(This sword is neither yours nor mine; put it down.) So I put it down, but said to myself, `The Prophet might give this sword to another man who did not fight as fiercely as I did.' I heard a man calling me from behind and I said, `Has Allah revealed something in my case' The Prophet said,

«كُنْتَ سَأَلْتَنِي السَّيْفَ وَلَيْسَ هُوَ لِي، وَإِنَّهُ قَدْ وُهِبَ لِي، فَهُوَ لَكَ»

(You asked me to give you the sword, but it is not for me to decide about. However, it has been granted to me (by Allah), and I give it to you.) So Allah sent down this Ayah,

(They ask you about Al-Anfal. Say: "Al-Anfal are for Allah and the Messenger").

Abu Dawud, At-Tirmidhi and An-Nasa'i collected this Hadith, At-Tirmidhi said, "Hasan Sahih".

Another Reason behind revealing the Ayah 8:1

Imam Ahmad recorded that Abu Umamah said, "I asked `Ubadah about Al-Anfal and he said, `It was revealed about us, those who participated in (the battle of) Badr, when we disputed about An-Nafl and our dispute was not appealing. So Allah took Al-Anfal from us and gave it to the Messenger of Allah . The Messenger divided it equally among Muslims.'"

Imam Ahmad recorded that Abu Umamah said that `Ubadah bin As-Samit said, "We went with the Messenger of Allah to the battle of Badr. When the two armies met, Allah defeated the enemy and some of us pursued them inflicting utter defeat and casualties. Another group of us came to the battlefield collecting the spoils of war. Another group surrounded the Messenger of Allah , so that the enemy could not attack him suddenly. When it was night and the various army groups went back to our camp, some of those who collected the spoils said, `We collected it, so none else will have a share in it.' Those who went in pursuit of the enemy said, `No, you have no more right to it than us. We kept the enemy away from the war spoils and defeated them.' Those who surrounded the Messenger of Allah to protect him said, `You have no more right to it than us, we surrounded the Messenger of Allah for fear that the enemy might conduct a surprise attack against him, so we were busy.' The Ayah,

(They ask you about Al-Anfal (the spoils of war). Say: "Al-Anfal are for Allah and the Messenger." So fear Allah and settle all matters of difference among you.) was revealed and the Messenger of Allah divided the Anfal equally between Muslims.'"

(And Allah's Messenger would give a fourth for Anfal when there was a surprise attack in the land of the enemy, and when there was a confrontation then a third to the people who returned).

The Prophet used to dislike the Anfal and encouraged strong fighters to give some of their share to weak Muslim fighters. At-Tirmidhi and Ibn Majah collected a similar narration for this Hadith, and At-Tirmidhi said, "Hasan".

Allah said,

(So have Taqwa of Allah and settle all matters of difference among you,)

The Ayah commands, have Taqwa of Allah in all your affairs, settle matters of differences between you, do not wrong each other, do not dispute, and do not differ. Certainly, the guidance and knowledge that Allah has granted you is better than what you are disputing about (such as Al-Anfal),

(and obey Allah and His Messenger,) in the division that the Messenger makes according to Allah's order. The Prophet only divided according to what Allah ordained, which is perfectly just and fair. Ibn `Abbas commented on this Ayah, "This is a command from Allah and His Messenger to the believers, that they should have Taqwa of Allah and settle all matters of differences between them." A similar statement was reported from Mujahid. As-Suddi also commented on Allah's statement,

(So have Taqwa of Allah and settle all matters of difference among you), meaning "Do not curse each other."

Surah: 8 Ayah: 2, Ayah: 3 & Ayah: 4

﴿ إِنَّمَا ٱلْمُؤْمِنُونَ ٱلَّذِينَ إِذَا ذُكِرَ ٱللَّهُ وَجِلَتْ قُلُوبُهُمْ وَإِذَا تُلِيَتْ عَلَيْهِمْ ءَايَٰتُهُۥ زَادَتْهُمْ إِيمَٰنًا وَعَلَىٰ رَبِّهِمْ يَتَوَكَّلُونَ ۝ ﴾

2. The believers are only those who, when Allâh is mentioned, feel a fear in their hearts and when His Verses (this Qur'ân) are recited unto them, they (i.e. the Verses) increase their Faith; and they put their trust in their Lord (Alone);

﴿ ٱلَّذِينَ يُقِيمُونَ ٱلصَّلَوٰةَ وَمِمَّا رَزَقْنَٰهُمْ يُنفِقُونَ ۝ ﴾

3. Who perform As-Salât (Iqâmat-as-Salât) and spend out of that We have provided them.

﴿ أُوْلَٰٓئِكَ هُمُ ٱلْمُؤْمِنُونَ حَقًّا ۚ لَّهُمْ دَرَجَٰتٌ عِندَ رَبِّهِمْ وَمَغْفِرَةٌ وَرِزْقٌ كَرِيمٌ ۝ ﴾

4. It is they who are the believers in truth. For them are grades of dignity with their Lord, and Forgiveness and a generous provision (Paradise).

Transliteration

2. Innama almu/minoona allatheena itha thukira Allahu wajilat quloobuhum wa-itha tuliyat AAalayhim ayatuhu zadat-hum eemanan waAAala rabbihim yatawakkaloona 3. Allatheena yuqeemoona alssalata wamimma razaqnahum yunfiqoona 4. Ola-ika humu almu/minoona haqqan lahum darajatun AAinda rabbihim wamaghfiratun warizqun kareemun

Tafsir Ibn Kathir

Qualities of the Faithful and Truthful Believers

`Ali bin Abi Talhah reported that Ibn `Abbas said about the Ayah,

(The believers are only those who, when Allah is mentioned, feel a fear in their hearts)

"None of Allah's remembrance enters the hearts of the hypocrites upon performing what He has ordained. They neither believe in any of Allah's Ayat nor trust (in Allah) nor pray if they are alone nor pay the Zakah due on their wealth. Allah stated that they are not believers. He then described the believers by saying,

(The believers are only those who, when Allah is mentioned, feel a fear in their hearts) and they perform what He has ordained,

(and when His Ayat are recited unto them, they increase their faith) and conviction,

(and they put their trust in their Lord), having hope in none except Him. " Mujahid commented on,

(their hearts Wajilat), "Their hearts become afraid and fearful." Similar was said by As-Suddi and several others. The quality of a true believer is that when Allah is mentioned, he feels a fear in his heart, and thus implements His orders and abstains from His prohibitions. Allah said in a similar Ayah,

(And those who, when they have committed Fahishah (immoral sin) or wronged themselves with evil, remember Allah and ask forgiveness for their sins; -- and none can forgive sins but Allah -- and do not persist in what (wrong) they have done, while they know) (3:135), and,

(But as for him who feared standing before his Lord, and restrained himself from vain desires. Verily, Paradise will be his abode.) (79:40-41)

Sufyan Ath-Thawri narrated that As-Suddi commented,

(The believers are only those who, when Allah is mentioned, feel a fear in their hearts)

"A man might be thinking of committing injustice or a sin. But he abstains when he is told, `Have Taqwa of Allah', and his heart becomes fearful.'"

Faith increases when the Qur'an is recited

Allah's statement,

(And when His Ayat are recited unto them, they increase their faith;) is similar to His statement,

(And whenever there comes down a Surah, some of them (hypocrites) say: "Which of you has had his faith increased by it" As for those who believe, it has increased their faith, and they rejoice) (9:124).

Al-Bukhari and other scholars relied on this Ayah (8:2) and those similar, as evidence that faith increases and varies in strength from heart to heart. This is also the view of the majority of the scholars of Islam, prompting some scholars, such as Ash-Shafi`i, Ahmad bin Hanbal and Abu `Ubayd to declare that this is the consensus of the Ummah, as we mentioned in the beginning of the explanation of Sahih Al-Bukhari. All the thanks and praises are due to Allah.

The Reality of Tawakkul

Allah said,

(And they put their trust in their Lord.)

Therefore, the believers hope in none except Allah, direct their dedication to Him alone, seek refuge with Him alone, invoke Him alone for their various needs and supplicate to Him alone. They know that whatever He wills, occurs and that whatever He does not will never occurs, that He alone is the One Who has the decision in His kingdom, without partners; none can avert the decision of Allah and He is swift in reckoning. Hence the statement of Sa`id bin Jubayr, "Tawakkul of Allah is the essence of faith."

Deeds of Faithful Believers

Allah said next,

(Who perform the Salah and spend out of what We have provided them.)

Allah describes the actions of the believers after He mentioned their faith. The acts mentioned here include all types of righteous acts, such as establishing prayer, which is Allah's right. Qatadah said, "Establishing the prayer requires preserving its times, making ablution for it, bowing down and prostrating." Muqatil bin Hayyan said, "Establishing the prayer means to preserve its times, perform perfect purity for it, perform perfect bowings and prostrations, recite the Qur'an during it, sitting for Tashahhud and reciting the Salah (invoking Allah's blessings) for the benefit of the Prophet."

Spending from what Allah has granted includes giving the Zakah and the rest of the what is due from the servant, either what is obligatory or recommended. All of the servants are Allah's dependents, and the most beloved among them to Him are the most beneficial to His creation.

The Reality of Faith

Allah's statement,

(It is they who are the believers in truth.) means, those who have these qualities are the believers with true faith.

The Fruits of Perfect Faith

Allah said,

(For them are grades of dignity with their Lord) meaning, they have different grades, ranks and status in Paradise,

(They are in varying grades with Allah, and Allah is All-Seer of what they do.)(3:163)

Next, Allah said,

(and forgiveness), therefore, Allah will forgive them their sins and reward them for their good deeds. In the Two Sahihs, it is recorded that the Messenger of Allah said,

«إِنَّ أَهْلَ عِلِّيِّينَ لَيَرَاهُمْ مَنْ أَسْفَلَ مِنْهُمْ كَمَا تَرَوْنَ الْكَوْكَبَ الْغَابِرَ فِي أُفُقٍ مِنْ آفَاقِ السَّمَاءِ»

(The residents of `Illiyyin (in Paradise) are seen from those below them, just as you see the distant planet in the horizon of the sky.)

They said, "O Allah's Messenger! They are the grades of the Prophets that none except them would attain." The Prophet said,

«بَلَى وَالَّذِي نَفْسِي بِيَدِهِ، لِرِجَالٍ آمَنُوا بِاللهِ وَصَدَّقُوا الْمُرْسَلِينَ»

(Rather, by He in Whose Hand is my soul! They are for men who have faith in Allah and believed in the Messengers.)

In a Hadith recorded by Imam Ahmad and the collectors of Sunan, Abu `Atiyyah said that Ibn Abu Sa`id said that the Messenger of Allah said,

«إِنَّ أَهْلَ الْجَنَّةِ لَيَتَرَاءَوْنَ أَهْلَ الدَّرَجَاتِ الْعُلَى كَمَا تَرَاءَوْنَ الْكَوْكَبَ الْغَابِرَ فِي أُفُقِ السَّمَاءِ وَإِنَّ أَبَا بَكْرٍ وَعُمَرَ مِنْهُمْ وَأَنْعَمَا»

(Residents of Paradise see the residents of the highest grades just as you see the distant planet in the horizon of the sky. Verily, Abu Bakr and `Umar are among them (in the highest grades), and how excellent they are.)

Surah: 8 Ayah: 5, Ayah: 6, Ayah: 7 & Ayah: 8

﴿كَمَا أَخْرَجَكَ رَبُّكَ مِنْ بَيْتِكَ بِالْحَقِّ وَإِنَّ فَرِيقًا مِّنَ ٱلْمُؤْمِنِينَ لَكَٰرِهُونَ ۝﴾

5. As your Lord caused you (O Muhammad (peace be upon him)) to go out from your home with the truth; and verily, a party among the believers disliked it,

﴿تُجَدِلُونَكَ فِى ٱلْحَقِّ بَعْدَ مَا تَبَيَّنَ كَأَنَّمَا يُسَاقُونَ إِلَى ٱلْمَوْتِ وَهُمْ يَنظُرُونَ ۝﴾

6. Disputing with you concerning the truth after it was made manifest, as if they were being driven to death, while they were looking (at it).

﴿وَإِذْ يَعِدُكُمُ ٱللَّهُ إِحْدَى ٱلطَّآئِفَتَيْنِ أَنَّهَا لَكُمْ وَتَوَدُّونَ أَنَّ غَيْرَ ذَاتِ ٱلشَّوْكَةِ تَكُونُ لَكُمْ وَيُرِيدُ ٱللَّهُ أَن يُحِقَّ ٱلْحَقَّ بِكَلِمَـٰتِهِۦ وَيَقْطَعَ دَابِرَ ٱلْكَـٰفِرِينَ ۝﴾

7. And (remember) when Allâh promised you (Muslims) one of the two parties (of the enemy i.e. either the army or the caravan) that it should be yours; you wished that the one not armed (the caravan) should be yours, but Allâh willed to justify the truth by His Words and to cut off the roots of the disbelievers (i.e. in the battle of Badr).

﴿لِيُحِقَّ ٱلْحَقَّ وَيُبْطِلَ ٱلْبَـٰطِلَ وَلَوْ كَرِهَ ٱلْمُجْرِمُونَ ۝﴾

8. That He might cause the truth to triumph and bring falsehood to nothing, even though the Mujrimûn (disbelievers, polytheists, sinners, criminals, etc.) hate it.

Transliteration

5. Kama akhrajaka rabbuka min baytika bialhaqqi wa-inna fareeqan mina almu/mineena lakarihoona 6. Yujadiloonaka fee alhaqqi baAAda ma tabayyana kaannama yusaqoona ila almawti wahum yanthuroona 7. Wa-ith yaAAidukumu Allahu ihda altta-ifatayni annaha lakum watawaddoona anna ghayra thati alshshawkati takoonu lakum wayureedu Allahu an yuhiqqa alhaqqa bikalimatihi wayaqtaAAa dabira alkafireena 8. Liyuhiqqa alhaqqa wayubtila albatila walaw kariha almujrimoona

Tafsir Ibn Kathir

Following the Messenger is Better for the Believers

Allah said,

(As your Lord caused you to go out...) After Allah described the believers as fearing their Lord, resolving matters of dispute between themselves and obeying Allah and His Messenger , He then said here, "since you disputed about dividing war spoils and differed with each other about them, Allah took them away from you. He and His Messenger then divided them in truth and justice, thus ensuring continued benefit for all of you. Similarly, you disliked meeting the armed enemy in battle, who marched in support of their religion and to protect their caravan. You disliked fighting, so Allah decided that battle should occur and made you meet your enemy, without planning to do so on your part.' This incident carried guidance, light, victory and triumph. Allah said;

(Jihad is ordained for you though you dislike it, and it may be that you dislike a thing which is good for you, and that you like a thing which is bad for you. Allah knows but you do not know.) (2:216)

As-Suddi commented,

(And verily, a party among the believers disliked) to meet (the armed) idolators. "

(Disputing with you concerning the truth after it was made manifest,)

Some have commented, "(Allah says:) they ask and argue with you about Al-Anfal just as they argued with you when you went out for the battle of Badr, saying, `You marched with us to confiscate the caravan. You did not inform us that there will be fighting and that we should prepare for it.'"

(but Allah willed to justify the truth by His Words)

Allah says, `He willed for you to meet the armed enemy (rather than the caravan) so that He makes you prevail above them and gain victory over them, making His religion apparent and Islam victorious and dominant above all religions. He has perfect knowledge of the consequences of all things, you are surrounded by His wise planning, although people only like what appears favorable to them,'

(Jihad (fighting in Allah's cause) is ordained for you (Muslims) though you dislike it, and it may be that you dislike a thing which is good for you and that you like a thing which is bad for you) (2:216).

Muhammad bin Ishaq reported that `Abdullah bin `Abbas said, "When the Messenger of Allah heard that Abu Sufyan had left the Sham area (headed towards Makkah with Quraysh's caravan), he encouraged the Muslims to march forth to intercept them, saying,

«هَذِهِ عِيرُ قُرَيْشٍ فِيهَا أَمْوَالُهُمْ، فَاخْرُجُوا إِلَيْهَا لَعَلَّ اللهَ أَنْ يُنَفِّلَكُمُوهَا»

(This is the caravan of Quraysh carrying their property, so march forth to intercept it, Allah might make it as war spoils for you.)

The people started mobilizing Muslims, although some of them did not mobilize, thinking that the Prophet would not have to fight. Abu Sufyan was cautiously gathering information on the latest news spying on travelers he met, out of fear for the caravan, especially upon entering the area of Hijaz (Western Arabia). Some travelers told him that Muhammad had mobilized his companions for his caravan. He was anxious and hired Damdam bin `Amr Al-Ghifari to go to Makkah and mobilize the Quraysh to protect their caravan, informing them that Muhammad had mobilized his Companions to intercept the caravan. Damdam bin `Amr went in a hurry to Makkah.

Meanwhile, the Messenger of Allah marched with his companions until he reached a valley called Dhafiran. When he left the valley, he camped and was informed that the Quraysh had marched to protect their caravan. The Messenger of Allah consulted the people for advice and conveyed the news about Quraysh to them. Abu Bakr stood up and said something good, and so did `Umar. Al-Miqdad bin `Amr stood up and said, `O Allah's Messenger! March to what Allah has commanded you, for we are with you. By Allah! We will not say to you what the Children of Israel said to Musa,

("So go you and your Lord and fight you two, we are sitting right here") (5:24). Rather, go you and Your Lord and fight, we will be fighting along with you both. By He Who has sent you with Truth! If you decide to take us to Birk-ul-Ghimad, we will fight along with you until you reach it.' The Messenger of Allah said good words to Al-Miqdad and invoked Allah for his benefit. The Messenger of Allah again said,

》أَشِيرُوا عَلَيَّ أَيُّهَا النَّاسُ《

(Give me your opinion, O people!) wanting to hear from the Ansar. This is because the majority of the people with him then were the Ansar. When the Ansar gave the Prophet their pledge of obedience at Al-`Aqabah, they proclaimed, `O Allah's Messenger! We are not bound by this pledge unless, and until, you arrive in our land. When you have arrived in our area, you are under our protection, and we shall protect you in the same manner we protect our children and wives.' The Messenger of Allah feared that the Ansar might think that they are not obliged to support him except from his enemies who attack Al-Madinah, not to march with him to an enemy in other areas. When the Prophet said this, Sa`d bin Mu`adh asked him, `O Allah's Messenger! Is it us whom you meant' The Prophet answered in the positive. Sa`d said, `We have faith and believed in you, testified that what you brought is the truth, and gave you our pledges and promises of allegiance and obedience. Therefore, march, O Allah's Messenger, for what Allah has commanded you. Verily, by He Who has sent you in Truth, if you decided to cross this sea (the Red Sea), we will follow you in it, and none among us would stay behind. We do not dislike that we meet our enemy tomorrow. Verily, we are patient in war, fierce in battle. May Allah make you witness what makes your eyes pleased with us. Therefore, march with us with the blessing of Allah.' The Messenger of Allah was pleased with what Sa`d said and was encouraged by it. He proclaimed,

》سِيرُوا عَلَى بَرَكَةِ اللهِ وَأَبْشِرُوا فَإِنَّ اللهَ قَدْ وَعَدَنِي إِحْدَى الطَّائِفَتَيْنِ وَاللهِ لَكَأَنِّي الْآنَ أَنْظُرُ إِلَى مَصَارِعِ الْقَوْمِ《

(March with the blessing of Allah and receive the good news. For Allah has indeed promised me one of the two camps (confiscating the caravan or defeating the Quraysh army). By Allah! It is as if I am now looking at the demise of the people (the Quraysh).)"

Al-`Awfi reported similar from Ibn `Abbas. As-Suddi, Qatadah, `Abdur-Rahman bin Zayd bin Aslam; and several others among the Salaf and later generations mentioned similarly, We have just summarized the story as Muhammad bin Ishaq briefed it.

Surah: 8 Ayah: 9 & Ayah: 10

﴿ إِذْ تَسْتَغِيثُونَ رَبَّكُمْ فَٱسْتَجَابَ لَكُمْ أَنِّي مُمِدُّكُم بِأَلْفٍ مِّنَ ٱلْمَلَٰٓئِكَةِ مُرْدِفِينَ ۞ ﴾

9. (Remember) when you sought help of your Lord and He answered you (saying): "I will help you with a thousand of the angels each behind the other (following one another) in succession."

﴿ وَمَا جَعَلَهُ ٱللَّهُ إِلَّا بُشْرَىٰ وَلِتَطْمَئِنَّ بِهِ قُلُوبُكُمْ وَمَا ٱلنَّصْرُ إِلَّا مِنْ عِندِ ٱللَّهِ إِنَّ ٱللَّهَ عَزِيزٌ حَكِيمٌ ۞ ﴾

10. Allâh made it only as glad tidings, and that your hearts be at rest therewith. And there is no victory except from Allâh. Verily, Allâh is All-Mighty, All-Wise.

Transliteration

9. Ith tastagheethoona rabbakum faistajaba lakum annee mumiddukum bi-alfin mina almala-ikati murdifeena 10. Wama jaAAalahu Allahu illa bushra walitatma-inna bihi quloobukum wama alnnasru illa min AAindi Allahi inna Allaha AAazeezun hakeemun

Tafsir Ibn Kathir

Muslims invoke Allah for Help, Allah sends the Angels to help Them

Al-Bukhari wrote in the book of battles (in his Sahih) under "Chapter; Allah's statement,

((Remember) when you sought help of your Lord and He answered you) until,

(then verily, Allah is severe in punishment)" that Ibn Mas`ud said, "I was a witness to something that Al-Miqdad bin Al-Aswad did, that I would like more than almost anything else to have been the one who did it. Al-Miqdad came to the Prophet while he was invoking Allah against the idolators and proclaimed, `We will not say as the people of Musa said, "So go you and your Lord and fight you two."

Rather, we will fight to your right, to your left, before you and behind you.' I saw the Prophet's face beaming with pleasure because of what Al-Miqdad said to him." Al-Bukhari next narrated from Ibn `Abbas that on the day of Badr, the Prophet said,

«اللَّهُمَّ أَنْشُدُكَ عَهْدَكَ وَوَعْدَكَ، اللَّهُمَّ إِنْ شِئْتَ لَمْ تُعْبَدْ»

Chapter 8: Al-Anfal (Spoils of War, Booty), Verses 001-040

(O Allah! I invoke You for Your covenant and promise (victory). O Allah! If You decide so (cause our defeat), You will not be worshipped.)

Abu Bakr held the Prophet's hand and said, "Enough." The Prophet went out proclaiming,

«سَيُهْزَمُ الْجَمْعُ وَيُوَلُّونَ الدُّبُرَ»

(Their multitude will be put to flight, and they will show their backs.)

An-Nasa'i also collected this Hadith. Allah's statement,

(with a thousand of the angels Murdifin) means, they follow each other in succession, according to Harun bin Hubayrah who narrated this from Ibn `Abbas about,

(Murdifin), meaning each behind the other in succession. `Ali bin Abi Talhah Al-Walibi reported that Ibn `Abbas said, "Allah supported His Prophet and the believers with a thousand angels, five hundred under the leadership of Jibril on one side and five hundred under the leadership of Mika'il on another side." Imams Abu Ja`far bin Jarir At-Tabari and Muslim recorded that Ibn `Abbas said that `Umar said, "While a Muslim man was pursuing an idolator (during the battle of Badr), he heard the sound of a whip above him and a rider saying, `Come, O Hayzum!' Then he looked at the idolator, who fell to the ground. When he investigated, he found that the idolator's nose had wound and his face torn apart, just as if he received a strike from a whip on it, and the entire face had turned green. The Ansari man came to the Messenger of Allah and told him what had happened and the Messenger replied,

«صَدَقْتَ، ذَلِكَ مِنْ مَدَدِ السَّمَاءِ الثَّالِثَةِ»

(You have said the truth, that was from the reinforcements from the third heaven.)

The Muslims killed seventy (pagans) in that battle and captured another seventy.

Al-Bukhari also wrote a chapter in his Sahih about the participation of the angels in Badr. He collected a Hadith from Rifa`h bin Rafi` Az-Zuraqi, who participated in Badr, Jibril came to the Prophet and asked him, "How honored are those who participated in Badr among you" The Prophet said,

«مِنْ أَفْضَلِ الْمُسْلِمِين»

(Among the best Muslims.) Jibril said, "This is the case with the angels who participated in Badr." Al-Bukhari recorded this Hadith. At-Tabarani also collected it in Al-Mu`jam Al-Kabir, but from Rafi` bin Khadij, which is an apparent mistake. The correct narration is from Rifa`h, as Al-Bukhari recorded it. In the Two Sahihs, it is recorded that the Messenger of Allah said to `Umar, when `Umar suggested that the Prophet have Hatib bin Abi Balta`ah executed,

«إِنَّهُ قَدْ شَهِدَ بَدْرًا وَمَا يُدْرِيكَ لَعَلَّ اللَّهَ قَدِ اطَّلَعَ عَلَى أَهْلِ بَدْرٍ فَقَالَ: اعْمَلُوا مَا شِئْتُمْ فَقَدْ غَفَرْتُ لَكُمْ»

(He (Hatib) participated in Badr. How do you know that Allah has not looked at the people of Badr and proclaimed, `Do whatever you want, for I have forgiven you.')

Allah said next,

(Allah made it only as glad tidings. ..)

Allah made sending down the angels and informing you of this fact as glad tidings,

(and that your hearts be at rest therewith.)

Surely, Allah is able to give you (O Muslims) victory over your enemies, and victory only comes from Him, without need to send the angels,

(And there is no victory except from Allah.)

Allah said in another Ayah,

(So, when you meet (in fight in Allah's cause) those who disbelieve, smite (their) necks till when you have killed and wounded many of them, then bind a bond firmly (on them, take them as captives). Thereafter (is the time) either for generosity (free them without ransom), or ransom (according to what benefits Islam), until war lays down its burden. Thus, but if it had been Allah's will, He Himself could certainly have punished them (without you). But (He lets you fight) in order to test some of you with others. But those who are killed in the way of Allah, He will never let their deeds be lost. He will guide them and set right their state. And admit them to Paradise which He has made known to them.) (47:4-6)

and,

(And so are the days (good and not so good), that We give to men by turns, that Allah may test those who believe, and that He may take martyrs from among you. And Allah likes not the wrongdoers. And that Allah may test (or purify) the believers (from sins) and destroy the disbelievers.) (3:140-141)

These are points of wisdom for which Allah has legislated performing Jihad, by the hands of the believers against the disbelievers. Allah used to destroy the previous nations that denied the Prophets, using various disasters that encompassed these rebellious nations. For instance, Allah destroyed the people of Nuh with the flood, `Ad with the wind, Thamud with the scream, the people of Lut with an earthquake and the people of Shu`ayb by the Day of the Shadow. After Allah sent Musa and destroyed his enemy Fir`awn and his soldiers by drowning, He sent down the Tawrah to him in which He legislated fighting against the disbelievers, and this legislation remained in the successive Laws. Allah said,

(And indeed We gave Musa -- after We had destroyed the generations of old -- the Scripture as an enlightenment.) (28:43)

It is more humiliating for the disbeliever and more comforting to the hearts of the faithful that the believers kill the disbelievers by their own hands. Allah said to the believers of this Ummah,

(Fight against them so that Allah will punish them by your hands, and disgrace them, and give you victory over them, and heal the breasts of a believing people.)(9:14)

This is why killing the disbelievers of Quraysh by the hand of their enemies, whom they used to despise, was more humiliating to the disbelievers and comforting to the hearts of the party of faith. Abu Jahl, for instance, was killed in battle and this was more humiliating for him than dying in his bed, or from lightening, wind, or similar afflictions. Also, Abu Lahab died from a terrible disease (that caused him to stink) and none of his relatives could bear approaching him. They had to wash him with water by sprinkling it from a distance, then threw stones over his corpse, until it was buried under them! Allah said next,

(Verily, Allah is All-Mighty,), the might is His, His Messengers and the believers, both in this life and the Hereafter. Allah said in another Ayah,

(We will indeed make victorious Our Messengers and those who believe, in this world's life and on the Day when the witnesses will stand forth (Day of Resurrection).)(40:51)

Allah said next,

(All-Wise.), in that He legislated fighting the disbeliever, even though He is able to destroy them and bring their demise by His will and power, all praise and honor is due to Him.

Surah: 8 Ayah: 11, Ayah: 12, Ayah: 13 & Ayah: 14

﴿ إِذْ يُغَشِّيكُمُ ٱلنُّعَاسَ أَمَنَةً مِّنْهُ وَيُنَزِّلُ عَلَيْكُم مِّنَ ٱلسَّمَاءِ مَآءً لِّيُطَهِّرَكُم بِهِۦ وَيُذْهِبَ عَنكُمْ رِجْزَ ٱلشَّيْطَٰنِ وَلِيَرْبِطَ عَلَىٰ قُلُوبِكُمْ وَيُثَبِّتَ بِهِ ٱلْأَقْدَامَ ﴾ ⑪

11. (Remember) when He covered you with a slumber as a security from Him, and He caused water (rain) to descend on you from the sky, to clean you thereby and to remove from you the Rijz (whispering, evil-suggestions) of Shaitân (Satan), and to strengthen your hearts, and make your feet firm thereby.

﴿ إِذْ يُوحِى رَبُّكَ إِلَى ٱلْمَلَٰٓئِكَةِ أَنِّى مَعَكُمْ فَثَبِّتُوا۟ ٱلَّذِينَ ءَامَنُوا۟ سَأُلْقِى فِى قُلُوبِ ٱلَّذِينَ كَفَرُوا۟ ٱلرُّعْبَ فَٱضْرِبُوا۟ فَوْقَ ٱلْأَعْنَاقِ وَٱضْرِبُوا۟ مِنْهُمْ كُلَّ بَنَانٍ ﴾ ⑫

12. (Remember) when your Lord revealed to the angels, "Verily, I am with you, so keep firm those who have believed. I will cast terror into the hearts of those who

have disbelieved, so strike them over the necks, and smite over all their fingers and toes."

﴿ ذَٰلِكَ بِأَنَّهُمْ شَاقُّوا۟ ٱللَّهَ وَرَسُولَهُۥ ۚ وَمَن يُشَاقِقِ ٱللَّهَ وَرَسُولَهُۥ فَإِنَّ ٱللَّهَ شَدِيدُ ٱلْعِقَابِ ﴿١٣﴾ ﴾

13. This is because they defied and disobeyed Allâh and His Messenger. And whoever defies and disobeys Allâh and His Messenger, then verily, Allâh is Severe in punishment.

﴿ ذَٰلِكُمْ فَذُوقُوهُ وَأَنَّ لِلْكَافِرِينَ عَذَابَ ٱلنَّارِ ﴿١٤﴾ ﴾

14. This is (the torment), so taste it; and surely for the disbelievers is the torment of the Fire.

Transliteration

11. Ith yughashsheekumu alnnuAAasa amanatan minhu wayunazzilu AAalaykum mina alssama-i maan liyutahhirakum bihi wayuthhiba AAankum rijza alshshaytani waliyarbita AAala quloobikum wayuthabbita bihi al-aqdama 12. Ith yoohee rabbuka ila almala-ikati annee maAAakum fathabbitoo allatheena amanoo saolqee fee quloobi allatheena kafaroo alrruAAba faidriboo fawqa al-aAAnaqi waidriboo minhum kulla bananin 13. Thalika bi-annahum shaqqoo Allaha warasoolahu waman yushaqiqi Allaha warasoolahu fa-inna Allaha shadeedu alAAiqabi 14. Thalikum fathooqoohu waanna lilkafireena AAathaba alnnari

Tafsir Ibn Kathir

Slumber overcomes Muslims

Allah reminds the believers of the slumber that He sent down on them as security from the fear they suffered from, because of the multitude of their enemy and the sparseness of their forces. They were given the same favor during the battle of Uhud, which Allah described,

(Then after the distress, He sent down security for you. Slumber overtook a party of you, while another party was thinking about themselves.) (3:154)

Abu Talhah said, "I was among those who were overcome by slumber during (the battle of) Uhud. The sword fell from my hand several times, and I kept picking it up again, several times. I also saw the Companions' heads nodding while in the rear guard." Al-Hafiz Abu Ya`la narrated that `Ali said, "Only Al-Miqdad had a horse during Badr, and at some point, I found that all of us fell asleep, except the Messenger of Allah . He was praying under a tree and crying until dawn." `Abdullah bin Mas`ud said, "Slumber during battle is security from Allah, but during prayer, it is from Shaytan." Qatadah said, "Slumber affects the head, while sleep affects the heart."

Slumber overcame the believers on the day of Uhud, and this incident is very well-known. As for this Ayah (8:11), it is describing the battle of Badr, indicating that slumber also overcame the believers during Badr. Therefore, it appears that this will occur for the believers, whenever they are in distress, so that their hearts feel safe and sure of Allah's aid, rewards, favor and mercy from Allah with them. Allah said in another Ayah,

(Verily, along with every hardship is relief. Verily, along with every hardship is relief.) (94:5-6)

In the Sahih, it is recorded that on the day of Badr, while he was in the bunker with Abu Bakr, the Messenger and Abu Bakr were invoking Allah. Suddenly, slumber overcame the Messenger and he woke up smiling and declared,

«أَبْشِرْ يَا أَبَابَكْرٍ هَذَا جِبْرِيلُ عَلَى ثَنَايَاهُ النَّقْعِ»

("Good news, O Abu Bakr! This is Jibril with dust on his shoulders.")

He left the shade while reciting Allah's statement,

(Their multitude will be put to flight, and they will show their backs.) (54:45)

Rain falls on the Eve of Badr

Allah said next,

(and He caused rain to descend on you from the sky.)

`Ali bin Abi Talhah reported that Ibn `Abbas said, "When the Prophet arrived at Badr, he made camp. At the time, there was a sandy piece of land between the idolators and the water (the wells at Badr). Muslims felt weak and the Shaytan cast frustration into their hearts. He whispered to them, `You claim that you are Allah's supporters and that His Messenger is among you! However, the idolators have taken over the water resource from you, while you pray needing purity.' Allah sent down heavy rain, allowing the Muslims to drink and use it for purity. Allah also removed Shaytan's whisper and made the sand firm when rain fell on it, and the Muslims walked on the sand along with their animals, until they reached the enemy. Allah supported His Prophet and the believers with a thousand angels on one side, five hundred under the command of Jibril and another five hundred under the command of Mika'il on another side."

An even a better narration is that collected by Imam Muhammad bin Ishaq bin Yasar, author of Al-Maghazi, may Allah have mercy upon him. Ibn Ishaq narrated that, Yazid bin Ruwman narrated to him that, `Urwah bin Az-Zubayr said, "Allah sent rain down from the sky on a sandy valley. That rain made the area where the Messenger of Allah and his Companions camped firmer so that it did not hinder their movement. Meanwhile, the part that the Quraysh were camping on became difficult to move in." Mujahid said, "Allah sent down the rain on the believers before slumber overtook them, and the rain settled the dust, made the ground firmer, made them feel at ease and their feet firmer." Allah said next, (to clean you thereby) using it after answering the call of nature or needing to wash oneself, and this involves cleansing what is on the out side,

(and to remove from you the Rijz of Shaytan,) such as his whispers and evil thoughts, this involves sinner purification, whereas Allah's statement about the residents of Paradise,

(Their garments will be of fine green silk, and gold embroidery. They will be adorned with bracelets of silver) (76:21) involves outer appearance,

(and their Lord will give them a pure drink.) (76:21) that purifies the anger, envy and hatred that they might have felt. This is the inner purity. Next, Allah said,

(and to strengthen your hearts,) with patience and to encourage you to fight the enemies, and this is inner courage,

(and make your feet firm thereby). this involves outer courage. Allah know best.

Allah commands the Angels to fight and support the Believers

Allah said next,

((Remember) when your Lord revealed to the angels, "Verily, I am with you, so keep firm those who have believed.")

This is a hidden favor that Allah has made known to the believers, so that they thank Him and are grateful to Him for it. Allah, glorified, exalted, blessed and praised be He, has revealed to the angels -- whom He sent to support His Prophet, religion and believing group -- to make the believers firmer. Allah's statement,

(I will cast terror into the hearts of those who have disbelieved.) means, `you -- angels -- support the believers, strengthen their (battle) front against their enemies, thus, implementing My command to you. I will cast fear, disgrace and humiliation over those who defied My command and denied My Messenger, f

(so strike them over the necks, and smite over all their fingers and toes.) strike them on their foreheads to tear them apart and over the necks to cut them off, and cut off their limbs, hands and feet. It was said that,

(over the necks) refers to striking the forehead, or the neck, according to Ad-Dahhak and `Atiyyah Al-`Awfi. In support of the latter, Allah commanded the believers,

(So, when you meet (in fight Jihad in Allah's cause) those who disbelieve, smite (their) necks till when you have killed and wounded many of them, then bind a bond firmly (on them, take them as captives).) (47:4)

Ar-Rabi` bin Anas said, "In the aftermath of Badr, the people used to recognize whomever the angels killed from those whom they killed, by the wounds over their necks, fingers and toes, because those parts had a mark as if they were branded by fire." Allah said,

(and smite over all their fingers and toes.)

Ibn Jarir commented that this Ayah commands, "O believers! Strike every limb and finger on the hands and feet of your (disbelieving) enemies." Al-`Awfi reported, that Ibn `Abbas said about the battle of Badr that Abu Jahl said, "Do not kill them (the Muslims), but capture them so that you make known to them what they did, their ridiculing your religion and shunning Al-Lat and Al-`Uzza (two idols)." Allah than sent down to the angels,

(Verily, I am with you, so keep firm those who have believed. I will cast terror into the hearts of those who have disbelieved, so strike them over the necks, and smite over all their fingers and toes.)

In that battle, Abu Jahl (may Allah curse him) was killed along with sixty-nine men. `Uqbah bin Abu Mua`it was captured and then killed, thus bring the death toll of the pagans to seventy,

(This is because they defied and disobeyed Allah and His Messenger.) joining the camp that defied Allah and His Messenger not including themselves in the camp of Allah's Law and faith in Him. Allah said,

(And whoever defies and disobeys Allah and His Messenger, then verily, Allah is severe in punishment.) for He will crush whoever defies and disobeys Him. Nothing ever escapes Allah's grasp nor can anything ever stand against His anger. Blessed and exalted He is, there is no true deity or Lord except Him.

(This is (the torment), so taste it; and surely, for the disbelievers is the torment of the Fire.)

This Ayah addresses the disbeliever, saying, taste this torment and punishment in this life and know that the torment of the Fire in the Hereafter is for the disbelievers.

Surah: 8 Ayah: 15 & Ayah: 16

﴿ يَـٰٓأَيُّهَا ٱلَّذِينَ ءَامَنُوٓاْ إِذَا لَقِيتُمُ ٱلَّذِينَ كَفَرُواْ زَحۡفٗا فَلَا تُوَلُّوهُمُ ٱلۡأَدۡبَارَ ﴾

15. O you who believe! When you meet those who disbelieve, in a battle-field, never turn your backs to them.

﴿ وَمَن يُوَلِّهِمۡ يَوۡمَئِذٖ دُبُرَهُۥٓ إِلَّا مُتَحَرِّفٗا لِّقِتَالٍ أَوۡ مُتَحَيِّزًا إِلَىٰ فِئَةٖ فَقَدۡ بَآءَ بِغَضَبٖ مِّنَ ٱللَّهِ وَمَأۡوَىٰهُ جَهَنَّمُۖ وَبِئۡسَ ٱلۡمَصِيرُ ﴾

16. And whoever turns his back to them on such a day - unless it be a stratagem of war, or to retreat to a troop (of his own), - he indeed has drawn upon himself wrath from Allâh. And his abode is Hell, and worst indeed is that destination!

Transliteration

15. Ya ayyuha allatheena amanoo itha laqeetumu allatheena kafaroo zahfan fala tuwalloohumu al-adbara 16. Waman yuwallihim yawma-ithin duburahu illa mutaharrifan liqitalin aw mutahayyizan ila fi-atin faqad baa bighadabin mina Allahi wama/wahu jahannamu wabi/sa almaseeru

Tafsir Ibn Kathir

Fleeing from Battle is prohibited, and its Punishment

Allah said, while warning against fleeing from the battlefield and threatening those who do it with the Fire,

(O you who believe! When you meet those who disbelieve, in a battlefield,) when you get near the enemy and march towards them,

(never turn your backs to them.) do not run away from battle and leave your fellow Muslims behind,

(And whoever turns his back to them on such a day -- unless it be a stratagem of war...)

The Ayah says, whoever flees from the enemy by way of planning to pretend that he is afraid of the enemy, so that they follow him and he takes the chance and returns to kill the enemy, then there is no sin on him. This is the explanation of Sa`id bin Jubayr and As-Suddi. Ad-Dahhak also commented, "Whoever went ahead of his fellow Muslims to investigate the strength of the enemy and make use of it,

(or to retreat to a troop (of his own)), meaning he leaves from here to another troop of Muslims to assist them or be assisted by them. So that is allowed for him, or even during the battle if he flees from his brigade to the commander. Or going to the grand Imam, would also fall under this permission."

`Umar bin Al-Khattab, may Allah be pleased with him, said about Abu `Ubayd when he was fighting on the bridge in the land of the Persians, because of the many Zoroastrian soldiers, "If he retreated to me then I would be as a troop for him."

This is how it was reported by Muhammad bin Sirin from `Umar. In the report of Abu `Uthman An-Nahdi from `Umar, he said: When Abu `Ubayd was fighting, `Umar said, "O people! We are your troop." Mujahid said that `Umar said, "We are the troop of every Muslim." Abdul-Malik bin `Umayr reported from `Umar, "O people! Don't be confused over this Ayah, it was only about the day of Badr, and we are a troop for every Muslim." Ibn Abi Hatim (recorded) that Nafi` questioned Ibn `Umar, "We are people who are not stationary when fighting our enemy, and we may not know where our troop is, be it that of our Imam or our army."

So he replied, "The troop is Allah's Messenger ." I said but Allah said,

(when you meet those who disbelieve in the battlefield) to the end of the Ayah . So he said; "This Ayah was about Badr, not before it nor after it."

Ad-Dahhak commented that Allah's statement,

(or to retreat to a troop), refers to "Those who retreat to the Messenger of Allah and his Companions (when the Messenger was alive), and those who retreat in the present time to his commander or companions." However, if one flees for any other reason than those mentioned here, then it is prohibited and considered a major sin. Al-Bukhari and Muslim recorded that Abu Hurayrah said that the Messenger of Allah said,

»اِجْتَنِبُوا السَّبْعَ الْمُوبِقَاتِ«

("Shun the seven great destructive sins.")

The people inquired, "O Allah's Messenger! What are they" He said,

»الشِّرْكُ بِاللهِ وَالسِّحْرُ وَقَتْلُ النَّفْسِ الَّتِي حَرَّمَ اللهُ إِلَّا بِالْحَقِّ وَأَكْلُ الرِّبَا وَأَكْلُ مَالِ الْيَتِيمِ وَالتَّوَلِّي يَوْمَ الزَّحْفِ وَقَذْفُ الْمُحْصَنَاتِ الْغَافِلَاتِ الْمُؤْمِنَاتِ«

((They are:) Joining others in worship with Allah, magic taking life which Allah has forbidden, except for a just cause (according to Islamic law), consuming Riba, consuming an orphan's wealth, fleeing the battlefield at the time of fighting, and false accusation to chaste women, who never even think of anything touching chastity and are good believers.)

This is why Allah said here,

(he indeed has drawn upon himself...), and returned with,

(wrath from Allah. And his abode...), destination, and dwelling place on the Day of Return,

(is Hell, and worst indeed is that destination!)

Surah: 8 Ayah: 17 & Ayah: 18

﴿ فَلَمْ تَقْتُلُوهُمْ وَلَـكِنَّ ٱللَّهَ قَتَلَهُمْ وَمَا رَمَيْتَ إِذْ رَمَيْتَ وَلَـكِنَّ ٱللَّهَ رَمَىٰ وَلِيُبْلِيَ ٱلْمُؤْمِنِينَ مِنْهُ بَلَآءً حَسَنًا إِنَّ ٱللَّهَ سَمِيعٌ عَلِيمٌ ۝ ﴾

17. You killed them not, but Allâh killed them. And you (Muhammad (peace be upon him)) threw not when you did throw, but Allâh threw, that He might test the believers by a fair trial from Him. Verily, Allâh is All-Hearer, All-Knower.

﴿ ذَٰلِكُمْ وَأَنَّ ٱللَّهَ مُوهِنُ كَيْدِ ٱلْكَـٰفِرِينَ ۝ ﴾

18. This (is the fact) and surely, Allâh weakens the deceitful plots of the disbelievers.

Transliteration

17. Falam taqtuloohum walakinna Allaha qatalahum wama ramayta ith ramayta walakinna Allaha rama waliyubliya almu/mineena minhu balaan hasanan inna Allaha sameeAAun AAaleemun 18. Thalikum waanna Allaha moohinu kaydi alkafireena

Tafsir Ibn Kathir

Allah's Signs displayed during Badr, And throwing Sand in the Eyes of the Disbelievers

Allah states that He creates the actions that the servants perform and that whatever good actions they take, it is He Who should be praised for them, for He directed and helped them perform these actions. Allah said,

(You killed them not, but Allah killed them.) meaning, it is not because of your power and strength that you killed the pagans, who were many while you were few. Rather, it is He Who gave you victory over them, just as He said in another Ayah,

(And Allah has already made you victorious at Badr, when you were a weak little force.) (3:123), and,

(Truly, Allah has given you victory on many battlefields, and on the day of Hunayn when you rejoiced at your great number, but it availed you naught and the earth, vast as it is, was straitened for you, then you turned back in flight.) (9:25)

Allah, the Exalted and Ever High, states that victory does not depend on numbers or collecting weapons and shields. Rather, victory is from Him, Exalted He is.

(How often has a small group overcome a mighty host by Allah's leave" And Allah is with the patient.) (2:249)

Allah then mentioned the handful of sand that His Prophet threw at the disbelievers during the day of Badr, when he went out of his bunker. While in the bunker, the Prophet invoked Allah humbly and expressing his neediness before Allah. He then threw a handful of sand at the disbelievers and said,

«شَاهَتِ الْوُجُوه»

(Humiliated be their faces.) He then commanded his Companions to start fighting with sincerity and they did. Allah made this handful of sand enter the eyes of the idolators, each one of them were struck by some of it and it distracted them making each of them busy. Allah said,

(And you threw not when you did throw, but Allah threw.)

Therefore, it is Allah Who made the sand reach their eyes and busied them with it, not you (O Muhammad).

Chapter 8: Al-Anfal (Spoils of War, Booty), Verses 001-040

Muhammad bin Ishaq said that Muhammad bin Ja`far bin Az-Zubayr narrated to him that `Urwah bin Az-Zubayr said about Allah's statement,

(that He might test the believers by a fair trial from Him.) "So that the believers know Allah's favor for them by giving them victory over their enemy, even though their enemy was numerous, while they were few. They should thus know His right and express gratitude for His favor on them." Similar was said by Ibn Jarir. It is stated in a Hadith,

«وَكُلَّ بَلَاءٍ حَسَنٍ أَبْلَانَا»

(Every trail (from Allah) is a favor for us.)

Allah said next,

(Verily, Allah is All-Hearer, All-Knower.)

Allah hears the supplication and knows those who deserve help and triumph. Allah said,

(This (is the fact) and surely Allah weakens the deceitful plots of the disbelievers.) This is more good news, aside from the victory that the believers gained. Allah informed them that He will weaken the plots of the disbelievers in the future, degrade them and make everything they have perish and be destroyed, all praise and thanks are due to Allah.

Surah: 8 Ayah: 19

﴿ إِن تَسْتَفْتِحُواْ فَقَدْ جَاءَكُمُ ٱلْفَتْحُ وَإِن تَنتَهُواْ فَهُوَ خَيْرٌ لَّكُمْ وَإِن تَعُودُواْ نَعُدْ وَلَن تُغْنِىَ عَنكُمْ فِئَتُكُمْ شَيْـًٔا وَلَوْ كَثُرَتْ وَأَنَّ ٱللَّهَ مَعَ ٱلْمُؤْمِنِينَ ﴾

19. (O disbelievers) if you ask for a judgement, now has the judgement come unto you; and if you cease (to do wrong), it will be better for you, and if you return (to the attack), so shall We return, and your forces will be of no avail to you, however numerous they be; and verily, Allâh is with the believers.

Transliteration

19. In tastaftihoo faqad jaakumu alfathu wa-in tantahoo fahuwa khayrun lakum wa-in taAAoodoo naAAud walan tughniya AAankum fi-atukum shay-an walaw kathurat waanna Allaha maAAa almu/mineena

Tafsir Ibn Kathir

The Response to the Disbelievers Who ask for a Judgement

Allah says to the disbeliever,

(If you ask for a judgement), you invoked Allah for victory, judgement and a decision between you and your believing nemesis, and you got what you asked for. Muhammad bin Ishaq and several others reported from Az-Zuhri from `Abdullah bin Tha`labah bin Su`ayr who said that Abu Jahl said on the day of Badr, "O Allah! Whichever of the two camps (pagans and Muslims) severed the relation of the womb and brought us what is not familiar, then destroy him this day." This Ayah was later on revealed,

(If you ask for a judgement, then now has the judgement come unto you,) until the end of the Ayah. Imam Ahmad recorded that `Abdullah bin Tha`labah said, "Abu Jahl asked for (Allah's judgment) when he said upon facing the Muslims, `O Allah! Those among us who severed the relations of the womb and brought forth what we do not recognize, then destroy him this day.'" This was also recorded by An-Nasa'i in the Book of Tafsir (of his Sunan) and Al-Hakim in his Mustadrak, and he said, "It is Sahih according to the criteria of the Two Shaykhs, and they did not record it. ". Similar statements were reported from Ibn `Abbas, Mujahid, Ad-Dahhak, Qatadah, Yazid bin Ruwman and several others. As-Suddi commented, "Before the idolators left Makkah for Badr, they clung to the curtains covering the Ka`bah and supplicated to Allah for victory, `O Allah! Give victory to the exalted among the two armies, the most honored among the two groups, and the most righteous among the two tribes.' Allah revealed the Ayah, F

(If you ask for a judgement, then now has the judgement come unto you.) Allah says here, `I accepted your supplication and Muhammad gained the victory.'"

`Abdur-Rahman bin Zayd bin Aslam said; "This is Allah the Most High's answer to their supplication;

(And (remember) when they said: "O Allah! If this is indeed the truth from you..)" (8:32)

Allah said next,

(and if you cease...) from your disbelief and rejection of Allah and His Messenger ,

(it will be better for you), in this life and the Hereafter. Allah said,

(and if you return, so shall We return...) This is similar to another Ayah,

(but if you return (to sins), We shall return (to Our punishment).) (17:8) meaning, `if you persist in your disbelief and misguidance, We shall repeat the defeat that you suffered,'

(and your forces will be of no avail to you, however numerous they be...) for even if you gather whatever forces you can, then know that those whom Allah is with cannot be defeated,

(and verily, Allah is with the believers.) in reference to the Prophet's group, the side of the chosen Messenger .

Surah: 8 Ayah: 20, Ayah: 21, Ayah: 22 & Ayah: 23

﴿ يَٰٓأَيُّهَا ٱلَّذِينَ ءَامَنُوٓا۟ أَطِيعُوا۟ ٱللَّهَ وَرَسُولَهُۥ وَلَا تَوَلَّوْا۟ عَنْهُ وَأَنتُمْ تَسْمَعُونَ ۝ ﴾

20. O you who believe! Obey Allâh and His Messenger, and turn not away from him (i.e. Messenger Muhammad (peace be upon him)) while you are hearing.

﴿ وَلَا تَكُونُوا۟ كَٱلَّذِينَ قَالُوا۟ سَمِعْنَا وَهُمْ لَا يَسْمَعُونَ ۝ ﴾

21. And be not like those who say: "We have heard," but they hear not.

﴿ ۞ إِنَّ شَرَّ ٱلدَّوَآبِّ عِندَ ٱللَّهِ ٱلصُّمُّ ٱلْبُكْمُ ٱلَّذِينَ لَا يَعْقِلُونَ ۝ ﴾

22. Verily! The worst of (moving) living creatures with Allâh are the deaf and the dumb, those who understand not (i.e. the disbelievers).

﴿ وَلَوْ عَلِمَ ٱللَّهُ فِيهِمْ خَيْرًا لَّأَسْمَعَهُمْ وَلَوْ أَسْمَعَهُمْ لَتَوَلَّوا۟ وَّهُم مُّعْرِضُونَ ۝ ﴾

23. Had Allâh known of any good in them, He would indeed have made them listen; and even if He had made them listen, they would but have turned away with aversion (to the truth).

Transliteration

20. Ya ayyuha allatheena amanoo ateeAAoo Allaha warasoolahu wala tawallaw AAanhu waantum tasmaAAoona   21. Wala takoonoo kaallatheena qaloo samiAAna wahum la yasmaAAoona   22. Inna sharra alddawabbi AAinda Allahi alssummu albukmu allatheena la yaAAqiloona   23. Walaw AAalima Allahu feehim khayran laasmaAAahum walaw asmaAAahum latawallaw wahum muAAridoona

Tafsir Ibn Kathir

The Command to obey Allah and His Messenger

Allah commands His believing servants to obey Him and His Messenger and warns them against defying him and imitating the disbelievers who reject him. Allah said,

(and turn not away from him...), neither refrain from obeying him or following his commands nor indulge in what he forbade,

(while you are hearing.) after you gained knowledge of his Message,

(And be not like those who say: "We have heard," but they hear not.)

Ibn Ishaq said that this Ayah refers to the hypocrites, who pretend to hear and obey, while in fact they do neither. Allah declares that these are the most wicked creatures among the Children of Adam,

(Verily, the worst of living creatures with Allah are the deaf) who do not hear the truth,

(and the dumb) who cannot comprehend it,

(who understand not.) These indeed are the most wicked creatures, for every creature except them abide by the way that Allah created in them. These people were created to worship Allah, but instead disbelieved. This is why Allah equated them to animals, when He said,

(And the example of those who disbelieve is as that of him who shouts to those that hear nothing but calls and cries.) (2:171), and,

(They are like cattle, nay even more astray; those! They are the heedless ones.) (7:179)

It was also said that the Ayah (8:22) refers to some of the pagans of Quraysh from the tribe of Bani `Abd Ad-Dar, according to Ibn `Abbas, Mujahid and Ibn Jarir. Muhammad bin Ishaq said that this Ayah refers to hypocrites, as we stated. There is no contradiction here, because both disbelievers and hypocrites are devoid of sound comprehension, in addition to having lost the intention to do good. Allah states here that such are those who neither have sound understanding nor good intentions, even if they have some type of reason,

(Had Allah known of any good in them, He would indeed have made them listen.)

He would have helped them understand. However, this did not happen because there is no goodness in such people, for Allah knows that,

(even if He had made them listen...) and allowed them to understand,

(they would but have turned...), intentionally and out of stubbornness, even after they comprehend,

(with aversion.), to the truth.

Surah: 8 Ayah: 24

﴿ يَٰٓأَيُّهَا ٱلَّذِينَ ءَامَنُوا۟ ٱسْتَجِيبُوا۟ لِلَّهِ وَلِلرَّسُولِ إِذَا دَعَاكُمْ لِمَا يُحْيِيكُمْ ۖ وَٱعْلَمُوٓا۟ أَنَّ ٱللَّهَ يَحُولُ بَيْنَ ٱلْمَرْءِ وَقَلْبِهِۦ وَأَنَّهُۥٓ إِلَيْهِ تُحْشَرُونَ ﴾

24. O you who believe! Answer Allâh (by obeying Him) and (His) Messenger when he (peace be upon him) calls you to that which will give you life, and know that Allâh comes in between a person and his heart (i.e. He prevents an evil person to decide anything). And verily to Him you shall (all) be gathered.

Transliteration

24. Ya ayyuha allatheena amanoo istajeeboo lillahi walilrrasooli itha daAAakum lima yuhyeekum waiAAlamoo anna Allaha yahoolu bayna almar-i waqalbihi waannahu ilayhi tuhsharoona

Tafsir Ibn Kathir

The Command to answer and obey Allah and His Messenger

Al-Bukhari said,

"(Answer), obey,

(that which will give you life) that which will make your affairs good." Al-Bukhari went on to narrate that Abu Sa`id bin Al-Mu`alla said, "I was praying when the Prophet passed by and called me, but I did not answer him until I finished the prayer. He said,

«مَا مَنَعَكَ أَنْ تَأْتِيَنِي؟ أَلَمْ يَقُلِ اللَّهُ:

(What prevented you from answering me Has not Allah said:

(يأَيُّهَا الَّذِينَ ءَامَنُواْ اسْتَجِيبُواْ لِلَّهِ وَلِلرَّسُولِ إِذَا دَعَاكُمْ لِمَا يُحْيِيكُمْ)

(O you who believe! Answer Allah and (His) Messenger when he calls you to that which will give you life)' He then said:

«لَأُعَلِّمَنَّكَ أَعْظَمَ سُورَةٍ فِي الْقُرْآنِ قَبْلَ أَنْ أَخْرُجَ»

(I will teach you the greatest Suah in the Qur'an before I leave.) When he was about to leave, I mentioned what he said to me. He said,

(الْحَمْدُ لِلَّهِ رَبِّ الْعَلَمِينَ)

(All the praises and thanks are to Allah, the Lord of all that exists...) (1:1-6).

«هِيَ السَّبْعُ الْمَثَانِي»

(Surely, it is the seven oft-repeated verses.)'" Muhammad bin Ishaq narrated that Muhammad bin Ja`far bin Az-Zubayr said that `Urwah bin Az-Zubayr explained this Ayah,

(O you who believe! Answer Allah and (His) Messenger when he calls you to that which will give you life,) "Answer when called to war (Jihad) with which Allah gives you might after meekness, and strength after weakness, and shields you from the enemy who oppressed you."

Allah comes in between a Person and His Heart

Allah said,

(and know that Allah comes in between a person and his heart.)

Ibn `Abbas commented, "Allah prevents the believer from disbelief and the disbeliever from faith." Al-Hakim recorded this in his Mustadrak and said, "It is Sahih and they did not record it." . Similar was said by Mujahid, Sa`id, `Ikrimah, Ad-Dahhak, Abu Salih `Atiyyah, Muqatil bin Hayyan and As-Suddi. In another report from Mujahid, he commented;

(...comes in between a person and his heart.) "Leaves him without comprehension," As-Suddi said, "Prevents one self from his own heart, so he will neither believe nor disbelieve except by His leave." There are several Hadiths that conform with the meaning of this Ayah. For instance, Imam Ahmad recorded that Anas bin Malik said, "The Prophet used to often say these words,

«يَا مُقَلِّبَ الْقُلُوبِ ثَبِّتْ قَلْبِي عَلَى دِينِكَ»

(O You Who changes the hearts, make my heart firm on Your religion.) We said, `O Allah's Messenger! We believed in you and in what you brought us. Are you afraid for us' He said,

«نَعَمْ، إِنَّ الْقُلُوبَ بَيْنَ إِصْبَعَيْنِ مِنْ أَصَابِعِ اللهِ تَعَالَى يُقَلِّبُهَا»

(Yes, for the hearts are between two of Allah's Fingers, He changes them (as He wills).)"

This is the same narration recorded by At-Tirmidhi in the Book of Qadar in his Jami' (Sunan), and he said, "Hasan." Imam Ahmad recorded that An-Nawwas bin Sam`an Al-Kilabi said that he heard the Prophet saying,

«مَا مِنْ قَلْبٍ إِلَّا وَهُوَ بَيْنَ أُصْبُعَيْنِ مِنْ أَصَابِعِ الرَّحْمَنِ رَبِّ الْعَالَمِينَ إِذَا شَاءَ أَنْ يُقِيمَهُ أَقَامَهُ وَإِذَا شَاءَ أَنْ يُزِيغَهُ أَزَاغَهُ»

(Every heart is between two of the Fingers of the Most Beneficent (Allah), Lord of all that exists, if He wills, He makes it straight, and if He wills, He makes it stray.)

And he said:

«يَا مُقَلِّبَ الْقُلُوبِ ثَبِّتْ قَلْبِي عَلَى دِينِكَ»

(O You Who changes the hearts! keep my heart firm on Your religion) And he would say;

«وَالْمِيزَانُ بِيَدِ الرَّحْمَنِ يَخْفِضُهُ وَيَرْفَعُهُ»

(The Balance is in the Hand of Ar-Rahman, He raises and lowers it.)

This was also recorded by An-Nasai and Ibn Majah.

Surah: 8 Ayah: 25

﴿ وَاتَّقُوا۟ فِتْنَةً لَّا تُصِيبَنَّ ٱلَّذِينَ ظَلَمُوا۟ مِنكُمْ خَآصَّةً ۖ وَٱعْلَمُوٓا۟ أَنَّ ٱللَّهَ شَدِيدُ ٱلْعِقَابِ ﴿٢٥﴾ ﴾

25. And fear the Fitnah (affliction and trial) which affects not in particular (only) those of you who do wrong (but it may afflict all the good and the bad people), and know that Allâh is Severe in punishment.

Translation

25. And fear the Fitnah (affliction and trial, etc.) which affects not in particular (only) those of you who do wrong (but it may afflict all the good and the bad people), and know that Allâh is Severe in punishment.

Tafsir Ibn Kathir

Warning against an encompassing Fitnah

Allah warns His believing servants of a Fitnah, trial and test, that encompasses the wicked and those around them. Therefore, such Fitnah will not be restricted to the sinners and evildoers. Rather, it will reach the others if the sins are not stopped and prevented. Imam Ahmad recorded that Mutarrif said, "We asked Az-Zubayr, `O Abu `Abdullah! What brought you here (for the battle of Al-Jamal) You abandoned the Khalifah who was assassinated (`Uthman, may Allah be pleased with him) and then came asking for revenge for his blood' He said, `We recited at the time of the Messenger of Allah , and Abu Bakr, `Umar and `Uthman,

(And fear the Fitnah (affliction and trial) which affects not in particular (only) those of you who do wrong,) We did not think that this Ayah was about us too, until it reached us as it did.'" `Ali bin Abi Talhah reported that Ibn `Abbas said that the Ayah,

(And fear the Fitnah (affliction and trial) which affects not in particular (only) those of you who do wrong,) refers to the Companions of the Prophet in particular. In another narration from Ibn `Abbas, he said, "Allah commanded the believers to stop evil from flourishing among them, so that Allah does not encompass them all in the torment (Fitnah). " This, indeed, is a very good explanation, prompting Mujahid to comment about Allah's statement,

(And fear the Fitnah (affliction and trial) which affects not in particular (only) those of you who do wrong,)

"Is for you too!" Several said similarly, such as Ad-Dahhak and Yazid bin Abi Habib and several others. Ibn Mas`ud said, "There is none among you but there is something that represents a Fitnah for him, for Allah said,

(Your wealth and your children are only a trial (Fitnah)...) (64:15). Therefore, when you seek refuge, seek it with Allah from the Fitnah that causes misguidance." Ibn Jarir collected this Hadith. The view that the warning in this Ayah addresses the Companions and all others is true, even though the speech in the Ayah was directed at the Companions. There are Hadiths that warn against Fitnah in general, thus providing the correctness of this explanation. Similarly there will be a separate book in which this subject will be discussed, Allah willing, as also is the case with the Imams, there being a number of writings about this. Of the most precise things that have been mentioned under this topic, is what was recorded by Imam Ahmad from Hudhayfah bin Al-Yaman that the Messenger of Allah said,

«وَالَّذِي نَفْسِي بِيَدِهِ لَتَأْمُرُنَّ بِالْمَعْرُوفِ وَلَتَنْهَوُنَّ عَنِ الْمُنْكَرِ أَوْ لَيُوشِكَنَّ اللهُ أَنْ يَبْعَثَ عَلَيْكُمْ عِقَابًا مِنْ عِنْدِهِ ثُمَّ لَتَدْعُنَّهُ فَلَا يَسْتَجِيبُ لَكُم»

(By He in Whose Hand is my soul! You will enjoin righteousness and forbid evil, or Allah will send a punishment upon you from Him; you will supplicate then to Him, but He will not answer your supplication.)

Imam Ahmad recorded that Abu Ar-Riqad said, "I heard Hudhayfah saying, `A person used to utter one word during the time of the Messenger of Allah and become a hypocrite on account of it. I now hear such words from one of you four times in the same sitting. Surely, you will enjoin good, forbid evil and encourage each other to do good or Allah will surround you all with torment, or make the wicked among you become your leaders. The righteous among you will then supplicate, but their supplication will not be accepted.'" sImam Ahmad recorded that An-Nu`man bin Bashir said that the Prophet gave a speech in which he said, while pointing to his ears with two of his fingers,

«مَثَلُ الْقَائِمِ عَلَى حُدُودِ اللهِ وَالْوَاقِعِ فِيهَا وَالْمُدَاهِنِ فِيهَا كَمَثَلِ قَوْمٍ رَكِبُوا سَفِينَةً فَأَصَابَ بَعْضُهُمْ أَسْفَلَهَا وَأَوْعَرَهَا وَشَرَّهَا وَأَصَابَ بَعْضُهُمْ أَعْلَاهَا فَكَانَ الَّذِينَ فِي أَسْفَلِهَا إِذَا اسْتَقَوُا الْمَاءَ مَرُّوا عَلَى مَنْ فَوْقَهُمْ فَآذَوْهُمْ فَقَالُوا:

«لَوْ خَرَقْنَا فِي نَصِيبِنَا خَرْقًا فَاسْتَقَيْنَا مِنْهُ وَلَمْ نُؤْذِ مَنْ فَوْقَنَا: فَإِنْ تَرَكُوهُمْ وَأَمْرَهُمْ هَلَكُوا جَمِيعًا وَإِنْ أَخَذُوا عَلَى أَيْدِيهِمْ نَجَوْا جَمِيعًا»

(The parable of the person abiding by Allah's order and restrictions in comparison to those who violate them, or sit idle while they are being violated, is that of those who drew lots for their seats in a boat. Some of them got seats in the lower part, which is the most rough and worst part, and the others in the upper. When the former needed water, they had to go up to bring water and that troubled the others, so they said, `Let us make a hole in our share of the ship and get water, saving those who are above us from troubling them, so, if the people in the upper part let the others do what they suggested, all the people of the ship would be destroyed, but if they prevented them, both parties would be safe.)

This was recorded by Al-Bukhari, but not Muslim, in the Book of Partnerships and the Book of Witnesses. It was also recorded by At-Tirmidhi through a different route of narration.

Imam Ahmad recorded that Umm Salamah, the Prophet's wife, said, "I heard the Messenger of Allah saying,

«إِذَا ظَهَرَتِ الْمَعَاصِي فِي أُمَّتِي عَمَّهُمُ اللهُ بِعَذَابٍ مِنْ عِنْدِهِ»

(If sins become apparent in my Ummah, Allah will surround them with punishment from Him.) I said, `O Allah's Messenger! Will they have righteous people among them then' He said,

«بَلَى»

(Yes.) I asked, `What will happen to them' He said,

«يُصِيبُهُمْ مَا أَصَابَ النَّاسَ ثُمَّ يَصِيرُونَ إِلَى مَغْفِرَةٍ مِنَ اللهِ وَرِضْوَانٍ»

(They will be striken as the people, but they will end up with Allah's forgiveness and pleasure.)"

Imam Ahmad recorded that Jarir said that the Messenger of Allah said,

«مَا مِنْ قَوْمٍ يُعْمَلُ فِيهِمْ بِالْمَعَاصِي هُمْ أَعَزُّ وَأَكْثَرُ مِمَّنْ يَعْمَلُونَ ثُمَّ لَمْ يُغَيِّرُوهُ إِلَّا عَمَّهُمُ اللهُ بِعِقَابٍ»

(Every people among whom sins are being committed, while they are mightier and more numerous than those who do wrong, yet they did nothing to stop them, then Allah will surround them all with punishment.)

Ibn Majah collected this Hadith.

Surah: 8 Ayah: 26

﴿ وَاذْكُرُواْ إِذْ أَنتُمْ قَلِيلٌ مُّسْتَضْعَفُونَ فِى ٱلْأَرْضِ تَخَافُونَ أَن يَتَخَطَّفَكُمُ ٱلنَّاسُ فَـَٔاوَىٰكُمْ وَأَيَّدَكُم بِنَصْرِهِۦ وَرَزَقَكُم مِّنَ ٱلطَّيِّبَـٰتِ لَعَلَّكُمْ تَشْكُرُونَ ﴾

26. And remember when you were few and were reckoned weak in the land, and were afraid that men might kidnap you, but He provided a safe place for you, strengthened you with His Help, and provided you with good things so that you might be grateful.

Transliteration

26. Waothkuroo ith antum qaleelun mustadAAafoona fee al-ardi takhafoona an yatakhattafakumu alnnasu faawakum waayyadakum binasrihi warazaqakum mina alttayyibati laAAallakum tashkuroona

Tafsir Ibn Kathir

Reminding Muslims of Their previous State of Weakness and Subjugation which changed into Might and Triumph

Allah, the Exalted, reminds His believing servants of His blessings and favors on them. They were few and He made them many, weak and fearful and He provided them with strength and victory. They were meek and poor, and He granted them sustenance and livelihood. He ordered them to be grateful to Him, and they obeyed Him and implemented what He commanded.

When the believers were still in Makkah they were few, practicing their religion in secret, oppressed, fearing that pagans, fire worshippers or Romans might kidnap them from the various parts of Allah's earth, for they were all enemies of the Muslims, especially since Muslims were few and weak. Later on, Allah permitted the believers to migrate to Al-Madinah, where He allowed them to settle in a safe resort. Allah made the people of Al-Madinah their allies, giving them refuge and support during Badr and other battles. They helped the Migrants with their wealth and gave up their lives in obedience of Allah and His Messenger . Qatadah bin Di`amah As-Sadusi commented,

(And remember when you were few and were reckoned weak in the land,)

"Arabs were the weakest of the weak, had the toughest life, the emptiest stomachs, the barest skin and the most obvious misguidance. Those who lived among them lived in misery; those who died went to the Fire. They were being eaten up, but unable to eat up others! By Allah! We do not know of a people on the face of the earth at that time who had a worse life than them. When Allah brought Islam, He made it dominant on the earth, thus bringing provisions and leadership for them over the necks of people. It is through Islam that Allah granted all what you see, so thank Him for His favors, for your Lord is One Who bestows favors and likes praise. Verily, those who thank Allah enjoy even more bounties from Him."

Surah: 8 Ayah: 27 & Ayah: 28

﴿ يَٰٓأَيُّهَا ٱلَّذِينَ ءَامَنُواْ لَا تَخُونُواْ ٱللَّهَ وَٱلرَّسُولَ وَتَخُونُوٓاْ أَمَٰنَٰتِكُمْ وَأَنتُمْ تَعْلَمُونَ ۝ ﴾

27. O you who believe! Betray not Allâh and His Messenger, nor betray knowingly your Amânât (things entrusted to you, and all the duties which Allâh has ordained for you).

﴿ وَٱعْلَمُوٓاْ أَنَّمَآ أَمْوَٰلُكُمْ وَأَوْلَٰدُكُمْ فِتْنَةٌ وَأَنَّ ٱللَّهَ عِندَهُۥٓ أَجْرٌ عَظِيمٌ ۝ ﴾

28. And know that your possessions and your children are but a trial and that surely with Allâh is a mighty reward.

Transliteration

27. Ya ayyuha allatheena amanoo la takhoonoo Allaha waalrrasoola watakhoonoo amanatikum waantum taAAlamoona 28. WaiAAlamoo annama amwalukum waawladukum fitnatun waanna Allaha AAindahu ajrun AAatheemun

Tafsir Ibn Kathir

Reason behind revealing This Ayah, and the prohibition of Betrayal

The Two Sahihs mention the story of Hatib bin Abi Balta`ah. In the year of the victory of Makkah he wrote to the Quraysh alerting them that the Messenger of Allah intended to march towards them. Allah informed His Messenger of this, and he sent a Companion to retrieve the letter that Hatib sent, and then he summoned him. He admitted to what he did. `Umar bin Al-Khattab stood up and said, "O Allah's Messenger! Should I cut off his head, for he has betrayed Allah, His Messenger and the believers" The Prophet said,

«دَعْهُ فَإِنَّهُ قَدْ شَهِدَ بَدْرًا، وَمَا يُدْرِيكَ لَعَلَّ اللهَ اطَّلَعَ عَلَى أَهْلِ بَدْرٍ فَقَالَ: اعْمَلُوا مَا شِئْتُمْ فَقَدْ غَفَرْتُ لَكُم»

(Leave him! He participated in Badr. How do you know that Allah has not looked at those who participated in Badr and said, Do whatever you want, for I have forgiven you.)

However, it appears that this Ayah is more general, even if it was revealed about a specific incident. Such rulings are dealt with by their indications, not the specific reasons behind revealing them, according to the majority of scholars.

Betrayal includes both minor and major sins, as well those that affect others. `Ali bin Abi Talhah said that Ibn `Abbas commented on the Ayah,

(nor betray your Amanat) "The Amanah refers to the actions that Allah has entrusted the servants with, such as and including what He ordained. Therefore, Allah says here,

(nor betray...), `do not abandon the obligations.'" `Abdur-Rahman bin Zayd commented, "Allah forbade you from betraying Him and His Messenger, as hypocrites do."

Allah said,

(And know that your possessions and your children are but a trial.) from Him to you. He grants these to you so that He knows which of you will be grateful and obedient to Him, or become busy with and dedicated to them instead of Him. Allah said in another Ayah,

(Your wealth and your children are only a trial, whereas Allah! With Him is a great reward.) (64:15),

(And We shall make a trial of you with evil and with good.) (21:35),

(O you who believe! Let not your properties or your children divert you from the remembrance of Allah. And whosoever does that, then they are the losers.)(63:9), and,

(O you who believe! Verily, among your wives and your children there are enemies for you (who may stop you from the obedience of Allah); therefore beware of them!) (64:14) Allah said next,

(And that surely with Allah is a mighty reward.) Therefore, Allah's reward, favor and Paradise are better for you than wealth and children. Certainly, among the wealth and children there might be enemies for you and much of them avail nothing. With Allah alone is the decision and sovereignty in this life and the Hereafter, and He gives tremendous rewards on the Day of Resurrection. In the Sahih, there is a Hadith in which the Messenger of Allah said,

«ثَلَاثٌ مَنْ كُنَّ فِيهِ، وَجَدَ بِهِنَّ حَلَاوَةَ الْإِيمَانِ: مَنْ كَانَ اللهُ وَرَسُولُهُ أَحَبَّ إِلَيْهِ مِمَّا سِوَاهُمَا، وَمَنْ كَانَ يُحِبُّ الْمَرْءَ لَا يُحِبُّهُ إِلَّا لِلَّهِ، وَمَنْ كَانَ أَنْ يُلْقَى فِي النَّارِ أَحَبَّ إِلَيْهِ مِنْ أَنْ يَرْجِعَ إِلَى الْكُفْرِ بَعْدَ إِذْ أَنْقَذَهُ اللهُ مِنْهُ»

(There are three qualities for which whomever has them, he will have tasted the sweetness of faith. (They are:) whoever Allah and His Messenger are dearer to him than anyone else, whoever loves a person for Allah's sake alone, and whoever prefers to be thrown in fire rather than revert to disbelief, after Allah has saved him from it.)

Therefore, loving the Messenger of Allah comes before loving children, wealth and oneself. In the Sahih, it is confirmed that he said,

»وَالَّذِي نَفْسِي بِيَدِهِ لَا يُؤْمِنُ أَحَدُكُمْ حَتَّى أَكُونَ أَحَبَّ إِلَيْهِ مِنْ نَفْسِهِ وَأَهْلِهِ وَمَالِهِ وَالنَّاسِ أَجْمَعِينَ«

(By He in Whose Hand is my soul! None of you will have faith unless I become dearer to him than himself, his family, his wealth and all people.)

Surah: 8 Ayah: 29

﴿ يَٰٓأَيُّهَا ٱلَّذِينَ ءَامَنُوٓاْ إِن تَتَّقُواْ ٱللَّهَ يَجْعَل لَّكُمْ فُرْقَانًا وَيُكَفِّرْ عَنكُمْ سَيِّـَٔاتِكُمْ وَيَغْفِرْ لَكُمْ ۗ وَٱللَّهُ ذُو ٱلْفَضْلِ ٱلْعَظِيمِ ﴾

29. O you who believe! If you obey and fear Allâh, He will grant you Furqân ((a criterion to judge between right and wrong), or (Makhraj, i.e. a way for you to get out from every difficulty)) and will expiate for you your sins, and forgive you; and Allâh is the Owner of the Great Bounty.

Transliteration

29. Ya ayyuha allatheena amanoo in tattaqoo Allaha yajAAal lakum furqanan wayukaffir AAankum sayyi-atikum wayaghfir lakum waAllahu thoo alfadli alAAatheemi

Tafsir Ibn Kathir

Ibn `Abbas, As-Suddi, Mujahid, `Ikrimah, Ad-Dahhak, Qatadah, Muqatil bin Hayyan and several others said that,

(Furqan), means, `a way out'; Mujahid added, "In this life and the Hereafter." In another narration, Ibn `Abbas is reported to have said, `Furqan' means `salvation' or -- according to another narration -- `aid'. Muhammad bin Ishaq said that `Furqan' means `criterion between truth and falsehood'. This last explanation from Ibn Ishaq is more general than the rest that we mentioned, and it also includes the other meanings. Certainly, those who have Taqwa of Allah by obeying what He ordained and abstaining from what he forbade, will be guided to differentiate between the truth and the falsehood. This will be a triumph, safety and a way out for them from the affairs of this life, all the while acquiring happiness in the Hereafter. They will also gain forgiveness, thus having their sins erased, and pardon, thus having their sins covered from other people, as well as, being directed to a way to gain Allah's tremendous rewards,

(O you who believe! Have Taqwa of Allah, and believe in His Messenger, He will give you a double portion of His mercy, and He will give you a light by which you shall walk (straight). And He will forgive you. And Allah is Oft-Forgiving, Most Merciful.) (57:28).

Surah: 8 Ayah: 30

﴿ وَإِذْ يَمْكُرُ بِكَ ٱلَّذِينَ كَفَرُوا۟ لِيُثْبِتُوكَ أَوْ يَقْتُلُوكَ أَوْ يُخْرِجُوكَ ۚ وَيَمْكُرُونَ وَيَمْكُرُ ٱللَّهُ ۖ وَٱللَّهُ خَيْرُ ٱلْمَـٰكِرِينَ ﴾

30. And (remember) when the disbelievers plotted against you (O Muhammad (peace be upon him)) to imprison you, or to kill you, or to get you out (from your home, i.e. Makkah); they were plotting and Allâh too was plotting; and Allâh is the Best of those who plot .

Transliteration

30. Wa-ith yamkuru bika allatheena kafaroo liyuthbitooka aw yaqtulooka aw yukhrijookawayamkuroona wayamkuru Allahu waAllahu khayru almakireena

Tafsir Ibn Kathir

The Makkans plot to kill the Prophet , imprison Him or expel Him from Makkah

Ibn `Abbas, Mujahid and Qatadah said,

(Liyuthbituka) means "to imprison you." As-Suddi said, "Ithbat is to confine or to shackle."

Imam Muhammad bin Ishaq bin Yasar, the author of Al-Maghazi, reported from `Abdullah bin Abi Najih, from Mujahid, from Ibn `Abbas, "Some of the chiefs of the various tribes of Quraysh gathered in Dar An-Nadwah (their conference area) and Iblis (Shaytan) met them in the shape of an eminent old man. When they saw him, they asked, `Who are you' He said, `An old man from Najd. I heard that you are having a meeting, and I wished to attend your meeting. You will benefit from my opinion and advice.' They said, `Agreed, come in.' He entered with them. Iblis said, `You have to think about this man (Muhammad)! By Allah, he will soon overwhelm you with his matter (religion).' One of them said, `Imprison him, restrained in chains, until he dies just like the poets before him all died, such as Zuhayr and An-Nabighah! Verily, he is a poet like they were.' The old man from Najd, the enemy of Allah, commented, `By Allah! This is not a good idea. His Lord will release him from his prison to his companions, who will liberate him from your hands. They will protect him from you and they might expel you from your land.' They said, `This old man said the truth. Therefore, seek an opinion other than this one.'

Another one of them said, `Expel him from your land, so that you are free from his trouble! If he leaves your land, you will not be bothered by what he does or where he goes, as long as he is not among you to bring you troubles, he will be with someone else.' The old man from Najd replied, `By Allah! This is not a good opinion. Have you forgotten his sweet talk and eloquency, as well as, how his speech captures the hearts By Allah! This way, he will collect even more followers among Arabs, who will gather against you and attack you in your own land, expel you and kill your chiefs.' They said, `He has said the truth, by Allah! Therefore, seek an opinion other than this one.' hAbu Jahl, may Allah curse him, spoke next, `By Allah! I have an idea that no one else has suggested yet, and I see no better opinion for you. Choose a strong, socially elevated young man from each tribe, and give each one of them a sharp sword. Then they would all strike Muhammad at the same time with their swords and kill him. Hence, his blood would be shed by all tribes. This way, his tribe, Banu Hashim, would realize that they cannot wage war against all of the Quraysh tribes and would be forced to agree to accept the blood money; we would have brought comfort to ourselves and stopped him from bothering us.'

The old man from Najd commented, `By Allah! This man has expressed the best opinion, and I do not support any other opinion.' They quickly ended their meeting and started preparing for the implementation of this plan.

Jibril came to the Prophet and commanded him not to sleep in his bed that night and conveyed to him the news of their plot. The Messenger of Allah did not sleep in his house that night, and Allah gave him permission to migrate. After the Messenger migrated to Al-Madinah, Allah revealed to him Suat Al-Anfal reminding him of His favors and the bounties He gave him,

(And (remember) when the disbelievers plotted against you to imprison you, or to kill you, or to expel you (from Makkah); they were plotting and Allah too was plotting; and Allah is the best of plotters.)

Allah replied to the pagans' statement that they should await the death of the Prophet , just as the poets before him perished, as they claimed,

(Or do they say: "He is a poet! We await for him some calamity by time!") (52:30)

As-Suddi narrated a similar story.

Muhammad bin Ishaq reported from Muhammad bin Ja`far bin Az-Zubayr, from `Urwah bin Az-Zubayr who commented on Allah's statement,

(...they were plotting and Allah too was plotting, and Allah is the best of plotters.) "I (Allah) plotted against them with My sure planning, and I saved you (O Muhammad) from them."

Surah: 8 Ayah: 31, Ayah: 32 & Ayah: 33

﴿ وَإِذَا تُتْلَىٰ عَلَيْهِمْ ءَايَٰتُنَا قَالُوا۟ قَدْ سَمِعْنَا لَوْ نَشَآءُ لَقُلْنَا مِثْلَ هَٰذَآ إِنْ هَٰذَآ إِلَّآ أَسَٰطِيرُ ٱلْأَوَّلِينَ ۝ ﴾

31. And when Our Verses (of the Qur'ân) are recited to them, they say: "We have heard this (the Qur'ân); if we wish we can say the like of this. This is nothing but the tales of the ancients."

﴿ وَإِذْ قَالُوا۟ ٱللَّهُمَّ إِن كَانَ هَـٰذَا هُوَ ٱلْحَقَّ مِنْ عِندِكَ فَأَمْطِرْ عَلَيْنَا حِجَارَةً مِّنَ ٱلسَّمَآءِ أَوِ ٱئْتِنَا بِعَذَابٍ أَلِيمٍ ۝ ﴾

32. And (remember) when they said: "O Allâh! If this (the Qur'ân) is indeed the truth (revealed) from You, then rain down stones on us from the sky or bring on us a painful torment."

﴿ وَمَا كَانَ ٱللَّهُ لِيُعَذِّبَهُمْ وَأَنتَ فِيهِمْ ۚ وَمَا كَانَ ٱللَّهُ مُعَذِّبَهُمْ وَهُمْ يَسْتَغْفِرُونَ ۝ ﴾

33. And Allâh would not punish them while you (Muhammad (peace be upon him)) are amongst them, nor will He punish them while they seek (Allâh's) Forgiveness.

Transliteration

31. Wa-itha tutla AAalayhim ayatuna qaloo qad samiAAna law nashao laqulna mithla hatha in hatha illa asateeru al-awwaleena 32. Wa-ith qaloo allahumma in kana hatha huwa alhaqqa min AAindika faamtir AAalayna hijaratan mina alssama-i awi i/tina biAAathabin aleemin 33. Wama kana Allahu liyuAAaththibahum waanta feehim wama kana Allahu muAAaththibahum wahum yastaghfiroona

Tafsir Ibn Kathir

The Quraysh claimed They can produce Something similar to the Qur'an

Allah describes the disbelief, transgression, rebellion, as well as misguided statements that the pagans of Quraysh used to utter when they heard Allah's Ayat being recited to them,

("We have heard (the Qur'an); if we wish we can say the like of this.")

They boasted with their words, but not with their actions. They were challenged several times to bring even one chapter like the Qur'an, and they had no way to meet this challenge. They only boasted in order to deceive themselves and those who followed their falsehood. It was said that An-Nadr bin Al-Harith, may Allah curse him, was the one who said this, according to Sa`id bin Jubayr, As-Suddi, Ibn Jurayj and others. An-Nadr visited Persia and learned the stories of some Persian kings, such as Rustum and Isphandiyar. When he went back to Makkah, He found that the Prophet was sent from Allah and reciting the Qur'an to the people. Whenever the Prophet would leave an audience in which An-Nadr was sitting, An-Nadr began narrating to them the stories that he learned in Persia, proclaiming afterwards, "Who, by Allah, has better tales to narrate, I or Muhammad" When Allah allowed the Muslims to capture

An-Nadr in Badr, the Messenger of Allah commanded that his head be cut off before him, and that was done, all thanks are due to Allah. The meaning of,

(...tales of the ancients) meaning that the Prophet has plagiarized and learned books of ancient people, and this is what he narrated to people, as they claimed. This is the pure falsehood that Allah mentioned in another Ayah,

(And they say: "Tales of the ancients, which he has written down:, and they are dictated to him morning and afternoon." Say: "It (this Qur'an) has been sent down by Him (Allah) Who knows the secret of the heavens and the earth. Truly, He is Oft-Forgiving, Most Merciful.") (25:5-6) for those who repent and return to Him, He accepts repentance from them and forgives them.

The Idolators ask for Allah's Judgment and Torment!

Allah said,

(And (remember) when they said: "O Allah! If this (the Qur'an) is indeed the truth (revealed) from You, then rain down stones on us from the sky or bring on us a painful torment.")

This is indicative of the pagans' enormous ignorance, denial, stubbornness and transgression. They should have said, "O Allah! If this is the truth from You, then guide us to it and help us follow it." However, they brought Allah's judgment on themselves and asked for His punishment. Allah said in other Ayat,

(And they ask you to hasten on the torment (for them), and had it not been for a term appointed, the torment would certainly have come to them. And surely, it will come upon them suddenly while they perceive not!) (29:53),

(They say: "Our Lord! Hasten to us Qittana (our record of good and bad deeds so that we may see it) before the Day of Reckoning!") (38:16), and,

(A questioner asked concerning a torment about to befall. Upon the disbelievers, which none can avert. From Allah, the Lord of the ways of ascent.) (70:1-3)

The ignorant ones in ancient times said similar things. The people of Shu`ayb said to him,

("So cause a piece of the heaven to fall on us, if you are of the truthful!")(26:187) while the pagans of Quraysh said,

("O Allah! If this (the Qur'an) is indeed the truth (revealed) from You, then rain down stones on us from the sky or bring on us a painful torment.")

Shu`bah said from `Abdul-Hamid that Anas bin Malik said that it was Abu Jahl bin Hisham who uttered this statement,

("O Allah! If this (the Qur'an) is indeed the truth (revealed) from You, then rain down stones on us from the sky or bring on us a painful torment.")

So Allah revealed this Ayah,

(And Allah would not punish them while you are among them, nor will He punish them while they seek (Allah's) forgiveness.)

Al-Bukhari recorded it.

The Presence of the Prophet, and the Idolators' asking For forgiveness, were the Shelters against receiving Allah's immediate Torment

Allah said,

(And Allah would not punish them while you are among them, nor will He punish them while they seek (Allah's) forgiveness.)

Ibn Abi Hatim recorded that Ibn `Abbas said, "Pagans used to go around the House in Tawaf and proclaim, `We rush to Your obedience, O Allah, there is no partner with You,' and the Prophet would tell them,

《قَدٍ، قَد》

(Enough, enough.) But they would go on, `We rush to Your obedience, O Allah, there is no partner with You except a partner who is with You, You own Him but he does not own! They also used to say, `O Allah, Your forgiveness, Your forgiveness.' Allah revealed this verse;

(And Allah would not punish them while you are among them...)"'

Ibn `Abbas commented, "They had two safety shelters: the Prophet, and their seeking forgiveness (from Allah). The Prophet went away, and only seeking forgiveness remained." At-Tirmidhi recorded that Abu Musa said that the Messenger of Allah said,

《أَنْزَلَ اللهُ عَلَيَّ أَمَانَيْنِ لِأُمَّتِي》

("Allah sent down to me two safe shelters for the benefit of my Ummah)

(And Allah would not punish them while you are among them, nor will He punish them while they seek (Allah's) forgiveness.)

《فَإِذَا مَضَيْتُ تَرَكْتُ فِيهِمُ الِاسْتِغْفَارَ إِلَى يَوْمِ الْقِيَامَة》

(When I die, I will leave the seeking of forgiveness with them, until the Day of Resurrection.)

What testifies to this Hadith, is the Hadith that Ahmad recorded in his Musnad and Al-Hakim in his Mustadrak, that Abu Sa`id narrated that the Messenger of Allah said,

«إِنَّ الشَّيْطَانَ قَالَ: وَعِزَّتِكَ يَا رَبِّ لَا أَبْرَحُ أُغْوِي عِبَادَكَ مَا دَامَتْ أَرْوَاحُهُمْ فِي أَجْسَادِهِمْ. فَقَالَ الرَّبُّ: وَعِزَّتِي وَجَلَالِي لَا أَزَالُ أَغْفِرُ لَهُمْ مَا اسْتَغْفَرُونِي»

(Shaytan said, `By Your might, O Lord! I will go on luring Your servants as long as their souls are still in their bodies.' The Lord said, `By My might and majesty! I will keep forgiving them, as long as they keep invoking Me for forgiveness.')

Al-Hakim, "Its chain is Sahih and they did not record it."

Surah: 8 Ayah: 34 & Ayah: 35

﴿ وَمَا لَهُمْ أَلَّا يُعَذِّبَهُمُ ٱللَّهُ وَهُمْ يَصُدُّونَ عَنِ ٱلْمَسْجِدِ ٱلْحَرَامِ وَمَا كَانُوٓاْ أَوْلِيَآءَهُۥٓ إِنْ أَوْلِيَآؤُهُۥٓ إِلَّا ٱلْمُتَّقُونَ وَلَٰكِنَّ أَكْثَرَهُمْ لَا يَعْلَمُونَ ﴾

34. And why should not Allâh punish them while they stop (men) from Al-Masjid-al-Harâm, and they are not its guardians? None can be its guardian except Al-Muttaqûn (the pious - see V.2:2), but most of them know not.

﴿ وَمَا كَانَ صَلَاتُهُمْ عِندَ ٱلْبَيْتِ إِلَّا مُكَآءً وَتَصْدِيَةً فَذُوقُواْ ٱلْعَذَابَ بِمَا كُنتُمْ تَكْفُرُونَ ﴾

35. Their Salât (prayer) at the House (of Allâh, i.e. the Ka'bah at Makkah) was nothing but whistling and clapping of hands. Therefore taste the punishment because you used to disbelieve.

Transliteration

34. Wama lahum alla yuAAaththibahumu Allahu wahum yasuddoona AAani almasjidi alharami wama kanoo awliyaahu in awliyaohu illa almuttaqoona walakinna aktharahum la yaAAlamoona 35. Wama kana salatuhum AAinda albayti illa mukaan watasdiyatan fathooqoo alAAathaba bima kuntum takfuroona

Tafsir Ibn Kathir

The Idolators deserved Allah's Torment after Their Atrocities

Allah states that the idolators deserved the torment, but He did not torment them in honor of the Prophet residing among them. After Allah allowed the Prophet to migrate away from them, He sent His torment upon them on the day of Badr. During that battle, the chief pagans were killed, or captured. Allah also directed them to seek forgiveness for the sins, Shirk and wickedness they indulged in. If it was not for the fact that there were some weak Muslims living among the Makkan pagans, those

Muslims who invoked Allah for His forgiveness, Allah would have sent down to them the torment that could never be averted. Allah did not do that on account of the weak, ill-treated, and oppressed believers living among them, as He reiterated about the day at Al-Hudaybiyyah,

(They are the ones who disbelieved and hindered you from Al-Masjid Al-Haram (at Makkah) and detained the sacrificial animals from reaching their place of sacrifice. Had there not been believing men and believing women whom you did not know, that you may kill them and on whose account a sin would have been committed by you without (your) knowledge, that Allah might bring into His mercy whom He wills if they (the believers and the disbelievers) had been apart, We verily, would have punished those of them who disbelieved with painful torment.) (48:25)

Allah said here,

(And why should not Allah punish them while they hinder (men) from Al-Masjid Al-Haram, and they are not its guardians None can be its guardians except those who have Taqwa, but most of them know not.)

Allah asks, `why would not He torment them while they are stopping Muslims from going to Al-Masjid Al-Haram, thus hindering the believers, its own people, from praying and performing Tawaf in it' Allah said,

T(And they are not its guardians None can be its guardians except those who have Taqwa,) meaning, the Prophet and his Companions are the true dwellers (or worthy maintainers) of Al-Masjid Al-Haram, not the pagans. Allah said in other Ayah,

(It is not for the polytheists, to maintain the Masjids of Allah, while they witness disbelief against themselves. The works of such are in vain and in the Fire shall they abide. The Masjids of Allah shall be maintained only by those who believe in Allah and the Last Day; perform the Salah, and give the Zakah and fear none but Allah. It is they who are on true guidance.) (9:17-18), and,

(But a greater (transgression) with Allah is to prevent mankind from following the way of Allah, to disbelieve in Him, to prevent access to Al-Masjid Al-Haram (at Makkah), and to drive out its inhabitants,) (2:217).

`Urwah, As-Suddi and Muhammad bin Ishaq said that Allah's statement,

(None can be its guardians except those who have Taqwa,) refers to Muhammad and his Companions, may Allah be pleased with them all. Mujahid explained that this Ayah is about the Mujahidin (in Allah's cause), whomever and wherever they may be.

Allah then mentioned the practice of the pagans next to Al-Masjid Al-Haram and the respect they observed in its vicinity,

(Their Salah (prayer) at the House was nothing but Muka' and Tasdiyah.)

`Abdullah bin `Umar, Ibn `Abbas, Mujahid, `Ikrimah, Sa`id bin Jubayr, Abu Raja' Al-Utardi, Muhammad bin Ka`b Al-Qurazi, Hujr bin `Anbas, Nubayt bin Sharit, Qatadah and `Abdur-Rahman bin Zayd bin Aslam said that this part of the Ayah refers to whistling. Mujahid added that the pagans used to place their fingers in their mouth (while whistling). Sa`id bin Jubayr said that Ibn `Abbas commented on Allah's statement,

(Their Salat at the House was nothing but Muka' and Tasdiyah.)

"The Quraysh used to perform Tawaf (encircling the Ka`bah) while naked, whistling and clapping their hands, for Muka' means `whistling', while, Tasdiyah means `clapping the hands.'" This meaning was also reported from Ibn `Abbas, by `Ali bin Abi Talhah and Al-`Awfi. Similar was recorded from Ibn `Umar, Mujahid, Muhammad bin Ka`b, Abu Salamah bin `Abdur-Rahman, Ad-Dahhak, Qatadah, `Atiyyah Al-`Awfi, Hujr bin `Anbas and Ibn Abza. Ibn Jarir recorded that Ibn `Umar explained the Ayah,

(Their Salat at the House was nothing but Muka' and Tasdiyah.) "Muka' means `whistling', while, `Tasdiyah' means `clapping the hands.'" Sa`id bin Jubayr and `Abdur-Rahman bin Zayd said that,

(and Tasdiyah), means, they hindered from the path of Allah, the Exalted and Most Honored. Allah said,

(Therefore taste the punishment because you used to disbelieve.)

This refers to the death and capture that they suffered during the battle of Badr, according to Ad-Dahhak, Ibn Jurayj and Muhammad bin Ishaq.

Surah: 8 Ayah: 36 & Ayah: 37

﴿ إِنَّ ٱلَّذِينَ كَفَرُوا۟ يُنفِقُونَ أَمْوَٰلَهُمْ لِيَصُدُّوا۟ عَن سَبِيلِ ٱللَّهِ ۚ فَسَيُنفِقُونَهَا ثُمَّ تَكُونُ عَلَيْهِمْ حَسْرَةً ثُمَّ يُغْلَبُونَ ۗ وَٱلَّذِينَ كَفَرُوٓا۟ إِلَىٰ جَهَنَّمَ يُحْشَرُونَ ۝ ﴾

36. Verily, those who disbelieve spend their wealth to hinder (men) from the Path of Allâh, and so will they continue to spend it; but in the end it will become an anguish for them. Then they will be overcome. And those who disbelieve will be gathered unto Hell.

﴿ لِيَمِيزَ ٱللَّهُ ٱلْخَبِيثَ مِنَ ٱلطَّيِّبِ وَيَجْعَلَ ٱلْخَبِيثَ بَعْضَهُۥ عَلَىٰ بَعْضٍ فَيَرْكُمَهُۥ جَمِيعًا فَيَجْعَلَهُۥ فِى جَهَنَّمَ ۚ أُو۟لَـٰٓئِكَ هُمُ ٱلْخَـٰسِرُونَ ۝ ﴾

37. In order that Allâh may distinguish the wicked (disbelievers, polytheists and doers of evil deeds) from the good (believers of Islâmic Monotheism and doers of righteous deeds), and put the wicked (disbelievers, polytheists and doers of evil deeds) one over another, heap them together and cast them into Hell. Those! it is they who are the losers.

Transliteration

36. Inna allatheena kafaroo yunfiqoona amwalahum liyasuddoo AAan sabeeli Allahi fasayunfiqoonaha thumma takoonu AAalayhim hasratan thumma yughlaboona waallatheena kafaroo ila jahannama yuhsharoona 37. Liyameeza Allahu alkhabeetha mina alttayyibi wayajAAala alkhabeetha baAAdahu AAala baAAdin fayarkumahu jameeAAan fayajAAalahu fee jahannama ola-ika humu alkhasiroona

Tafsir Ibn Kathir

The Disbelievers spend Their Wealth to hinder Others from Allah's Path, but this will only cause Them Grief

Muhammad bin Ishaq narrated that Az-Zuhri, Muhammad bin Yahya bin Hibban, `Asim bin `Umar bin Qatadah, and Al-Husayn bin `Abdur-Rahman bin `Amr bin Sa`id bin Mu`adh said, "The Quraysh suffered defeat at Badr and their forces went back to Makkah, while Abu Sufyan went back with the caravan intact. This is when `Abdullah bin Abi Rabi`ah, `Ikrimah bin Abi Jahl, Safwan bin Umayyah and other men from Quraysh who lost their fathers, sons or brothers in Badr, went to Abu Sufyan bin Harb. They said to him, and to those among the Quraysh who had wealth in that caravan, `O people of Quraysh! Muhammad has grieved you and killed the chiefs among you. Therefore, help us with this wealth so that we can fight him, it may be that we will avenge our losses.' They agreed." Muhammad bin Ishaq said, "This Ayah was revealed about them, according to Ibn `Abbas,

(Verily, those who disbelieve spend their wealth...) until,

(they who are the losers.)" Mujahid, Sa`id bin Jubayr, Al-Hakam bin `Uyaynah, Qatadah, As-Suddi and Ibn Abza said that this Ayah was revealed about Abu Sufyan and his spending money in Uhud to fight the Messenger of Allah. Ad-Dahhak said that this Ayah was revealed about the idolators of Badr. In any case, the Ayah is general, even though there was a specific incident that accompanied its revelation. Allah states here that the disbelievers spend their wealth to hinder from the path of truth. However, by doing that, their money will be spent and then will become a source of grief and anguish for them, availing them nothing in the least. They seek to extinguish the Light of Allah and make their word higher than the word of truth. However, Allah will complete His Light, even though the disbelievers hate it. He will give aid to His religion, make His Word dominant, and His religion will prevail above all religions. This is the disgrace that the disbelievers will taste in this life; and in the Hereafter, they will taste the torment of the Fire. Whoever among them lives long, will witness with his eyes and hear with his ears what causes grief to him. Those among them who are killed or die will be returned to eternal disgrace and the everlasting punishment. This is why Allah said,

(And so will they continue to spend it; but in the end it will become an anguish for them. Then they will be overcome. And those who disbelieve will be gathered unto Hell.)

Allah said,

(In order that Allah may distinguish the wicked from the good.), meaning recognize the difference between the people of happiness and the people of misery, according to Ibn `Abbas, as `Ali bin Abi Talhah reported from him. Allah distinguishes between those believers who obey Him and fight His disbelieving enemies and those who disobey Him. Allah said in another Ayah,

(Allah will not leave the believers in the state in which you are now, until He distinguishes the wicked from the good. Nor will Allah disclose to you the secrets of the Ghayb (Unseen).) (3:179), and,

(Do you think that you will enter Paradise before Allah (tests) those of you who fought (in His cause) and (also) tests those who are the patient)(3:142).

Therefore, the Ayah (8:37) means, `We tried you with combatant disbelievers whom We made able to spend money in fighting you,'

(in order that Allah may distinguish the wicked from the good, and put the wicked one over another, heap them together) put in a pile on top of each other,

(and cast them into Hell. Those! It is they who are the losers.) (8:37), in this life and the Hereafter.

Surah: 8 Ayah: 38, Ayah: 39 & Ayah: 40

﴿ قُل لِّلَّذِينَ كَفَرُوٓاْ إِن يَنتَهُواْ يُغۡفَرۡ لَهُم مَّا قَدۡ سَلَفَ وَإِن يَعُودُواْ فَقَدۡ مَضَتۡ سُنَّتُ ٱلۡأَوَّلِينَ ۝ ﴾

38. Say to those who have disbelieved, if they cease (from disbelief) their past will be forgiven. But if they return (thereto), then the examples of those (punished) before them have already preceded (as a warning).

﴿ وَقَٰتِلُوهُمۡ حَتَّىٰ لَا تَكُونَ فِتۡنَةٌ وَيَكُونَ ٱلدِّينُ كُلُّهُۥ لِلَّهِ ۚ فَإِنِ ٱنتَهَوۡاْ فَإِنَّ ٱللَّهَ بِمَا يَعۡمَلُونَ بَصِيرٌ ۝ ﴾

39. And fight them until there is no more Fitnah (disbelief and polytheism, i.e. worshipping others besides Allâh) and the religion (worship) will all be for Allâh Alone (in the whole of the world). But if they cease (worshipping others besides Allâh), then certainly, Allâh is All-Seer of what they do.

﴿ وَإِن تَوَلَّوۡاْ فَٱعۡلَمُوٓاْ أَنَّ ٱللَّهَ مَوۡلَىٰكُمۡ ۚ نِعۡمَ ٱلۡمَوۡلَىٰ وَنِعۡمَ ٱلنَّصِيرُ ۝ ﴾

40. And if they turn away, then know that Allâh is your Maulâ (Patron, Lord, Protector and Supporter), (what) an Excellent Maulâ, and (what) an Excellent Helper!

Transliteration

38. Qul lillatheena kafaroo in yantahoo yughfar lahum ma qad salafa wa-in yaAAoodoo faqad madat sunnatu al-awwaleena 39. Waqatiloohum hatta la takoona fitnatun wayakoona alddeenu kulluhu lillahi fa-ini intahaw fa-inna Allaha bima yaAAmaloona baseerun 40. Wa-in tawallaw faiAAlamoo anna Allaha mawlakum niAAma almawla waniAAma alnnaseeru

Tafsir Ibn Kathir

Encouraging the Disbelievers to seek Allah's Forgiveness, warning Them against Disbelief

Allah commands His Prophet Muhammad ,

(Say to those who have disbelieved, if they cease...) the disbelief, defiance and stubbornness they indulge in, and embrace Islam, obedience and repentance.

(their past will be forgiven.) along with their sins and errors. It is recorded in the Sahih Al-Bukhari that Abu Wa'il said that Ibn Mas'ud said that the Messenger of Allah said,

«مَنْ أَحْسَنَ فِي الْإِسْلَامِ لَمْ يُؤَاخَذْ بِمَا عَمِلَ فِي الْجَاهِلِيَّةِ، وَمَنْ أَسَاءَ فِي الْإِسْلَامِ أُخِذَ بِالْأَوَّلِ وَالْآخِرِ»

(He who becomes good in his Islam, will not be punished for what he has committed during Jahiliyyah (before Islam). He who becomes bad in his Islam, will face a punishment for his previous and latter deeds.)

It is also recorded in the Sahih that the Messenger of Allah said,

«الْإِسْلَامُ يَجُبُّ مَا قَبْلَهُ وَالتَّوْبَةُ تَجُبُّ مَا كَانَ قَبْلَهَا»

("Islam erases what occurred before it, and repentance erases what occurs before it.")

Allah said,

(But if they return,) and remain on their ways,

(then the examples of those (punished) before them have already preceded.) (8:38) meaning, Our way with the nations of old is that when they disbelieve and rebel, We send down to them immediate torment and punishment.

The Order to fight to eradicate Shirk and Kufr

Allah said,

Chapter 8: Al-Anfal (Spoils of War, Booty), Verses 001-040

(And fight them until there is no more Fitnah, and the religion will all be for Allah alone.)

Al-Bukhari recorded that a man came to Ibn `Umar and said to him, "O Abu `Abdur-Rahman! Why do you not implement what Allah said in His Book,

(And if two parties (or groups) among the believers fall to fighting...)(49:9). What prevents you from fighting as Allah mentioned in His Book" Ibn `Umar said, "O my nephew! I prefer that I be reminded with this Ayah rather than fighting, for in the latter case, I will be reminded by the Ayah in which Allah, the Exalted and Most Honored, said,

(And whoever kills a believer intentionally...) (4:93)"

The man said, "Allah, the Exalted, said,

(And fight them until there is no more Fitnah...)." Ibn `Umar said, "We did that during the time of the Messenger of Allah, when Islam was weak and the man would be tried in religion, either tormented to death or being imprisoned. When Islam became stronger and widespread, there was no more Fitnah." When the man realized that Ibn `Umar would not agree to what he is saying, he asked him, "What do you say about `Ali and `Uthman" Ibn `Umar replied, "What do I say about `Ali and `Uthman! As for `Uthman, Allah has forgiven him, but you hate that Allah forgives him. As for `Ali, he is the cousin of the Messenger of Allah and his son-in-law," and he pointed with his hand saying, "And this is his house over there." Sa`id bin Jubayr said, "Ibn `Umar came to us and was asked, "What do you say about fighting during Fitnah" Ibn `Umar said, "Do you know what Fitnah refers to Muhammad was fighting against the idolators, and at that time, attending (or residing with) the idolators was a Fitnah (trial in religion). It is nothing like what you are doing, fighting to gain leadership!" All these narrations were collected by Al-Bukhari, may Allah the Exalted grant him His mercy. Ad-Dahhak reported that Ibn `Abbas said about the Ayah,

(And fight them until there is no more Fitnah...) "So that there is no more Shirk." Similar was said by Abu Al-`Aliyah, Mujahid, Al-Hasan, Qatadah, Ar-Rabi` bin Anas, As-Suddi, Muqatil bin Hayyan and Zayd bin Aslam. Muhammad bin Ishaq said that he was informed from Az-Zuhri, from `Urwah bin Az-Zubayr and other scholars that

(until there is no more Fitnah) the Fitnah mentioned here means, until no Muslim is persecuted so that he abandons his religion. Ad-Dahhak reported that Ibn `Abbas said about Allah's statement,

(and the religion (worship) will all be for Allah alone.) "So that Tawhid is practiced in sincerity with Allah." Al-Hasan, Qatadah and Ibn Jurayj said,

(and the religion will all be for Allah alone) "So that La ilaha illa-llah is proclaimed." Muhammad bin Ishaq also commented on this Ayah, "So that Tawhid is practiced in sincerity towards Allah, without Shirk, all the while shunning all rivals who (are being worshipped) besides Him."

`Abdur-Rahman bin Zayd bin Aslam said about,

(and the religion will all be for Allah alone) "So that there is no more Kufr (disbelief) with your religion remains." There is a Hadith collected in the Two Sahihs that testifies to this explanation. The Messenger of Allah said,

«أُمِرْتُ أَنْ أُقَاتِلَ النَّاسَ، حَتَّى يَقُولُوا: لَا إِلَهَ إِلَّا اللهُ، فَإِذَا قَالُوهَا عَصَمُوا مِنِّي دِمَاءَهُمْ وَأَمْوَالَهُمْ، إِلَّا بِحَقِّهَا، وَحِسَابُهُمْ عَلَى اللهِ عَزَّ وَجَلَّ»

(I was commanded to fight against the people until they proclaim, `There is no deity worthy of worship except Allah.' If and when they say it, they will preserve their blood and wealth from me, except for its right (Islamic penal code), and their reckoning is with Allah, the Exalted and Most Honored.)

Also, in the Two Sahihs, it is recorded that Abu Musa Al-Ash`ari said, "The Messenger of Allah was asked about a man who fights because he is courageous, in prejudice with his people, or to show off. Which of these is for the cause of Allah He said,

«مَنْ قَاتَلَ لِتَكُونَ كَلِمَةُ اللهِ هِيَ الْعُلْيَا فَهُوَ فِي سَبِيلِ اللهِ عَزَّ وَجَلَّ»

(Whoever fights so that Allah's Word is the supreme, is in the cause of Allah, the Exalted and Most Honored.)"

Allah said next,

(But if they cease), and desist from their Kufr as a result of your fighting them, even though you do not know the true reasons why they did so,

(then certainly, Allah is All-Seer of what they do.)

Allah said in similar Ayah,

(But if they repent and perform the Salah, and give Zakah, then leave their way free.) (9:5),

(...then they are your brethren in religion.) (9:11), and,

(And fight them until there is no more Fitnah and the religion (worship) is for Allah (alone). But if they cease, let there be no transgression except against the wrongdoers.) (2:193)

It is recorded in the Sahih that the Messenger of Allah said to Usamah bin Zayd when he overpowered a man with his sword, after that man proclaimed that there is no deity worthy of worship except Allah;

«أَقَتَلْتَهُ بَعْدَ مَا قَالَ لَا إِلَهَ إِلَّا اللهُ؟ وَكَيْفَ تَصْنَعُ بِلَا إِلَهَ إِلَّا اللهُ يَوْمَ الْقِيَامَةِ؟»

Chapter 8: Al-Anfal (Spoils of War, Booty), Verses 001-040 — 153

(Have you killed him after he proclaimed, `La Ilaha Illallah' What would you do with regard to `La Ilaha Illallah' on the Day of Resurrection.)

Usamah said, "O Allah's Messenger! He only said it to save himself." The Messenger replied,

«هَلَّا شَقَقْتَ عَنْ قَلْبِهِ؟»

(Did you cut his heart open)

The Messenger kept repeating,

«مَنْ لَكَ بِلَا إِلَهَ إِلَّا اللهُ يَوْمَ الْقِيَامَةِ؟»

(What would you do with regard to `La Ilaha Illallah' on the Day of Resurrection) until Usamah said, "I wished I had embraced Islam only that day." Allah said next,

(And if they turn away, then know that Allah is your protector, an excellent protector, and an excellent helper!)

Allah says, if the disbelievers persist in defying and fighting you, then know that Allah is your protector, master and supporter against your enemies. Verily, what an excellent protector and what an excellent supporter.

www.ingramcontent.com/pod-product-compliance
Lightning Source LLC
Chambersburg PA
CBHW081111080526
44587CB00021B/3538